THE ILLUSION

THE
ILLUSION

AN ESSAY ON POLITICS,
THEATRE AND THE NOVEL

David Caute

HARPER COLOPHON BOOKS
Harper & Row, Publishers
New York, Evanston, San Francisco, London

First HARPER COLOPHON edition published 1972

LIBRARY OF CONGRESS CATALOG CARD NUMBER: 73-186812

STANDARD BOOK NUMBER: 06-090268-X

*Dedicated with love
to the memory of my father
and to the future of my sons
Edward and Daniel*

Contents

Acknowledgments

George Steiner and John Willett were kind enough to read the manuscript. Their comments were of great benefit to me.

Thanks are due to Grove Press Inc. for permission to quote from *Selected Poems of Pablo Neruda*, edited and translated by Ben Belitt (Copyright © 1961 by Grove Press Inc.; English texts Copyright © 1961 by Ben Belitt, published by Grove Press Inc. 1961); and to The World Publishing Company for permission to quote from *The Bedbug and Selected Poetry* by Vladimir Mayakovsk translated by George Reavy and Max Hayward (Copyright © 1960 by The World Publishing Company.)

Introduction

ONE

The great Cervantes ridicules those authors who shelter their dull wits behind quotations from Authorities. But the practice remains a useful one. And if I begin with a remark made by Henry James it is because I need a Trojan horse to carry me through the defences of a highly fortified city . . . What Henry James did in 1884 was to make a rather punishing reference to English novels and English puddings. Until recently, he said, 'there was a comfortable, good-humoured feeling abroad that a novel is a novel, as a pudding is a pudding, and that our only business with it could be to swallow it.'

Of course nothing could be less true today. The philistine attitude towards creative writing is a thing of the past and unnumbered legions of academics, critics and graduate students have invested their lives in the study of the novel, poetry and the drama. Intelligence, learning and sensibility —none are lacking. What then is my complaint and why have I spoken of a highly fortified city?

A certain insularity prevails in the national bloodstream; a distrust of generalisations, abstractions, pretentiousness and jargon. Our collective cultural reaction to foreign aesthetic theories, particularly those which attempt to understand literature in a wider philosophical, sociological and political context, continues to resemble that of a Folkestone customs officer examining a suitcase brimming with Danish pornography. James noted this tendency in his own time (although such intemperate metaphors were alien to him) and once again I invoke his name on the assumption that it occupies a scarcely less authoritative place in the Anglo-Saxon literary Pantheon than did that of Aristotle among the scholars of the later Middle Ages. We have not lost our commonsensical pragmatism, our innate distrust of foreign hot air and of supermen intellectuals who apparently aspire to explain the whole of human experience in a single, exhaustive sentence. We know what is compatible with the great tradition and decent moderation.

If this is so, I personally regret it. By this prejudice we lose more than we gain.

I regret above all the hard-boiled British distrust of intellectuals and I make bold to declare myself at the outset an unrepentant intellectual and the pages which follow a typically intellectual search for synthesis and re-evaluation within the existing corpus of knowledge and observation.

Let me generalise and therefore exaggerate. By prevailing British cultural and academic criteria, the intellectual is jack of all trades and master of none. He lacks a sense of role, professional specialisation, division of function and mental discretion. Not knowing where to stop he naturally knows not where properly to start. He trades in extravagant affirmative generalisations where the only valid one would be that none can be safely made. As for the study of creative literature, he is a kind of destructive marauder, a predatory fox prowling the chicken coops and bringing havoc in his tracks. He fails to appreciate that the creative and critical processes are innately separate, confided by nature to two distinct species of men possessing radically different forms of mental life. The intellectual cannot grasp that the authentic creative writer is an inspired, imaginative journeyman whose job it is to *make* things (books, plays, poems) leaving it to others to explain what he has done and why. The intellectual wants to be writer, critic, reader and philosopher all in one. He does not understand that theoretical pretensions can be

purchased only at the cost of thwarted or dwindling creative
powers; that reason and the imagination are not only separate, but also incapable of a mutually healthy coexistence
within a single skull; that the creative writer is like a sleepwalker whose safety lies in the maintenance of an inspired
trance. Read any interview in a British cultural journal or
newspaper and you will invariably detect the genuine,
authentic creative writer by the fact that he is obviously
more naïve and unlettered than his interrogator. Of course
he is not stupid; he has an instinctive sense of how to shield
the crystal shrine of his creativity against the intrusions of
rude reason and cerebration. The genuine British writer
never has the vaguest idea as to how he achieved the effects
for which he is famous. He is justifiably reluctant to explore
any intellectual or artistic influences which may have shaped
his work; he would rather explain his life in terms of a series
of empirical reactions to a series of formative experiences.
And if by chance he should be asked his opinion of the latest
productions of the French, German or Italian avant-gardes,
he will very sensibly declare himself either entirely ignorant
of them or too primitive to understand them. Such a confession will invariably draw a sympathetic reaction from an
educated British audience — and the irony will not be lost
on them.

A whole national history, a whole heritage, a whole
complex of educational norms and assumptions are involved.
And it is precisely because the history, the norms and the
general pattern of cultural inquiry are different in many
countries of Europe that the creative writers there move
with more assurance from practice to theory, creativity to
criticism, art to analysis, from the role of writer to the role
of intellectual. (It is no doubt a glory of British civic enlightenment that the appearance here of a disruptive novel
is not treated as a threat to the very existence of the state —
and yet I cannot evade a faint feeling of deprivation that the
authorities here show no interest in what may be buried in
glass jars under my rose bushes.) Anyway, in this book I am

applying for a licence to import a cumbersome cargo of
foreign contraband, not because I am a fellow-traveller of
any particular Parisian school, sect, party or movement, not
because I have what Koestler once called 'the French flu',
and certainly not because I believe that the British public is
entirely ignorant of the names and ideas I shall discuss. In
point of fact I am as prone as any other Englishman to exas-
peration and bewilderment as I plough my way through un-
ending paragraphs of turgid, jargon-riddled, self-satisfied
European intellectual bombast. Then why the importation?
There is no point in anticipating the answer here, the chapters that follow will either justify or they will not. I am only
marginally hopeful; at this moment the gates of Troy look
formidable indeed, armoured with suspicion.

TWO

I confess to admiring Sartre and Brecht above all others.
And in this I am a Chinese, sharing my enthusiasm shoulder
to shoulder with millions of others. But be sure of one thing:
the pure love of the disciple contains the seeds of murder.
Today he mounts the master's massive back, tomorrow he
will kick the old man in the neck.

THREE

Consider this book a single motion in the choreography of a
wider folly . . .
    How reassuring to think of literature in terms of enter-
tainment and pleasure, for how demonstrably true! But
once you pose a wider question, once you consider literature
in its possible relationships to philosophy and politics, as a
contribution to social consciousness, as a stimulant to social
action, you begin to climb a hill which may not exist. The
experts remind us time and again that no concrete evidence

exists linking any obscene or pornographic novel to any particular act of sexual violence or aggression. Very well. And does not the same scepticism, the same lack of tangible proof, the same dependence on abstract speculation and normative assumption, equally apply to literature and politics as to literature and sex? A dirty book will certainly give a man an erection but will it lead him to rape a schoolgirl in a public park? A good radical novel will equally certainly bring the reader to a high state of social indignation, but will it carry his feet a step closer to the barricades? I am constantly shadowed by an unpleasant thought: that in the sphere of socio-political action, all artistic activity is surplus-activity.

In 1757 Rousseau wrote to d'Alembert. 'I hear it said that tragedy leads to pity through fear. So it does; but what is this pity? A fleeting and vain emotion which lasts no longer than the illusion which produced it . . . a sterile pity which feeds on a few tears and which has never produced the slightest act of humanity.' Rousseau was prejudiced, of course, but few men have had more illuminating prejudices. And then he goes on to a paradox: 'The more I think about it, the more I find that everything that is played in the theatre is not brought nearer to us but made more distant.' And why? Because, he says, the effect of art is usually ' . . . to present virtue to us as a theatrical game, good for amusing the public, but which it would be folly seriously to attempt introducing into society.'

Such words must darken the brow of every committed writer.

In my gloomier moments (they are numerous) I see it like this:

The advanced industrial societies, particularly those blessed by capitalist affluence, throw up a superfluous superstructure of writers, intellectuals, dons and pundits, all or most of them well cared for materially by colleges, institutions, grants, publishers' advances and stipends, and all engaged in mental activity which advances the productive

capacity of society little or nothing. Frustrated and sometimes enraged by their own irrelevancy, a proportion of these
scribes 'breaks away' and announces its unshakable intention of overthrowing the system which patronises it. A great
deal of talking, scribbling and junketing to and fro takes
place, manifestoes are signed, conferences on the 'Dialectics of Liberation', etc., are attended to the enormous advantage of the airlines, highly sophisticated yet obscure treatises
are lobbed like bombs at the octopus eye of 'the system',
and the air is full of noise. Meanwhile the real victims of
social oppression, the poor, or the workers, or the blacks,
or the natives or whatever, either know nothing of this
palaver in high places or observe it with uncomprehending
amazement.

. . . At Heathrow Airport I run into a fellow intellectual,
writer or academic. We are both bound for New York. Indeed we sit next to each other on the same plane, order the
same whisky and soda and consume the same carefully
packaged lunch. However I ought to tell you that this fellow
is a notorious liberal . . . and that during his two-week sojourn
at the University of California he will undoubtedly employ
every mendacious trick of rhetoric at his disposal to reinforce the values of the 'system'. But I am quite different. It is
true that I also am temporarily a visiting professor and that
our financial remuneration will be of similar proportions, but
there all resemblance ends (except perhaps for our accents,
educational backgrounds, cut of coat and size of domestic
establishment in London). For I — and this is the crux —
am taking the opportunity (a seminar on Kafka and Brecht,
by the way) to launch into the minds and hearts of my
students a set of values and propositions which can only
contribute to the radical and revolutionary overthrow of the
entire authoritarian, militaristic, monopolistic, post-industrial, neo-capitalist system.

I make this point, firmly, perhaps heatedly, to my liberal
colleague as our plane descends over Kennedy Airport. He
blinks at me with apparent contempt.

'You are being paid to masturbate,' he says.

What!

'Listen to me,' he says. 'No one is afraid of you. You may not know who you are but the system, as you call it, does. You evolve your own questions and then you answer them; you engage in the most elaborate charades, letting your tongue luxuriate in words like "revolution", "guerrilla warfare" and "contestation", while in fact all you are doing is chain-smoking in small seminar rooms or writing introverted books destined to be read by your fellow onanists. You are always on the verge of breaking out onto the parade ground of relevance, that concrete sierra where the word and the bullet are one. You never do. The circle remains closed.'

My colleague and I pass through immigration and customs.

'Care to share a taxi?' he asks, producing from his briefcase a well-thumbed volume of speeches by Germany's latter-day George Orwell, Günter Grass.

The taxi lurches along the dockland cobbles, then thrusts into the Hobbesian bedlam of the lower West Side.

My colleague now begins to quote Grass on leftist intellectuals: '"Dancing godlike over the exhaust fumes of our society, they diffuse their academic Marxism into the empyrean and turn their attention to the far-off misery of Indo-China and Persia, which, thanks to their intellectual elevation, they have no difficulty in understanding . . . And who would expect this fashionably cosmopolitan élite to rub shoulders with our *petit bourgeois* Social Democrats . . . ?"'

My friend closes the book and offers me a king-size cigarette.

FOUR

But, as Eric Bentley has said, 'an artist cannot give up

regarding himself as the conscience of mankind, even if
mankind pays no attention.'

On can reasonably suppose that socio-political action is
shaped by group consciousness. In so far as literature and
art are tributaries flowing to and from the great river of
ideology there is a *prima facie* case for their practical relevance. What we have to guard against — a central theme of
this book — is allowing these tributaries to become diversions. Once art assumes a therapeutic or cathartic function,
then energies, beliefs, passions and dreams which might
otherwise be translated into militant activism are siphoned
off, turned in on themselves, and encouraged to spawn
exotic foliage in a highly cultivated garden closed to the
general public. One gets this feeling on leaving a theatre
noted for its daring, avant-garde, anti-establishment productions. The mood of the audience can all too easily resemble that of a wealthy lady who has spent the afternoon
bringing comfort to the poor and the sick: she has done her
bit, she has been in holy communion with virtue, her guilt is
assuaged, her small thirst for a better world quenched, and
now she must hurry, for the real world, her world, is waiting.
When you close a book or the curtain comes down, the game
is over.

This sense of a termination, of a finality, of a self-contained illusion abruptly closed is what the committed writer
must oppose.

To do this, I suggest, we are by no means obliged to offer
violence to art; nor do I have in mind any device so clumsily
transparent as carrying the action from the auditorium into
the streets. (If this is the way, the novel becomes irrelevant.)
Even the most violently mobile novel, play or film achieves
in retrospect a quality of still-life, and therefore of 'apart-
ness' and irrelevance, if it encourages total illusion, empathy
and catharsis. The truth is, the finality of a text is a myth
encouraged by the majority of writers who believe that a
book or play justifies itself only if it effectively lays claim to
a self-contained existence. But a book has no absolute

moment of genesis and no absolute moment of completion
or self-fulfilment. What appears to be the 'final', printed
text is itself an arbitrary version 'frozen' by a number of contingent factors or compromises — a publisher's deadline, the
need for money, mental exhaustion. The text is 'caught' in
motion like a butterfly is caught in flight or a facial expression is caught by the flick of a camera shutter. The next
moment things would have been different. A radical committed literature, in order to break out of purdah, out of that
exotic yet secluded garden called 'art', in order to break
into the general group consciousness, must first shed its
pretensions to still-life and self-containment. It must display
itself in constant motion, as a process, as a transparency, as
something intransitive as well as transitive.

The Old Left — the broad socialist movement of a century
or more — has been greatly attached to literary realism. You
first take a social situation, an instance of class struggle and
exploitation, and you then present it in fictional or dramatic
form, as faithfully and realistically as possible. Literature
here is a means and not an end. I do not suggest that literature should become an end in itself, its own object, but I do
suggest that the view of literature as a vehicle for representational mimesis, working through illusion, self-containment
and empathy, is now historically obsolete and ideologically
retrograde. It is, in any case, a lie. It relies on tricks,
techniques, sleight of hand, magic, hypnotism, hidden persuasion. It defeats its own objective. It distinguishes between 'form' and 'content' in a way which is banal, philistine
and erroneous.

Let me offer an assertion which I shall instantly retract.
It is this: in our present situation, what counts about a
committed book is not what it says but how it says it. But I
take that back. The statement is internally contradictory.
Furthermore it implies a sympathy for ultra-modernism
which I do not possess.

What, then, am I saying? A distinguishing feature of our
age, of the late-industrial and post-industrial societies, is the

battle which rages within and around the means of communication. In the old revolutionary parlance the 'means of communication', to be instantly seized by the revolutionary power, meant railways, postal services, telegraph, telephone and radio. But in modern mass society the communications network is more complex and more ramified. It begins with the first book a child is offered, the first words he hears from his parents, the first lessons in school, and it ends with the maturing adult bombarded by every conceivable form of media, most of them regulated by partial and sectarian interests whose sole task (apart from making money) is to condition and manipulate a mass audience into conformity with the central values and behavioural norms of the system. It therefore seems clear to me that this fact, this syndrome of signals flashing from a few brains to millions of ears and eyes, offers the first area of confrontation for a radically committed literature and art. The battle is joined in the area of general consciousness and communications. A literature which aspires to combat false consciousness, mystification and noxious alienation, must take as its first point of consideration its own nature and possibilities as a form of communication. And this, I suggest, primarily involves *not* substituting one mystique for another, one illusion for another, one kind of magic for another, one form of hidden persuasion for another.

Which is precisely what the traditional realist left-wing novel or play does.

But if you wish to see it stated in less normative terms, it's a matter of not trying to reach the moon on a bicycle. A literature which invites its audience to question the prevailing social structure and social consciousness must constantly question and expose itself. The power of language reassociates itself with the perception of language. An honest literature will divorce itself from the contemporary obsession with manipulated *effects*. Allow me a touch of McLuhanesque glibness: the product is the process. Language and literature must revive their true identity — as the cutting edge of

perception. Creativity and the critical spirit must achieve a
new harmony and interdependence.

FIVE

If we divide all creative writing into 'public' and 'private' we
do something wild yet illuminating. Where does the distinction lie? Not — let this be clear — in the size of the
audience or the range of the medium involved. A nineteenth-
century Earl of Derby embarked on the immense labour of
translating the *Odyssey* and was afterwards content to show
his text to a small circle of friends. But these friends were
reading a public poem. Make Jane Austen available to
millions of viewers by adapting her novels for television and
you will still have a private writer. Nor can we simply say
that the public novel treats of public affairs (the corridors of
power) while the private novel treats of private affairs
(hearth, home and heart). If this held good, *Middlemarch*
would be an eminently private novel instead of an eminently
public one, which it is.

It was George Eliot who said that there is no private life
untouched by a wider public life. And this statement perhaps
sums up the central proposition or perspective of public
writing: no man is an island. Public writing gravitates from
the particular to the general, from the human interior to the
social exterior, from the core to the context, from the contingent to the predictable. Wells put the case for public
writing, but without using the word: 'You see now the
scope of the claim I am making for the novel; it is to be the
social mediator, the vehicle of understanding, the instrument of self-examination, the parade of morals and the exchange of manners, the factory of customs, the criticism of
laws and institutions and of social dogmas and ideas.' The
great Russian novelists are almost invariably public writers;
this holds good not only for the socialist realists but also for
their opponents, for Pasternak's *Dr Zhivago* or Solzhenitsyn's

The First Circle. Private writing, on the other hand, is distinguished by its preoccupation with the individual, the unique and idiosyncratic, with the obscure recesses of the mind and heart. The public writer points to the orchestra, the private writer to the soloist. The one is philosophical in tendency, the other psychological. The epic form is public, the lyric private. It is a matter of mood, sensibility and range of reference. Balzac, Dickens and Zola are obviously public writers, Keats, Baudelaire, Proust and Gide private ones. Ibsen is public, Chekhov private. Shaw, Brecht, Sartre and Snow public, Virginia Woolf, Nathalie Sarraute and Iris Murdoch private. Females tend towards the private, but there are exceptions. Mailer is public, Updike is private. Of course the model is not always easy to apply. The great writers (Shakespeare, Tolstoy, Joyce) span both sensibilities, both dimensions of reference with such masterful assurance that they threaten to explode the categories. One could argue all night whether Camus' novel, *The Fall*, was essentially public or private. Even so, I hold to the distinction as a useful working proposition. One could without too much strain and stretch reclassify Shakespeare's plays along these lines. The dichotomy lives and reverberates at the heart of the creative literary mind from Greek times to our own. I know of no title more private than *Sense and Sensibility*, of none more public than *USA*.

It is public writing and public writing alone that I shall discuss in this book. ('Shall discuss' is relevant only to the reader's time-scale, not my own; the introduction is written last of all.) The public writer need not be a radical or committed to political change, but I insist that the committed radical must be a public writer. (Ionesco would not agree.) That this kind of writing, with its special motivation and aims, is only one kind among many is a fact which I recognise without heartache. I do not aspire to join the ranks of those who, like Prynne, Praisegod Barebones and Rousseau, wanted to banish light and frivolous entertainment from the city of virtue. (Not that private writing is necessarily light or frivolous.) I am only discussing what interests me and I take it for granted that what interests me is interesting. The assumption is no doubt fragile, but without it writing would be impossible.

SIX

By way of a political memoir . . .

I first went up to Oxford in the autumn of 1956. A week or so later the Russian tanks entered Budapest and the Anglo-French paratroops dropped over Port Said. This was fortunate for us, for every generation of radical intellectuals needs a political crime whose cud they can chew for the rest of their lives. Our fathers, the young men of the thirties, have set an example, never relaxing the grip of their ageing jaws on the time of high historical temperature during which they grew into manhood. Three decades later they continue to derive their waning voltage from the dilemmas that history once inflicted upon them. They have carried the art of literary self-pity to a high peak: Spain, fascism, Munich, the Nazi-Soviet Pact — how terrible it all was for *them*.

I have to react against this. The significance of Hungary and Suez is not that they scarred our tender sheltered souls. But the long-term effects are worth noting. I say 'long-term' because we, raw and freshly panting from military service, were not yet capable of formulating our own positive response. I, for example, knew nothing of Khrushchev's February speech in the course of which he had shattered the myths and dreams of two generations of fellow-travellers; I knew nothing because at the time I had been playing soldier-games in the Ghanaian bush, pitting my ferocious black legions against an ever-absent foe. And now, in the dry, sunny weeks of this first Oxford autumn, the mind remained politically lazy and obtuse from parade grounds, bullshit and only recently abandoned dreams of having Nasser's balls. Every new institution keeps you on the move: now it was no longer klaxon-voiced sergeants trumpeting the reveille of fear, it was soft-voiced tutors with their more subtly persuasive demands that kept the legs constantly on the move, from library to lecture hall to tutorial, in pursuit of a neat, effective account of why Hengest and Horsa had conquered ancient England. In such conditions, the analysis of the two great contemporary imperialisms, the Communist and capitalist, would have to wait. In fact we waited until older voices, seasoned in pain and disappointment, told us what to think and how to begin again. We eventually adopted *their* new beginning, their New Left — and were thus destined to become the last of the old rather than the first of the new.

It did not seem so at the time. We adhered fervently and proudly to a New Left which combined a deepened anti-capitalism (hostility to war, nuclear weapons, colonialism, profiteering, social injustice, the false anti-values of commercialism) with a new, renovated, de-bureaucratised, non-authoritarian Marxism. When, not so long afterwards, the *real* change came, the real tidal wave, we were as bewildered and indignant as Danton and Kerensky had been when the Jacobins and Bolsheviks thrust them contemptuously aside. Little did we know that we were playing out, or rather joining in, a drama relevant only to older men; that this was the last scene in 'The God that Failed', an epic whose long run makes *The Mousetrap* seem by contrast a first-night flop.

But this was no accident. Those who are not ready to make their own philosophy borrow others'. Our radicalism was crippled by our life-style. We grew our hair long — long enough to dirty our collars. But when a few years and several carefully acquired degrees later, we caught sight of the first shoulder-length male locks bobbing down the High or up the Broad, we felt the soft glove of history on our shoulder. Of course we knew about doing things and not just talking: our fathers had gone to Spain, ought we not to follow them to Algeria to fight for the FLN? In the long vacation.

Nor did we eat South African fruit. And sometimes we would challenge authority to the extent of marching to an American airbase instead of reading an essay on Elizabethan foreign policy.

Nothing much had changed in thirty years. Fascism, Spain, Munich, the war, the cold war, Hungary, Suez — that algebraic sequence so emphasised by political historians, that series of profoundly disruptive and formative shocks, well, don't pay too much attention to it. Many animals change their pelts once a year: likewise the Old Left. We, like our fathers, anxiously climbed a ladder which we indulgently hacked to pieces with our tongues. Radical goldfish in a conservative bowl. We denounced the privileged basis of things but had little or no perception about the things themselves. The word 'structure' may today have been debased by fashionable exploitation, but it is a word we sorely lacked. We were long-distance radicals. Our consciences were born to be astronauts. As for what lay right there beneath our feet, those feet never ceased to hurry up and down the library steps. Academic curricula, academic learning, the tutorial, lecture and essay, these were validated by centuries of proven success. We had come to enjoy the best; this was the best. Alpha, beta, gamma; the magic, make-or-break symbols of introverted ambition, the judgments of Solomon. Excellence, success, prizes, ambition, careers: we could turn our backs on none. We were like servants: we groused about personalities in whispers below stairs. It did not occur to us to sabotage the staircase let alone call into question the house. Our Marxism was all in our essays and in the occasional causes we occasionally supported. We neither understood nor challenged the very structures within which we lived and worked — local structures of learning, social behaviour and authority. We never gave the Proctors any trouble except as individual miscreants to be fined or otherwise punished.

Rationality, knowledge, formal logic, evidence, analysis, proof . . . The feet would not and indeed should not move unless the head could provide six good reasons and counter all possible objections. We never ran up a road unless we knew where it led; consequently we hardly ever ran. We were good Oxford men, proud to be scholars, exhibitioners and commoners of our respective colleges, fired with group loyalty. Some of us happened to be Marxists as well. Or thought we were.

From 1956 until the present I have been working inside various universities, first as student, then as graduate and finally as teacher. In the mid-1960s the hurricane began to blow: the extent and rapidity of its impact depended on where you lived and worked. The shock has been profound: a whole life-style blown inside out; the academy in ruins. Judged and condemned like the petrified corpses of Pompeii, condemned to remain what, during a few formative years, we had become, all our assumptions, priorities and acquired traits of personality were mocked and buffeted by the howling winds of revolution. Like Panzer divisions, the profane principles of participation and collective dissent have penetrated the Holy Sanctuary of knowledge, culture, authority. (Eliot, Eliot, where art thou now?) The university teacher who travels stores his paper clips in a crash helmet. To be shouted down by one's pupils is a routine rite; to be physically barred from one's classroom by a solid wall of undergraduate bodies no longer occasions surprise. So much has changed. A few years back I resigned an Oxford Fellowship on a 'matter of principle' and subsequently published my reasons for doing so. At the time the gesture seemed to claim a place on the outer fringes of heroism. But a contemporary student, bandaged from head to toe, hobbling on crutches, his lungs sandpapered by tear gas, is most unlikely to be impressed by the fact that his teacher once wrote ten thousand words complaining about a fifteenth-century college's failures to institute sensible reforms. This student won't give a fuck, and he will say so. The word 'fuck' has become for the battered pedagogic eye the most familiar of missiles: 'We don't give a fuck for facts, not your facts, how

will your facts help us to become more human? Your
fucked-up facts are hang-ups, man, alienated facts, the system's facts, bourgeois facts. We don't give a fuck for them.'
Today action is the yardstick. Today they know us not by
our good intentions but by our actions — or non-actions;
we are what we do.

I have recently taught (a banished word in certain radical
circles) not only in several established universities but also
in two break-away affairs, the Free School of New York and
the Anti-University of London. If I were to let myself go
and to offer my crippled id a span of indulgence, I would
portray our far-out radical young something like this:

Lazy. Mentally ragged. Incoherent and ignorant. Unable
to be alone, dependent on the presence of other warm flesh,
therefore unable to study, to learn, to think in solitude.
Rhetorical and repetitive and derivative in their rhetoric.
Addicted to short cuts. An inexhaustible sense of virtue and
some self-pity — the universal wicked uncle, otherwise
known as 'the system', is held responsible for all evils, including the fact that being in love is not always easy. Drugs,
sure, but who drove us to them? Stop the world I want to
get off, no wait, I'd rather burn it down if it can happen not
later than tomorrow. Addicted to what is fast, zippy, theatrical, spontaneous; suspicious of what is slow, difficult, painstaking. We live today, history is for squares. Adam and Eve,
then the student revolution. Chiliastic mysticism: man is
good, society made him bad, tomorrow after the revolution
he will be good again. Love will resume its sovereignty
(sorry, too long a word). Slogans: the revolution is a theatre,
the theatre is a revolution. Take your dreams for realities. Is
is ought and ought is is. Facts which don't help aren't worth
knowing. The posture taken for the portrait. Lethargy,
frenzy, renewed lethargy.

And yet — I cannot deny that the New Left (this real
New Left) has achieved certain objectives in five years which
the Old Left ignored for fifty. (Do not remind me that the Old
Left, far from being a composite entity, was in fact composed

of widely disparate factions, Communists, Trotskyists, Social
Democrats, Fabians, revisionists, anarchists, syndicalists,
labourites, trade unionists . . . I know it. I'll stick by my
proposition.)

What do guerrilla tactics mean and why are they so impressive? They mean starting the clean-up wherever you find
yourself and then carrying on from one room to the next.
They mean accepting revolution as a way of life, a working
principle, and not something blueprinted on paper. The New
Left are termites constantly nibbling at the foundations; the
Old Left was forever waiting for the Day of the Bulldozer.
This is what is so shattering yet so impressive for a university teacher today: the revolution is no longer an abstraction
to be discussed, dissected and debated, it is suddenly a living
organism reaching out to you. Threatening you too. Eat well
at breakfast, you may never make it across the campus court-
yard to lunch. And what resource have we now, except for a
painful schizophrenia? Because they, the students, keep on
acting, taking practical initiatives, their feet are always running ahead of our minds and their own. We wring our hands
. . . on the one hand, on the other hand . . . we are driven to
a series of *ad hoc* negative expedients . . . we don't agree that
this action was well considered, indeed it may prove counter-
productive BUT the authorities are worse . . . yes it was
senseless vandalism BUT after all we can't let the students
down . . . If you watch the troubled, riot-torn campuses you
will observe an exodus of Old Leftist dons, first a trickle of
finks, then a positive waterfall of funks, escaping to what they
hope will be calmer provincial campuses. No one can blame
them. I admire the achievements, the bravado and the inspired madness of the New Left, but I nevertheless recoil.
(When one sadly recognises what one is and always will be,
then one has entered early middle age.)

These reflections, I hope, have some relevance to the
central theme of this book: the possible relationships of literature to political commitment. A writer always has some vague,
amorphous image of his potential audience, and I make no

secret of the fact that I would prefer this book to be read by the young radicals whose ranks are closed to me rather than by the middle-aged Hampstead Pinks whom — God help me — I am soon destined to join. But the reverse is the more likely outcome. Either way, there is no evading the fact that the vast majority of marriages contracted between the political and artistic avant-gardes have resulted in crippled offspring and rapid divorce. Obviously something new — a different approach — is needed.

The aesthetics of both the Old Left and the New Left reflect their general *Weltanschauung*. The one realist, rational, wedded to the Enlightenment and to particular nineteenth-century traditions; the other dynamic, obscene, physical, noisy, expressionistic, instinctual. In my opinion neither remotely meets the needs of a contemporary radical literature. Nor do I have in mind any compromising mixture or synthesis of the two. Realism is burnt-out, obsolete, a tired shadow of a once-living force. It has to go. As for the New Left, it has made little or no contribution to the novel (which is symptomatic of a prevailing illiteracy) but a great deal to the theatre. But the aesthetic style of the New Left burns with the desperate bright brevity of a sodium flare. Like the ads and coloured seductions of the world it opposes, it is dedicated to instant consumption, instant impact, subliminal techniques. Bright colours, loud sounds, strong sensations, spontaneous Effects. A throw-away art. Sometimes an anti-art.

Both the *Weltanschauung* and the aesthetics of the New Left are youthful; which is fine. But they also look suspiciously like a cult of the Young. As each generation passes over the deadly rubicon of twenty-five (or is it thirty?) what will become of them? With what will they be equipped? A long hang-over after the party? Private degeneration and despair, perhaps apathy and cynicism, the frustrated anger of those suddenly abandoned by the carnival of light? If the city guerrillas commit cultural and political hara-kiri when they reach the dateline, the others will not. By 'the others' I mean all those who continue wisely to groom themselves for success, who study hard, acquire degrees and diplomas, marry well, all those who look for footholds and a solid career leading to wealth and power. *They* are the System everywhere. They are the realists. And they will work on steadily, year after year, climbing from floor to floor until finally, grey-haired and fifty, they gaze down from the President's office on floor ninety at the swirling, ragged, youthful mobs battling with the police and running from the mace below. Gazing down on the perennial revolt of the children.

It may be that the revolution will come. But it may be that it will not; and that socialists will find themselves engaged in a long, protracted defensive struggle against the Iron Heel, whether military, political, economic or technological. In fact this struggle goes on all the time. The New Left does not notice it because it is insufficiently spectacular. Without education (ah, but what kind of education?), learning, knowledge, rationality and self-control this battle is inevitably lost.

The proposals I make in this book have the entirely immodest ambition of contributing towards the success of that defensive battle. And if the perspective is more optimistic, more positive, more revolutionary than I imagine, then they will neither hinder nor cramp it. At least I hope not. The proposals grew out of several related activities: reading, teaching, writing. As a creative writer they already work for me as positive principles. The kind of literature and theatre I have in mind is innovatory but not brand new; it already exists embryonically and occasionally in mature form. I mean a literature which is modern but not necessarily modernist; which is alive, experimental and in constant motion, yet which does not despise or discard coherence, rationality and balance of mind. A literature aware of itself but also oriented towards the radical culture and the mental impulses which generate social action. A literature of possibilities, one which gives grave consideration to the dialectic

of praxis and the practico-inert, of 'ought' and 'is'. A literature which is creative, critical and alienated in a special
sense. A dialectical literature.

Modesty some other time.

CHAPTER ONE

On Commitment

ONE

To begin with, another cruel thrust by Günter Grass: 'From the start, even before inserting his paper into the typewriter, the committed writer writes, not novels, poems or comedies, but committed literature . . . Everything else, which takes in a good deal, is disparaged as art for art's sake.' Many others subscribe to this derogatory view of the partisan writer as someone found shovelling commitment like crude salt into the clear champagne of belles lettres. The novel being a product of a peculiarly liberal love of plenitude, diversity and individuality, it is therefore (says W. J. Harvey) incompatible with monistic fanaticism. Where (he asks) is the truly great Christian or Marxist novel? And according to Lionel Trilling, the real threat to literature derives not from ideas but from ideology — ideology being, I suppose, a sinister black bomb of obsessions aimed by pale-faced, tight-lipped fanatics at the crystal palace of culture. (It is of course impossible to imagine that Jane Austen, for example, ever glimpsed an ideology outside her window, a system of beliefs and assumptions and preferences, latent perhaps, but expressing the world view of a particular social class . . .)

An American critic, Gerald Rabkin, has this to say: 'The *problem* of commitment arises when the artist is committed to values or actions extrinsic to the immediate concerns of his art, when the moral urgency of outside imperatives forces him as an artist into nonaesthetic areas of consideration.'

Here is our first encounter with the 'intrinsic' fallacy; Robbe-Grillet drives the fallacy into its own shadow when he asserts that the only valid commitment for the writer is to literature. *Poésie pure*, Honorary President of the Pantheon of Pure Literature. Is it a philistine heresy to suggest that novelists, even the better ones, occasionally write *about* something? Are the tribulations of Emma Bovary, or the sexual hang-ups of Leopold Bloom, or the running-on-the-spot of Beckett's heroes, somehow inherently aesthetic, somehow congruent with the immediate concerns of art, whereas the revolutionary activities of Gorky's Vlassova or Malraux's Kyo somehow fall into the danger zone of alien, extrinsic, outside imperatives? I am not persuaded that this is the case.

TWO

I have been taken apart, mauled and left for dead by the critic Martin Seymour Smith in the course of a general assault on the British literary Left. (Title: 'Thinking Pink'.) Apparently D. H. Lawrence was responsible for the unpleasant comment that the novelist 'is usually a dribbling liar', and this, in Mr Seymour Smith's opinion, 'nicely exposes the ghastly critical *naïveté* of the so-called committed writer in England.' A somewhat kangaroo-like *sequitur*, perhaps, but more is to come. I quote: '. . . although Sartre's philosophical arguments in favour of commitment are formidable, possessing an intellectual stamina that we are not used to from left-wing *littérateurs* in Great Britain, all his dramatic and fictional achievements have been made in spite of it. When Sartre is at his best, the novel — or the play — take over from the polemical intellect of the "dribbling" novelist himself: his imagination becomes engaged with its material.'

Oh well: certainly Sartre leads the way, but there is no reason why Nigeria should ignore atomic energy simply because Max Planck did not happen to be an African.

Notice also the adroit use of '*littérateurs*'; Mr Seymour
Smith is not the first English critic to give the impression
that only higher education saved him from the immigration
service. Meanwhile commitment becomes 'polemics' (long
live the proletariat and its vanguard the Communist Party!),
which are of course incompatible with art and the imagination. If Sartre meant something else by commitment, this
has obviously escaped our critic, who no doubt regards
Nausea as a pure work of the imagination and *Being and
Nothingness* as a pure product of the 'polemical intellect';
never the twain shall meet.

Now Mr Seymour Smith turns his guns on a very modest
novel of my own; if even Sartre cannot control his own
novels, if they 'take over', my own hopes of controlling my
creations are slender indeed. I quote: 'So far as Mr Caute's
conscious intentions are concerned, the successful parts of
The Decline of the West are accidental, one might say inci-
dental: sometimes, in individual scenes, the characters take
over, and behave independently of any theory. But Mr
Caute's view of history ultimately proves stronger than his
imagination: the result is a series of brilliant cameos, strung
too didactically together. You cannot write a novel to prove
something: if your novel succeeds, then you will inevitably
end by proving something else.'

What we have here is a fairly crude example of the fallacy
which assumes that the idiosyncratic behaviour of individual
characters springs from the author's imagination or subconscious, and is therefore compatible with art, while any
wider vision of how society works and how it might work
better emanates from theory, the intellect and the committed
conscious — all enemies of art. First we have a highly
schematic skeleton design, decided upon while the writer is
tuned in to the alien demon *logos*, and then, scattered about,
'brilliant cameos' of real flesh, blood and tears, born on to
the page when the writer has relaxed into an inspired trance
and surrendered himself to the glories of the 'imagination'.

I refer the reader to a later section of this book, which

attempts to deal with the problem of reason and imagination. I would only say here that, justified as Mr Seymour Smith may be in his value judgment of my novel, he completely misunderstands the complex oscillations, manœuvres, juxtapositions and mergers of the creative process. He makes this mistake because he wishes, like many critics, to seize upon one element in this process (social or political commitment), and to trap, corral and subdue it as if it were a mad dog run amok in a rose garden. He wishes to banish it from literature.

'You cannot write a novel to prove something: if your novel succeeds, then you will inevitably end by proving something else.' Of course the word 'prove' is misleading; literature is not physics. Illustrate or express or develop would be more helpful words. And since Camus' name now rings more harmoniously on the ear of English conservatives than that of Sartre, one might ask, comparing Camus' *Lettres à un ami allemand* (essays) with his *The Plague* (novel), did the latter not succeed in expressing, illustrating and developing many of the highly committed notions of the former? Does Camus' play, *The Just*, ultimately fail to express or illustrate the highly polemical anti-revolutionary arguments of his essay, *The Rebel*? Presumably not. Could it be that Sartre, rather than Camus, provides the whipping-boy for nine out of ten critics hostile to commitment, because Sartre's commitment tended in one political direction and Camus' in another?

My suspicions about this are deepened by the generally favourable Western reaction to the novels of Pasternak and Solzhenitsyn, both public, highly committed writers. I am not aware that the Western literary establishment accused either of vulgarising art by putting it at the service of socio-political commitment. On the contrary; their novels were hailed as devastating indictments of the Soviet, or Stalinist, system. I do not suggest that Solzhenitsyn is a right-wing or reactionary novelist; but I do suggest that *The First Circle* is as deliberately and systematically a committed novel as any

written by the literary champions of communism or revolution in the West. Yet no one complains; I am not aware that
any of these critics have chastised Solzhenitsyn for writing
a novel in which he tries to prove something; nor have they
suggested that by his very success as a novelist Solzhenitsyn
inevitably ends up by proving something else.

Consider the systematic, indeed almost obsessive manner
in which Solzhenitsyn uses *The First Circle* in order to
smash his fist into every aspect of the Stalinist system.
The ubiquitousness of fear at every level from those high
officials who tremble before Stalin in the small hours of the
night down to the simplest peasant; the cruel and passionate
depiction of the ageing Stalin, suspicious and megalomanic,
surrounded by absurd security precautions, a man aspiring
to be God; the derisive portraits of the Soviet upper classes,
fully confirming the analysis offered by Milovan Djilas in his
The New Class. 'They belonged to that circle of society
where such a thing as walking or taking the Metro is unknown . . . where there is never any worry about furnishing
a flat . . . They held that "you only live once" . . . Not a
breath of the sorrow of the world fanned the cheeks of
Innokenty and Datoma.' Elsewhere the Public Prosecutor's
daughter tells her father: 'Oh! Come off it, Father! You
don't belong to the working class. You were a worker once
for two years and you've been a prosecutor for thirty . . .
You live off the fat of the land!' We meet Abakumov, Minister of State Security, who 'had arrested and condemned
millions'. Solzhenitsyn harrowingly depicts the plight of the
wives of these millions: 'Her faced was lined, her voice rang
with the purity of intense suffering.' These were the women
who had 'to hear other people whispering they were traitors
to their country every time they went to the communal tap
for water.' And of course — a persistent theme in Solzhenitsyn's work — the vast majority of those condemned to ten
or twenty-five years hard labour were completely guiltless.
Take the story of Potapov, a designer of the Dnieper dam,
who *refused* to help the Germans reconstruct it. 'Not holding

this against him, the Soviet court gave him only ten years.'
Solzhenitsyn's indictment misses nothing: neither bogus
political trials, nor anti-semitism, nor the crudely concocted
campaign against Tito. Nor does he spare those Western
progressives who allowed themselves to be taken in by quick
white-wash façades put up for their benefit. On the last page
of the novel we find the Moscow correspondent of the Paris
Communist paper, *Libération*, in a car on his way to a hockey
match. He sees the word 'MEAT' written in four languages on
the side of a van, and makes a note to tell his readers about
the high standards of food hygiene in the Soviet Union. In
fact the van is loaded with the prisoners of Mavrino, the
men whose bitter misfortunes we have followed throughout
the novel, now on their way from the 'first circle' of hell to
the real inferno, the camps of Siberia.

I have introduced Solzhenitsyn's novel here not simply
because of its outstanding quality, not simply because I feel
myself in passionate sympathy with this persecuted writer
of genius, but more particularly because *The First Circle* is
one of the most politically committed novels ever written:
deliberately, subjectively, designedly committed. Yet, for
some reason, those Western critics who are most adamant
that art and politics don't mix raise no objections. Why?
Why is it that they reserve their condemnations for left-wing
Western writers who attack the evils of capitalism and
colonialism? Why is Mr Seymour Smith so scornful of
what happens when Sillitoe, myself and other left-wing
writers 'decide' to commit ourselves?

The word 'decide' is highly significant. It reinforces our
sense of the prevailing *logos*; commitment is depicted as
something the writer switches on and off, like the electric
heater which keeps him warm in winter. Did I 'decide' to
loathe apartheid, or the treatment of blacks in the United
States and Britain? Did I 'decide' to detest colonialism or the
exploitative manipulation of the working class under
modern capitalism? This may sound unduly rhetorical; the
critic would no doubt grant me the sincerity of my opinions

on such matters while reminding me that what is at issue is my approach to the novel, to fiction, to literature. Fair enough. It is of course true that I might, by an effort of will, or in the service of my sensibility, 'decide' to eschew all public issues in my 'artistic' writing, turning my pen to the tragic emotional consequences of loving a dog, or having a father, or being married to one lady while coveting another. I daresay that, given the time, I could turn out fifty sensitive pages on the strange alchemy of attraction and repulsion that I felt for a boy two years younger than myself while I was at school. It so happens that these themes do not seize my 'creative imagination'. It must be the case that when Marguerite Duras, whose work I admire, catches sight of two strangers seated in silence, several feet apart, on a park bench, her imagination is at once set to work — highly delightful and rewarding work. Me, I pass by. It is said that Dostoyevsky's novel, *The Possessed*, was originally inspired by a newspaper report of the execution of a handful of Russian terrorists. And I am prepared to bet that what stimulated Dostoyevsky's imagination was not the 'story-line' potential alone, but the catalytic effect of the real incident on a highly committed intelligence. It is this commitment, and not merely Dostoyevsky's craft as a novelist, which gives *The Possessed* its unity.

In England the assault on commitment is more often than not launched from the vantage point of moderation and good sense. The wild commitment mongers, intoxicated by Continental metaphysics, are brought to their senses by a healthy douche of cool empiricism (where is the truly great Christian or Marxist novel?). But on the reverse side of the empirical coin there lurks a certain mysticism. Here, once again, is Mr Seymour Smith: 'What prevents the English writer, as a writer if not as a man, from being committed to left, right, centre, or to anything else, is the genius of his native language. His beliefs are, of course, important to him; but the imagination is holy. The magnificently undefinable and unique entity of the English language exists to test the worth of, and to challenge, all dogmas and abstractions, the proponents of which often abuse it. The words take over; the purpose is truth. The right words in the right order destroy, or at least correct and modify, the predilections of the men who write them.'

I sit at my desk, re-reading this paragraph. It is a hot July day, my collar is sticking to my neck. I don't suppose that our critic feels that the genius of his native language has in a magnificently indefinable way thwarted his own case; or could it be that when this same unique entity passes from criticism, journalism, philosophy and history to 'art', to the novel, to the holy sphere of the imagination, that it undergoes an awe-inspiring metamorphosis, rising against its creator, asserting its own absolute autonomy? The words take over . . .

No. No.

THREE

Commitment, what is it?

The word came into Anglo-American critical usage during the decade following the Second World War. The impact of Sartre's thinking, particularly of his *Qu'est ce que la littérature?*, was paramount. 'Commitment' is a fairly precise, but not exact, translation of the French word *'engagement'*.

In essence, Sartre argued (a) that all writing is committed, willy-nilly, and (b) that it is the writer's duty to adopt a committed stance. The apparent contradiction here results from the attempt to make a single term service different notions. The same problem had arisen when Sartre argued (a) that all men are free by virtue of the human condition, and (b) that freedom is something a man has to choose and grasp. In the second instance Sartre employs a single word to cover both a potential and a reality; at the same time the word 'freedom' shifts semantically, meaning in the first instance the availability of choice and in the second a positive

way of life, an ethic. In the case of commitment, Sartre
transfers the word from a state of implicit ideological bias
to a strongly recommended, explicit radical philosophy. The
single word blurs the passage from the descriptive to the
prescriptive, masking the normative and ethical content it
acquires on the way.

It seems reasonable to distinguish between objective
commitment and subjective commitment; between the kind
of commitment which can be read into a book, or extracted
from it, by the reader, and the kind of commitment which
is inscribed at the outset by the writer. (Of course even in
the second case the reader has his own judgment to make;
the writer's position, as it emerges through the text, may
differ in certain respects from his own commentary on the
work.)

In the present essay, we are concerned (I am concerned)
with subjective commitment, particularly as it effects what
I have called public writing. We are dealing, therefore, with
writers for whom commitment is a positive value. What this
implies can perhaps best be illustrated by reference to extreme examples, in the supply of which the Russians have
generally been the most generous. The populist N. G.
Chernyshevsky, for example, made it painstakingly clear
that the main aim of his novel, *What Is To Be Done?* was to
propagandise the claims of Reason, Materialism, Utilitarianism, Knowledge, Enlightened Self-Interest and the 'new
men' of the 1860s who lived by these values. And then came
the whole tradition of socialist realism, set in motion by
Lenin's remark that 'Art . . . ought to unify the feeling,
thought and will of the masses, elevate them.' The Agitprop
novel was born. Extreme didactic commitment was demanded time and again by the official spokesmen for Stalinist
culture. Of these, A. A. Zhdanov deserves pride of place:
'The truthfulness and historical concreteness of the artistic
portrayal should be combined with the ideological remould-
ing and education of the toiling people in the spirit of
socialism.' Zhdanov called for 'revolutionary romanticism'.

Personally, I know of no more brazenly heuristic view of literature than this: 'At the same time as we select Soviet man's finest feelings and qualities and reveal his future to him, we must show our people what they should not be like and castigate the survivals from yesterday that are hindering the Soviet people's progress.' Meanwhile Maxim Gorky was prescribing suitable themes for budding Soviet novelists, including the cultivation of virgin lands, the moral regeneration of peasants in urban environments, and heroic construction on the White Sea. The mood in those days was tough, uncompromising. In 1930 Tretiakov had told the First Congress of Proletarian Writers: 'We can't wait forever while the professional writer tosses in his bed and gives birth to something known and useful to him alone. We assume that book production can be planned in advance like the production of textiles or steel.'

Unconscious humour was not in short supply; here is a writer called Avdennko addressing the Seventh Congress of Soviets in January 1935: 'I am strong. I cultivate in myself the best human sentiments: love, devotion, honesty, abnegation, heroism, disinterestedness — all these thanks to you, great teacher, Stalin . . .' This piety was not confined to the Soviet Union nor even to those nations where the Communists had acquired state power. In France, 'free', post-war bourgeois France, Communist writers like Aragon or Stil echoed the Zhdanovist mood to the letter. Here commitment descends to its crudest level. In Aragon's *Les Communistes*, for example, a young militant Communist recently conscripted (September '39) into the army and uncertain of his duty, happens to meet by accident the great Secretary-General of the Party, Maurice Thorez. To the young man's nervous inquiry Thorez replies: 'Nothing special. Be the best everywhere . . . do what your conscience as a Communist and as a Frenchman dictates.' The young hero, Aragon tells us sycophantically, 'blushed at the lesson'.

I could go on providing examples, but I won't. It has been my misfortune to read widely among the second- and third-rate writers of the French extreme Left. If my point is taken, I see no reason to bequeath this misfortune to my present readers. I would, however, draw their attention to modern Chinese literature, far and away the most didactic and nakedly committed in the contemporary world. The good Communist girl Chiu-lau is about to be married; but not before becoming propaganda officer of the Youth League, not before mastering the new marriage laws and not before encountering old Pai, the Party Secretary, on the eve of her wedding. Says she to the old man: 'Tell me more of my faults so that I can correct them.' Says he to the girl: 'Work hard and give your whole heart to the collective. The main thing is to be humble and learn from the people.' Or take the case of tank sergeant Hsia Kuo-yu who, although granted only twenty-five days' leave, volunteers to take messages and gifts to the families of no less than twelve comrades even though they live far apart. In the course of his journey the model tank sergeant (a) helps an old man weed his garden, (b) offers a wife and her mother-in-law a short sermon on their mutual obligations, (c) whitewashes a passing house, (d) encounters a girl called Peach who has organised a voluntary female washing brigade, and (e) even snatches a few selfish hours with his own mother before returning to his military unit and 'the offensive manœuvres he didn't want to be too late to join in'. We are back in the New Testament.

But instances of extreme dedication to political commitment are to be found in many national cultures. Among American writers of the 1930s, Clifford Odets led the way; he wanted to write plays that were 'immediately and dynamically useful'. (He did.) 'Art works', added Odets, 'should shoot like bullets.' As for the American novel, Howard Fast perhaps takes pride of place among those committed to the extreme Left. Of his novel *Spartacus* he commented: 'I wrote it so that those who read it, my children and others, may take strength for our own troubled future and that they may struggle against oppression and wrong — so that the dream of Spartacus may come to be in our own time.' In German literature, the tradition of didactic or committed writing is both old and honourable. Brecht noted in 1949 that his play *Mother Courage* should be staged in such a way as to demonstrate that 'in wartime big business is not conducted by small people. That war is a continuation of business by other means . . . That no sacrifice is too great for the struggle against war.' More recently Peter Weiss has completed a play whose very title must be among the most didactic ever invented: 'A Discourse on the Early History and the Course of the Long Lasting War of Liberation in Vietnam as an example of the Necessity for the Armed Struggle of the Oppressed against their Oppressors as also on the attempts of the United States of America to destroy the foundations of the Revolution.'

Sartre's original conception of the duties of the committed writer were not so different from those of Fast (although Sartre rejected Communist dogmas and the grosser crudities of socialist realism). In 1946 he told a UNESCO conference that the writer's responsibility — a key notion for Sartre — was to condemn injustice, whatever its source, and to throw his weight against violence, while distinguishing between violence as an end and violence as a means, between the violence instituted to sustain an oppressive regime and the violence required to overthrow it. For Sartre, the question of the age was: 'How can one make oneself a man in, by, and for history?' Could literature succeed in granting man his uniqueness, his freedom, while at the same time revealing him as a creature of situations — another key term — and of passing time? With this end in view, the writer must fashion a lucid and reflective commitment, attempting to embrace the totality of the human condition from within it. He must at all times make clear his position, adopting socialist principles, drawing attention to the predicament of the oppressed, transforming the reader's formal good will into a concrete determination to change the world by specific means. At the same time the writer must always avoid sterile dogmatism, always preserve his independence of judgment, always call a cat a cat.

Thus Sartre rejects a literature of *hexis*, one which produces a synthetic and explanatory view of life, in favour of a literature of *praxis*, one which attempts an active role in mediating between the world and man's capacity to change it. 'Literature has need of being universal', he wrote in 1964. 'The writer ought therefore to range himself on the side of the greatest number — of the two thousand million starving — if it wishes to address itself to all and to be read by all.'

FOUR

It is generally assumed that literary commitment is a special preserve of the Left. As for Right and Left, what they mean historically and in terms of political theory, your orator has already decisively resolved this question elsewhere . . . the arrogant mood of this remark to be attributed to an unduly protracted membership (ten years) of the Oxford History Club where local tribal logic insists that the more universally attacked one's theory, the more irrefutable it must be.

Left and Right are post-1789 concepts marked by the disposition of political battalions in a semi-circular parliamentary chamber, as viewed from the President's throne. The original Left (Jacobins, Chartists, etc) demanded *political* popular sovereignty: that was the central preoccupation behind the plethora of sects and programmes. The latter-day Left (socialists, Communists, etc) demand *economic* popular sovereignty as well. The dictatorial Left (Robespierre, Lenin, etc) are easy to assimilate into the concept of popular sovereignty if you (a) relax, and (b) distinguish between the long term and the short term, the final goal and the immediate necessity. (With Stalin, relaxation becomes admittedly difficult.) As for the Right, its posture is normally defensive and conservatory. It resists whatever the Left is demanding, feels nostalgic about the past and is nagged by the feeling that history is helping the other camp. The Right also has its own sects. United by its distrust of the mob and of popular sovereignty, it has been divided as to alternatives. One squad favoured divine right monarchy, another preferred a new-rich, oligarchical kingdom, a third could not forget Bonaparte, while a fourth equated equity and natural law with the enfranchisement of the £10 householders. Military rule provides the Super-answer. Leaving aside Spain, Portugal, Greece, South Africa, Rhodesia and much of Latin America, the Right in recent times has tended to concede the political struggle, granting each man his vote and concentrating instead on the preservation of economic privilege. This latter struggle is conducted in the name of free enterprise, rationalisation into larger and larger units, the rights of the individual, survival of the fittest, and other apparently compatible ideas.

The widespread belief that philosophers and writers almost invariably lean towards the Left is quite mistaken.

Early in 1871 Paris fell into the hands of an assortment of Jacobins, anarchists, socialists and Blanquists. They proclaimed a free Commune. Marx rallied to its defence, Thiers crushed it by force. This is what Gustave Flaubert had to say of the Communards: 'What retrogrades! What savages!' He suggested that the whole tribe of 'mad dogs' be sent to the galleys, but not before these 'bloody imbeciles' had been forced to clean up Paris with chains fastened to their necks. As for universal suffrage, it was in Flaubert's opinion worse than divine right, since 'the mass, the number, is always idiotic'. Anatole France described the Communard government as 'the Government of Crime and Madness'. Edmund de Goncourt concluded that a republic in France could only lead to 'the enslavement or death of the superior classes'. When Thiers' army captured Paris in a welter of bloodshed and pursued a policy of massacring suspects which shocked even the correspondent of the London *Times*, Goncourt was delighted: 'Good. There has been neither conciliation nor deals. The solution has been brutal — pure force.' Seventy-odd years later, Louis Ferdinand Céline, an undoubted genius and a future Nazi collaborator, showed that this tradition remained alive and kicking. 'The People . . . it swallows everything, it admires everything, it conserves everything, it defends everything, it understands nothing.' Barrès was a diehard conservative, Claudel was pleased to become ambassador to Franco's Spain. Drieu la Rochelle, Brasillach, Abel Bonnard, Alphonse de Chateaubriant and Rebatet embraced fascism. So also, in different styles, did the Italian writers d'Annunzio and Marinetti.

The case of Ezra Pound is well known. Yeats had tendencies too. Mr Eliot was certainly not a fascist, but he did have occasion to remark: 'On the whole, it would appear for the best that the great majority of human beings should go on living in the place where they were born.' It was Eliot's opinion that, 'in a healthily *stratified* society, public affairs would be a responsibility not equally borne: a greater responsibility would be inherited by those who inherited special advantages, and in whom self-interest, and interest for the sake of their families ("a stake in the country") should cohere with public spirit.' In Germany, the intellectuals expressed their detestation of the mob in terms less anaemic and whiggish. Stefan George dreamed of an élite leadership of the *Volk* in the style of the Knights Templar of the Crusading era — a time when the white God's burden had not yet become the white man's burden. Nietzsche said, simply: 'Life is a well of joy; but where the rabble drinks too, all wells are poisoned.' Fascism and neo-fascism held a strong appeal for the writers of Eastern Europe as well. To take only one example: the Hungarian writer Dezsó Szabó had a phenomenal popular success with his novel, *The Swept-Off Village*, which lashed out variously at the corrupt urban bourgeoisie, socialism, parliamentary democracy and the universal Jewish conspiracy.

I spent part of a summer in Bloomington, Indiana, a beautiful campus where the greenness of tree and parkland is sustained by water sprinklers rotating soothingly on

sunny evenings. It was 1967. Not many miles away Detroit
and Newark, broiled beyond endurance, crackled with gun-
fire. The cities were choking on arsonists' smoke, while
police sirens, ambulances, fire engines and panic swept
through the ghettoes and their environs. Here in Bloomington the students, big, healthy boys and girls dressed in sweat
shirts and tartan bermudas, had read the newspapers, seen
the photographs and decided (for the most part) that the
black case was a just one.

It was in this atmosphere that I went one evening to see a
film club showing of a classic of the silent cinema, *The Birth
of a Nation*. A mimeographed information sheet explained
that this film, made in 1915 by D. W. Griffith, 'is equal with
Brady's photographs, Whitman's war poems . . . it is equal,
in fact, to the best work that has been done in this country.'
A synopsis followed: the film covers the first period of the
Civil War, the era of Reconstruction and the birth of the
Ku Klux Klan. It depicts Negroes as shiftless, irresponsible,
violent, corrupt and lustful, while the upper class white Con-
federate families provide pure, chivalrous heroes and delicate,
romantic heroines. They are the defenders of what the film's
commentary calls the Aryan heritage.

The projector begins to hum, the lights go out, the screen
flickers and we, despite the air conditioning, begin to sweat.
Here, exquisitely photographed, smoke is seen drifting
above the battlefield of Gettysburg. The awkward, jerky
style of the early scenes, and the subtitles peppered with
exclamation marks, have the effect of alienating a modern
audience and permitting it to greet Griffith's denigratory
depiction of Negroes with derisive laughter.

The film lasts three hours. The cumulative, epic effect
begins to impress. It is a masterpiece. But Sartre has said
that there can be no great work of literature which does not
contribute to the liberation of man and surely this must hold
true of film as well . . . Griffith is now drawing his lines of
convergence. The white Cameron family, armed only with
faith and fortitude amidst the ruins of Southern civilisation,

are in flight from a rabble of drunken, lustful black soldiers. Form, content and meaning are now juxtaposed in an alarmingly unfamiliar and subversive combination. Our whole conditioning as spectators dictates that the heroine in flight, pale, panting, scrambling over rocks, glancing wildly over her shoulder, seeking sanctuary — she must find that sanctuary, she must escape. It is not simply that we have a prejudice against rape and murder, carried from the outer world to art: it is equally the case that we are attuned to *form*, that form and structure by means of persistent convention dictate a certain meaning, a certain empathy. The form is tripartite: heroine running, cut; frenzied rapists pursuing and gaining on her, cut; rescuers galloping in clouds of dust and banging coconut shells . . .

Now it is true that the more radical *illuminati* amongst us have long since pierced the sinister racial conventions of the Western. In theory, at least, we have reminded ourselves that it was not a case of white civilisation marooned and marauded by bad Indians, but rather a matter of white imperialism penetrating and plundering the land of a free people. In theory we know that the bad, savage, scalping, painted, lynx-eyed, hooting Indians were approximately what we would today call freedom fighters. And the good ones, the patient, dignified chiefs who kept their word, they were the collaborators, the village headmen of the South Vietnamese regime. But the work of a Griffith and your average Western do not belong to the same sphere of artistic and intellectual impact. Griffith is committed, engaged, he is an artist, he has the power to penetrate us at a fundamental level, to force a response.

Newark and Detroit are burning. Already the Black Power orators have insisted, and we have accepted, that the white race in America is not divided into the good and the bad, the Governor Wallaces and the liberals; we have accepted the proposition that American society as a whole is flawed by collective socio-economic racial domination and exploitation. And therefore the black looter, arsonist, rapist or sniper is to be understood not as a looter, arsonist, rapist or sniper, but as a Black . . . Yet the audience in the university cinema has fallen silent. The occasional snickers and jibes have died away. That nice young Cameron girl, trembling inside a frail wooden shack, doesn't she come from a slave-owning class, aren't her hands smooth and flawless from the toil of other women? The hooded Klansmen pounding to the rescue, is not their just fate failure and rout? But no, the audience, myself included, are shifting our feet and urgently digging our knees into the flanks of the Klansmen's horses . . . the girl is saved; embraces, tears, music, it had to be like that, the form, the convention has overwhelmed us, we emerge into the hot night the prisoners of reaction.

You say that I have been carried away by a delight in paradox. After all, an audience's perfectly natural repugnance at the prospect of a young girl being raped and murdered does not necessarily imply that they have swallowed the Aryan philosophy and the virtues of slavery wholesale. Agreed, yet not granted. Steinbeck said of *The Grapes of Wrath*: 'The ideal act of propaganda consists in identifying your cause with values that are unquestioned.' Correct. But this identification is achieved not simply by creating an *equation of content* (young virgin equals white civilisation, lustful drunkard equals black barbarity), but also by means of a particular harmony of form and rhythm. The forms employed by arts are symbolic by convention and association: they engender meaning symbolically. Imagine — make an image which is both pictorial and conceptual — a bourgeois audience in Paris, London, Vienna, or New York emerging from a cinema. They have just seen Eisenstein's *Potemkin* or *October* or Pudovkin's *The Last Days of St Petersburg*. Question them: you, sir, you, madam, have you been converted to Bolshevism by this film? No I have not, a gentleman says, looking for a taxi; oh no, nothing like that, a lady replies indignantly, searching for her escort. You have discovered how to ask the wrong question. You have placed yourself on a false axis of interrogation, you have compelled obeisance to the Reality Principle where in fact the Illusion Principle continues to dominate the inner landscape. You have, to draw what is more a metaphor than a parallel, asked a man who has just seen *Hamlet* whether the characters and action of the play are real. He is bound to say no; he is not a fool.

The higher the level of art, the more difficult it becomes to surrender to the aesthetic experience while staunchly resisting the message. The art of a Griffith or a Pudovkin should not be likened to an engine dragging a wagon loaded with political dynamite up a hill. The power of art is to present and impose a symbolic unity, a coherence of forms, a language of its own, a realignment of associations, an architecture of images, all of which cannot be immunised or dispersed by objections posed on a different level and in a different code. If I awake from a nightmare screaming, flooded by horror and fear, and I am then reassured by other members of the household that it was only a dream, that we are all quite safe and not, as I had supposed, in mortal peril — then I accept their assurances, I believe them, I recognise my dream for what it was. But the dream and its content, de-realised at the level of concept and knowledge, retains its reality, its meaning, at the level of symbol and image.

I have digressed from Griffith and right-wing commitment. But the digression, I hope, is a crescent leading back to the main road from which it came. I have already emphasised the extent to which conservative or avowedly reactionary socio-political attitudes have appealed to highly gifted representatives of the intellectual and artistic community both in Europe and America. Yet the notion of literary commitment remains tied, almost umbilically, to the Left. Why? Is it simply due to an accident of genetics — that Sartre and his friends who developed the theory of *engagement*, happened to be dedicated socialists? I doubt it. Sartre, after all, merely gave a particular philosophical expression to a widely prevalent left-wing doctrine, a doctrine articulated and hammered home even more forcefully and didactically by Zhdanov, Fadeyev and the Communist exponents of socialist realism. The left-wing literature of the 1930s, pre-Sartrian literature if you like, was furiously committed, not only in the Soviet Union but also in Europe and America. The 'accident' ceased to look accidental.

The root of the matter lies in the different nature of left- and right-wing ideologies. Right-wing ideology tends to be implicit, masked, refracted when it is conservative, and only explicit and self-aware when it is reactionary. The conservative wishes to preserve the fabric of the existing social order, whereas the reactionary aspires to turn the clock back, to reclaim a noble but forgotten age. The reactionary therefore has it in common with the socialist that he demands *change*. The aim of an ideology of change is to infuriate, activate and mobilise public sentiment; the aim of ideologies of conservatism is to pacify, refract and divert public opinion. And because ideology proves to be such a terrible weapon in the hands of the iconoclasts, conservatives have learned to distrust and disparage ideology as such. They claim to have none; only their radical enemies are victims of the virus. Even in moments of revolutionary ascendancy, in times of high historical temperature, the bourgeoisie never recognises itself as the bourgeoisie. It issues 'Declarations of Independence', proclaims the 'Rights of Man', and points out the universal benefits to be derived from free enterprise, free trade or individual liberty. The bourgeois calls himself, simply, Man. What benefits him will surely benefit everyone. (Low wages are in the interests of the worker if they ensure his continued employment.) Rationalism, utilitarianism, positivism or pragmatism are presented to society not as philosophical developments of a particular class ideology, but as contributions to universal truth.

The ideologies which give expression to the claims of the oppressed and exploited classes, when they achieve a *radical* form, are explicitly divisive; they refer to 'us' and 'them', they call for intensified class struggle, and they describe the rationality of the capitalist as the misery of the worker. (The whites of America, seriously challenged, now say: 'aren't we all men and women, can't we integrate and live together?' The blacks say, 'you are white, we are black'.) Between radical ideologies which are reactionary and those which are progressive (a loaded term, I admit), disparity of content is offset by certain similarities of form and tone. Whatever their mythical and mystifying content, radical reactionary ideologies like nazism and fascism aim to bring strife and incompatibility into the open, to set one man against another, to prepare for war. Thus, so long as the white slave-owning class of the American South felt secure in its property and way of life, its ideology was mainly implicit, an *ad hoc* conglomeration of racial assumptions and prejudices; it required the invading Union armies, the rebellion of the Negroes and the era of Reconstruction to engender the more coherent supremacist ideology of the Klan. In the context of rightist art, Griffith's *The Birth of a Nation* is unusually explicit; and this can be attributed to the director's retrospective bitterness at the extinction of the old Southern civilisation, his fierce determination to halt the process of nigger emancipation before it destroyed the whole society, and his residual dream of turning the clock back. If we were to extend the category of 'artist', as well we might, to writers like Nietzsche and Spengler, we would have more evidence of how the sense of an old, hierarchical and fundamentally noble order decaying engenders a vividly explicit commitment and a rhetoric which is not only passionate but often beautiful. In differing forms, one finds the same phenomenon in Hamsun, Céline, Yeats, Pound, Deszó Szabó and Faulkner. And in Eliot too, despite his avowed distrust of philosophical or heuristic poetry.

The general conservative distrust of ideology has as its close corollary a distrust of literary commitment, and its equation of commitment with explicit, subjective commitment. And so, in answer to the question posed earlier, conservative ideology tends to emerge from literature in an implicit form. It often passes unnoticed. The characteristics of this evasion are various, but familiar: an aversion to political themes or, alternatively, a depiction of politics as a self-contained power game divorced from society at large; a concentration on the individual and his psychology; a preference for the private as opposed to the public, for the microscope rather than the telescope. Finally, a view of art as a thing-in-itself, as something created, practised and enjoyed for its own particular pleasure.

FIVE

. . . On proletarian literature:

'There is no proletarian culture,' said Trotsky, 'and there never will be any. It is impossible to create a class culture behind the backs of a class.' (Substitute 'ideology' for 'culture' in Trotsky's statement, and you make a nonsense, you are pulling the hairs out of Marx's beard by the tuft.) Bogdanov and the proponents of the Proletkult disagreed. After all if the proletariat was inscribed on the tablet of history as *the* ultimate revolutionary class, and if, furthermore, Marxism, that is to say scientific socialism, represented proletarian ideology in its purest and most intransigent form — then did it not follow that the most revolutionary, didactic and committed art must be proletarian art? In fact the Bolshevik Party increasingly disassociated itself from this view, if largely because 'proletarianism' posed at an organisational level a challenge to Party control. The Proletkult was squashed and Bogdanov was despatched to the dog house. The small 'proletarian' groups which remained active in the late twenties squabbled among themselves and managed to antagonise many writers. Nevertheless an International Conference of Proletarian Writers was convened at Kharkov in 1930, attended by eminent foreign proletarians like Louis Aragon and Henri Barbusse. The Great Depression arrived, and now the spectre of proletarian art began to haunt America. In 1935 the Congress of American Writers met. Many of its members had been practising, perpetrating and propagandising proletarian literature, and all that now remained was to find out what it was. Should it be defined and consecrated in terms of (a) the class origins of the writer, (b) the *milieu* described in the play or novel, or (c) the ideological perspective of the work? The first option was clearly a non-starter; the horny hands of toil were somewhere else, down the pits or in the breadlines. The second option posed problems. Anyone familiar with Zola's novels or D. H. Lawrence's trilogy of plays about the Nottinghamshire mining community must have realised that a detailed, naturalistic and even warmly sympathetic description of working-class trials and tribulations did not guarantee a socialist perspective, let alone a revolutionary perspective. For the majority of writers attending the congress, the true formula resided in a synthesis of (b) and (c), of a faithful, densely documented portrait of working-class environments combined with an emphasis on class struggle and on the necessity of a revolutionary solution.

But the working class stubbornly refused to write or even read proletarian literature. The only exceptions were a minority of trade union militants, Communist activists, a sprinkling from the skilled trades, particularly in the Jewish sectors of New York. But the majority knew nothing about it.

Nowadays the younger Marxist critics are more sophisticated. They have banished proletarian art along with the cult of personality, dogmatism, Zhdanovism and all the other 'errors of the past'. Thus André Gisselbrecht, prominent among the new wave of Communist critics in France, writes: 'We do not for our part acknowledge some (literary) forms which might be "bourgeois" and some which might be "proletarian". We quite simply distinguish between intentions which are revolutionary and others which are not: between those who question the world and others who accommodate to it.' It seems to me, however, that one must go further; that if the notion of a proletarian culture or art is

meaningless, so equally must be the notion of a proletarian
ideology. To paraphrase Trotsky: 'It is impossible to create
a class ideology behind the backs of a class.'

But this is precisely what Marxists have attempted to do
for more than a century. The notion of 'proletarian art' is
part of a wider fallacy. The vocabulary of Marxist aesthetics
is pervaded by socio-normative confusions which in turn
originate in Marx's refusal to distinguish between the descriptive and the prescriptive, the 'is' and the 'ought'. Thus
the basic sociological vocabulary (aristocracy, bourgeoisie,
petty-bourgeoisie, proletariat, peasantry) is wrenched from
its moorings in an observable, measurable reality and assigned
a particular teleology. A necessary dualism gives way to a
mystifying monism. Instead of saying, 'the proletariat is
conservative today, we must work to make it revolutionary
tomorrow', the Marxist first equates proletarian ideology
with the ideal mission and then describes as 'bourgeois' all
instances of proletarian consciousness which do not corre-
spond to the ideal mission. An astonishing paradox ensues.
On the one hand we are given a materialist formula: 'life
determines consciousness'; we are then left with the task of
explaining how the working class, clearly proletarians in
terms of their structural relationship to capital and to the
means of production, continue for decades to share very
largely the consciousness of the bourgeoisie. The moment of
authentic proletarian consciousness, the moment when the
proletariat becomes truly itself, is always one step into the
future. Marxists will explain their monist vocabulary in
terms of the fact that scientific socialism is not only a system
of explaining the world, it is also a crucial weapon in changing
it. Hence the emergence of an ideal vocabulary, sculptured
not out of a limited, empirical perception of reality in the
short term, but out of the deeper truth of the historical dialectic, out of the ultimate trajectory of those famous orbiting
twins, freedom and necessity.

Unfortunately such self-enclosed systems of thought
become obsessively reductionist. All particularities and

peculiarities have to be seized, melted down like scrap metal and then poured into the great categorical moulds of the system. Lenin told Gorky, when speaking of Tolstoy: 'Until this nobleman came along, there was no real peasant in our literature.' Lenin did not mean that Tolstoy was sympathetic to the plight of the Russian peasantry, he meant that Tolstoy's Christian-pacifist socialism represented 'objectively' the ideology of the discontented but still obscurantist peasant class. George Lukács, the most celebrated Marxist critic of this century, absurdly refers to Tolstoy's ideas on aesthetics as 'peasant and plebeian humanism'. Every individual tree and shrub in the landscape of literature is thus bulldozed by two steel caterpillars, Deduction and Reduction. Ralph Fox summed up the entire adventure of romanticism by calling it the most pernicious form of bourgeois illusion. The Austrian Marxist, Ernst Fischer, writes: 'Romanticism, in terms of the petty-bourgeois consciousness, is the most complete reflection in philosophy, literature and art of the contradictions of a developing capitalist society.' Well, now you know. But wait; two pages later we read this: 'What all the Romantics had in common was an antipathy to capitalism (some viewing it from an aristocratic angle, some from a plebeian) . . .' And then, after two more pages, this: 'Despite its invocation of the Middle Ages, Romanticism was an eminently bourgeois movement . . .' So there you have it. Romanticism was petty-bourgeois, aristocratic, plebeian and anti-capitalist — it was nevertheless 'eminently bourgeois'. Pass on. According to Christopher Caudwell, Byron's poetry represents the work of an aristocrat determined 'to go over to the bourgeoisie'. Caudwell called the French surrealists 'the last bourgeois revolutionaries'. Caudwell on G. B. Shaw: 'a study of the bourgeois superman'. Caudwell on D. H. Lawrence: 'A study of the bourgeois artist'. As for poor Wells, no thanks is accorded him for Mr Polly or *The Time Machine* or *The War of the Worlds* or *Kipps*; no, Wells 'is a *petit bourgeois*, and of all the products of capitalism, none is more unlovely than this class'. Another Marxist critic of the 1930s, Edward Upward, pronounced judgment that Proust, Joyce and Lawrence had 'failed' because 'they shared the life of a social class which has passed its prime . . .' Later, after the war, in the Vichinsky-Zhdanov-Fadeyev era of maximum (overkill) vituperation, a leading French Communist hatchetman, Roger Garaudy (subsequently disgraced), observed: 'Every class has the literature it deserves. The big bourgeoisie in decay delights in the erotic obsessions of a Henry Miller or the intellectual fornications of a Jean-Paul Sartre.'

So: Sartre, bourgeois writer;

Aragon, proletarian writer . . ?

We have at our disposal two distinct categorical axes, and nothing but confusion and hypocrisy can ensue from blurring this distinction. The one is sociological: aristocratic, bourgeois, petty-bourgeois, peasant, plebeian, proletarian; the other is ideological and programmatic: conservative, reactionary, liberal, socialist, Communist, anarchist, etc. Every equation between the elements of the two axes should be empirically tested and verified in each specific context. Marx decided to make the proletariat the Agent, Instrument and Subject of the transition from pre-history to history; but if we hold up every novel, play or poem to the Cosmos of this Objectified Teleological Ultimate, these humble plants will die of too much sunlight.

A committed literature of the Left remains, in one shape or another, a socialist literature. And it will do so until our changing perception of social dialectics offers us a new perspective and a new vision. But the relationship of the proletariat or any other class to socialism must always remain a question, a perpetual interrogation. When Lukács writes that 'the object of proletarian humanism is to reconstruct the complete human personality and free it from the distortion and dismemberment to which it has been subjected in class society', we are entitled to call for evidence beyond the passion of his affirmation. Trotskyists deny it with impressive sincerity, and Communists deny it with mechanical tenacity, but all the evidence points inescapably to this — the industrial proletariat has shed its revolutionary potential, its vulnerability to absolute pauperisation, its brief claim to occupy the last avenue of history. The Trotskyists blame it all on the revisionism, reformism, bureaucratism and corruption of the Communist and Social Democratic parties. Thus, given revolutionary leadership . . . leadership . . . leadership. The Communists blame it all on the insidious power of bourgeois ideology and the capacity of the capitalist state to offer seductive concessions. Very well. But all this has gone on for too long. A theory such as Marx's cannot survive for more than a century the series of 'accidents' and 'betrayals' which have apparently thwarted its realisation; for the theory itself claimed to have unearthed socio-economic impulsions powerful enough to grind such accidents and betrayals to powder.

The most radical and impoverished class is today the peasantry of the third world. In the period of contested decolonisation, in Kenya, Indo-China and Algeria, the Western proletariat joined forces with the bourgeoisie to crush the black, brown and yellow peasant. In the great guerrilla campaigns in China, Vietnam, Algeria and Cuba, the rifles have been shouldered by peasants, by Fanon's *damnés de la terre*. As the disparity of wealth between the post-industrial, industrial and pre-industrial nations increases year by year, and as the great divide between the haves and have-nots assumes the luminous, coloured glow of racial animosity, so the conflict between worker and capitalist, between him who sells his labour power and him who exploits it, pales in significance. Globally, the proletarian becomes psychologically integrated with the bourgeoisie. The old myths of race and nation are revived to animate the new frontiers of confrontation. Within the syndrome of scarcity and need (the primary motor of the historical process) only the starving peasantry experience a true desperation; they alone have nothing to lose.

I am not canvassing the beneficence of capitalism. The European worker remains poorly paid, poorly educated, poorly housed, poorly guaranteed against unemployment, poorly endowed with status and dignity, poorly shielded from alienation and a cretinising boredom in his work. I thank God that I am not a proletarian. Above all, the function of the worker under capitalism is now, as it was in Marx's time, to make money for other people. Nevertheless, the class struggle in the West has increasingly assumed the milder contours of a family quarrel. When the crunch comes, the worker and his representatives are cautious, and caution is never the child of desperation — *pace*, the events of May 1968 in France. In the constant realignment of social stratification, the proletarian loses his special status, his unique historical mission. Instead he takes his place in a broader stream, in a popular front of democratic forces, in a coalition of black collar and white, of town and country, a coalition in which his own ranks are in a minority. Nor, to take up once again Marx's vision of the future, can we any longer believe in the 'dictatorship of the proletariat'. The proletariat is a class, but Sartre is quite correct in his insistence that whole classes do not rule. Groups rule on their behalf and then, increasingly, on their own behalf. Three theoretical spanners (each based upon historical experience) have been thrown into the Marxian mechanism: (a) the sociology of élites, of technocracy, of bureaucracy and of a constantly renewed tendency towards oligarchy; (b) the re-recognition of power-lust and aggression as a cause rather than simply a product of exploitative social systems; and (c) the socio-political consequences of affluence.

Socialism is the brain-child of the intellectuals. The earliest socialists were dreamers, 'utopians' like Owen, Saint-Simon, Fourier and Cabet who presented to the world paper blueprints of the perfect society. Sometimes, as with Owen and Cabet, they attempted experimentally to create model settlements, the embryonic nuclei of paradise on earth. Marx and Engels adopted the dream of paradise, discarded the details, denounced utopians, insisted that socialism would be achieved neither by 'reason' nor persuasion, inscribed socialism-communism on the tablet of history, endowing it with the weight of destiny, and allocated to the working class the privileged mission of bringing it all about. There was a hint of double-talk in Marx; his theory, he would persuade us, was less *his* theory than the scientific truth which he had discovered; the theory really belonged to the proletariat, and it only remained to sell it to its rightful owners. Therefore Marx's work contains no coherent account of the socio-historical function of the intelligentsia. Lenin was more frank. The proletariat, he said, could not develop a revolutionary-socialist ideology without the assistance of the radicalised intellectuals and of the Party. But Lenin makes this observation empirically, without facing or developing its theoretical consequences. With the writings of the Italian Marxist Gramsci, the historical function (or functions) of the intelligentsia becomes more explicit and more plausible. Classes exist, and their basic interests and attitudes are rooted in their socio-economic foundations. But between those interests and attitudes on the one hand, and a mature, elaborated class ideology on the other, there is always a nascent gap; it is the intellectuals who bridge the gap. According to Gramsci, it is the intellectuals who, as philosophers, political theorists, sociologists, historians, writers and artists offer to each class a highly elaborated case for its own supremacy. The intellectual is like a lawyer (not Gramsci's image, but mine); he first briefs himself as to his client's situation and ambitions, and then employs his own resources of knowledge, rationality and rhetoric to make out a case which will convince the courts. Some intellectuals achieve status and equilibrium within the great institutions, as servants of the Church, the State, the Academy. Others, the alienated and disaffected, the *déraciné* bourgeoisie, wander in perpetual search of clients, a constituency, a cause. For many, anomic solitude proves an unbearable source of anguish; they grasp at a stable context, they search frantically for the comforts of family and tribe. They return to the establishment; or they join the Communist Party.

However — when we consider the political positions adopted by creative writers it would be foolish to account for them solely in terms of the sociological roles and functions I have just outlined. There is always something else left over. I mean, of course, the writer himself. Grandiose analyses of global socio-economic patterns, and bold prognoses about ascending, revolutionary classes and doomed, assimilated classes, leave unaltered the fact not merely that the writer speaks only for himself but that writing itself is a middle-class activity. Between the creative writer and the classes or causes he wishes to 'represent' or 'express' *there is always a gap*: the gap between the book and the world, between my pen at this moment and the miner's drill at this moment, the gap between a superfluous, middle-class game (literature) and those forms of necessary, concrete activity by which we stay alive. This gap brings a renewed anguish to the intellectuals generation after generation; and generation after generation the impulse to 'go to the people' (in the Russian phrase) is renewed. This impulse is both noble and futile; I know of no better account of it than the one on pp. 388–9 of the Collins-Harvill English edition of *The First Circle*, by Alexander Solzhenitsyn.

SIX

What are the proper limits of commitment? At what point do art and propaganda collide in an irreconcilable confrontation? University lecturers (to their undying shame!) today refer to their teaching 'load': how great a 'load' of commitment can a novel or play carry before it grinds to a halt?

It must be obvious at once that no exact answer is possible to such questions. We lack yardsticks.

Different circumstances dictate different struggles. In conditions of strict censorship, such as prevailed in nineteenth-century Russia, the committed writer must of necessity adopt codes of conveyance which are both cunning and

oblique. Art becomes a favoured weapon, offering oppor-
tunities for masking the message, for wrapping it in the
diverting garments of character portrayal, or for presenting
it in symbolical or allegorical form. The writer's scope is
limited; the censor, the Holy Office, some idiot careerist
bureaucrat in the Kremlin, casts a shadow over his desk.
But there are compensations. In a 'closed' society, the
audience is quicker on the uptake than in an 'open' society —
they make a habit of reading between the lines; the slightest
wink or nod and they are with you to a man. In some countries like Poland this tradition is so highly developed that it
is quite useless for a writer to state an opinion explicitly; the
audience will automatically assume he means the opposite.
We therefore have to seriously consider purchasing a paradox
— that the political impact of art increases in proportion to
the inexorability of the censorship. (Serious proviso: the art
which *reaches* the public.) In an open and permissive society,
like contemporary Britain and the United States, the audience resembles a rich child satiated and numbed by too
abundant an offering of presents. Since the artist is free to
say virtually anything, and since he usually does, he unwittingly assumes the old licence and the old ineffectuality of
the court jester or fool. Scurrilous irresponsibility is taken
to be his social function; no one takes him seriously.

The political impact of art is always unpredictable. Particularly in the theatre, where the public nature of the performance and the collective nature of the audience increase
the potential voltage, the author is liable to be astonished by
the impact of his work. When *Coriolanus* was staged in Paris
in the late 1930s, Fascists and Communists rioted outside
the theatre. Today no one would turn a political hair. Stanislavsky recalls how a performance of Ibsen's *The Enemy of the
People*, presented in St Petersburg immediately after the
massacre in Kazansky Square, brought the house down, the
whole audience surging forward in a wave of euphoria to
shake 'Dr Stockman's' hand. (Stanislavsky was disgusted.)
When the same author's *Ghosts* was first performed in

London, a large part of the audience and most of the critics
took it to be an attack on marriage as the useless sacrifice of
people to an ideal. Uproar ensued. It is not unusual for a
play to cause a riot in one capital city and hardly a stir in the
next. The English critic Harold Hobson wrote of Albee's
A Delicate Balance (a non-political, uncommitted, private
play if ever there was one): 'Great and moving dramas have a
way of taking on a specific meaning that their author never
dreamed of; and *A Delicate Balance* is today a commentary
on the policy of Mr Enoch Powell, of whom at the time he
wrote it Mr Albee had almost certainly never heard.' It
would be idle to pretend that Hochhuth's play, *The Repre-
sentative*, carries the same 'meaning' in Presbyterian Edinburgh as in Catholic Liverpool. Everyone knows that in the
Soviet Union the work of so-and-so will be hailed as 'positive' today and attacked as 'negative' tomorrow.

Novels too are subject to the vagaries of public preoccupation and passion. One recent example of this is William
Styron's novel, *The Confessions of Nat Turner*. Although
himself a white Southerner, Styron is a man of progressive
views; while writing his novel he can scarcely have expected,
even less desired, to become overnight Enemy Number One
for the radical black intelligentsia of America. Styron's Nat
Turner, a fictionalised, re-created hero drawn from real life,
leads a slave revolt (1831) in the course of which he murders
the white girl whom he loves. At the end of the novel, as he
faces execution, Nat, in Styron's account, reflects: 'I would
have done it all again. I would have destroyed them all. Yet
I would have spared one. I would have spared her that
showed me Him whose presence I had not fathomed or
maybe never even known.' Styron's black critics pounced
on these elements in Nat's make-up — his innate pacifism,
his Christianity, his capacity to love a girl from the race of
white oppressors. But Styron's hero does not regret the
revolt itself and it is clearly the author's purpose to empha-
sise the absolute legitimacy of such a revolt, however bloody,
by drawing a contrast between Nat's natural moral and

temperamental inclinations and what slave-owning society drove him ultimately to do. If a social system turns men such as this to violence, is it not all the more irreprievably condemned?

We see that Styron's didactic purpose is also balanced by his sense of history. The black slave rebels of 1831, we can assume, were fashioned out of different clay than the urban militants of 1968. But the militant critic will indulge no such latitude; for him, a book must address itself in the most immediate, agitational and familiar way to the contemporary reader. It was not a Negro, but a white critic, Stephen Vizinczey, who began his review of Styron's novel in *The Times* with these words: '*The Times* reported on 27th April (1968) that New York City Hall had approved a plan to build a sewage treatment plant in Harlem, against the protest of the only Negro member of the Board of Estimates . . .' What has this to do with Nat Turner? Wait — Mr Vizinczey will soon turn to Styron's portrait: 'What a reassuring dream of a Negro rebel, so full of sex and piety even as he is being executed — and just shortly before his skin is turned into a purse, if not a lampshade. Such people will forgive us our sewage plants.' Evidently *The Times*' reviewer is determined to be no less radical than the most crazed black sniper perched dizzily on a burning Detroit rooftop. In fact, such mental juxtapositions are symptomatic of a general infantile disorder — nor do they ring true.

They say that when space capsules return from the moon they must either enter the earth's atmosphere through a narrow funnel or else burn up. With committed literature it is generally the opposite; the broader the point of entry, the more comprehensive and complex the appeal to the reader's intelligence and emotions, the less likely is the heat-shield to sustain damage or disintegration. However — and this is the minor point I have been advancing — the writer, unlike the space scientist, is aiming at an elastic 'atmosphere' whose contours and dimensions change by the hour. Whatever cargo of commitment he launches into literary space, he can have no certainty as to what will return to earth. Accidents are the rule rather than the exception.

SEVEN

The broader the funnel of entry, the less likely a burn-up. But I exaggerate. Unless we are careful the whole notion of commitment will evaporate in the ether of Pure Art. I have already referred to the riotous scenes following Stanislavsky's production of *The Enemy of the People* in St Petersburg. Stanislavsky's own comment on the affair was one with which I am out of sympathy: ' . . . but we, who knew the true nature of the Theatre, understood that the boards of the stage could never become a platform for the spread of propaganda, for the simple reason that the very least utilitarian purpose or tendency, brought into the realm of pure art, kills art instantly.' (In which case, it is rather surprising that he undertook this particular play in the first case.) However, the message is clear: 'the very least utilitarian tendency . . . kills art'. By 'utilitarian' Stanislavsky does not of course mean the secular social philosophy associated with Bentham, Chernyshevsky *et al*; he means any purpose which is didactic, programmatic or directed towards inspiring some practical action. But what of religious art, the art which not only expresses devotion but seeks to inspire it — does it not have a utilitarian basis? Do not devotion and revivalism coexist within the Passion Plays, the Corpus Christi cycle? Were the cathedrals of Chartres, Notre Dame, Ulm and St Peter's raised and lovingly decorated in the name of art for art's sake? And what of the stone and wooden gods of Africa, Asia, Mexico and Peru — are they really without utilitarian purpose?

I am out of sympathy with Stanislavsky here. I am more convinced by Camus' formulation: 'The great novelists are the philosophical novelists, that is to say the opposite of the thesis writers. Thus Balzac, Sade, Melville, Stendhal,

Proust, Malraux, Kafka, to name only a few.' The word
'philosophical' suggests a funnel broad and rich, whereas
'thesis' invokes a sense of narrow aridity. The Czech playwright Václav Havel translates the same broad-based proposition into a more concrete idiom: '. . . the best theatre is
and always has been naturally political. Political, I repeat, in
the *broadest and truly serious sense of the term*: in other words,
in no sense as an instrument of propaganda for this or that
political ideology, conception, power, party or group but as
something which has the innate characteristic that it is not
indifferent to the fate of the human *polis*, that it has a live,
committed and penetrative relationship with its country and
its time . . .'

Yevtushenko adds:

> *in Russia the poet is more than a poet.*
> *There only those are born poets*
> *in whom a proud civic spirit dwells*
> *for whom there is no comfort, no peace.*
> *The poet is the image of his own age*
> *and the phantom herald of the future.*

This sense of commitment has traditionally been stronger
in Eastern Europe than in the Western part. The persistence
of censorship has endowed the indirect, camouflaged voice of
the artist with a special vocation; at the same time the writer
shares with other members of the intelligentsia an acute sense
of guilt, and therefore of responsibility, in the face of the
prehistoric peasant poverty and inertia which surrounds him.

But the Oder-Neisse line does not divide Hades from
Heaven.

Sartre was quite right: the writer should address himself to
his contemporaries, and not to posterity. On the other hand
Bernard Shaw remarked wisely that when a play deals only
with a specific social question, nothing can prolong its life
beyond the life of that question. The agitational literature of
the 'living newspaper' tradition is worthy of respect and
attention, but its built-in limitations are enormous. Here

planned obsolescence is carried to extremes. Chekhov was once asked to write a play about the Russo-Japanese War. He felt insulted. 'Listen,' he said, 'it is necessary that twenty years should pass. It is impossible to speak of it now. It is necessary that the soul should be in repose. Only then can the author be unprejudiced.' Chekhov spoils one good point (perspective) with two bad ones (repose and unprejudiced); nevertheless it is a point worth making.

In the autumn of 1966 the Royal Shakespeare Company staged a kind of collage play called *US*. The theme of the play was Vietnam and the mood was one of high commitment. One of the participants, Michael Kustow, recalls that during rehearsals a few members of the company went one lunch time to a meeting sponsoring the forthcoming Russell War Crimes Tribunal. According to Kustow's account, Russell's secretary, Ralph Schoenman, recited a list of the chemicals used by the U.S. in Vietnam, and then, turning to practical action and what ordinary citizens could do, he suggested petitioning M.P.s, supporting the Tribunal financially, and staging demonstrations. Kustow comments: 'Here we were stranded again . . . now we were being handed the same woefully inadequate prescriptions for action we had been handed so many times before. Here, perhaps, was the point at which the theatre — the right kind of theatre — could speak with a special voice.' Why? Was the theatre about to propose new, more imaginative, more efficacious solutions? Hardly. The problem for Schoenman and the Tribunal was not, repeat not, that they were operating in an irrelevant medium, but rather that true power lay beyond their reach. The artist, the man of the theatre, is entitled to recognise this and to approach the Vietnam war tuned in to a different medium, but it is foolish to pretend that this medium can ever provide immediately practicable solutions to immediately pressing problems. After the first night of *US*, Alan Brien wrote very sensibly: 'But it is at least arguable that anyone who has seen monks in flames, legless children, mutilated corpses, charred countryside, through

the electronic immediacy of television may find the sight of
well-fed actors hobbling and gibbering an impressive illusion rather than an unbearable reality.' Arnold Wesker commented: 'You cannot stand on the sidewalk and attack others
who do the same; and that play stands on the sidewalk
because the Aldwych Theatre is on the sidewalk, all theatre
is on the sidewalk.' Wesker is right, but he has put his words
together a trifle hastily: the *extent* to which a theatre stands
on a sidewalk depends on the nature and scope of the
commitment.

A comic episode . . . Paris, the early 1930s, and the surrealist poets (Breton, Aragon, etc) are on the revolutionary
drug for the time being. They pose as ultras — no compromise. Aragon delivers himself of a fiery poem called *Front
Rouge,* in which he invites the comrades to 'bring down the
cops, bring down the cops . . .' and to 'fire on the trained
bears of social democracy' such as Blum, Frossard and Bon-
cour. The poem proclaims, among other things, 'the violent
domination of the Proletariat over the Bourgeoisie.' Unfortunately for Aragon, the 'bourgeoisie' takes him seriously —
a legal prosecution for incitement is put in hand. The surrealists now have a heaven-sent (?) opportunity to publicise
their struggle against capitalism and to make an eloquent,
rousing defence of the revolutionary ethic in the courts.
But this is not the course they chose. Instead, Breton quotes
Hegel to the effect that a poem incarnates a general idea and
should not be judged in its component phrases. A petition is
circulated, not a political petition, but an appeal to all civi-
lised men in the name of the special immunity of literature.

I have myself posed (at the Royal Court Theatre) two
successive questions to a panel of distinguished left-wing
writers, critics and directors. Question One: do you favour
the Race Relations Act which makes incitement to racial
hatred a prosecutable offence? Unanimous verdict: Yes!
Second question: imagine that a fascistic, openly racist
play has just opened in London. In your opinion, should
those responsible be prosecuted or the play censored?

Pause: such a play, someone replies, would not last two nights. Well, let us suppose it proved popular. Pause: no, art should never be censored.

Admittedly the two cases (the French surrealists and the Royal Court episode) are slightly different. In the one, the writers are defending one of their own comrades in practice; in the second, the writers are defending one of their enemies in theory. But essentially the same contradiction is evident in both cases. The writers avow in one breath (their political seriousness and the political relevance of literature) what they disavow in the next. By bowing to the legendary fetish of ART, the privileged sanctuary of the muse, they effectively jettison the claims of art to be taken seriously in the corridors of power. Ultimately, however, there is an in-built contradiction from which there is no escape. The extent to which the artist can claim special freedoms is proportionate to the extent that art is ineffective in the sphere where freedom is grudgingly rationed out. Art retains its relative freedom from the reality principle at the cost of a relative impotence within the sphere of reality.

John Berger has explained very well the difference between short-term and long-term art: 'The new totality which reality represents is by its nature ambiguous. These ambiguities must be allowed in long-term art. The purpose of such art is not to iron out the ambiguities, but to contain and define the totality in which they exist. In this way art becomes an aid to increasing self-consciousness instead of an immediate and limited guide to direct action.' What Berger says here is highly perceptive; its relevance to the problem of politically committed literature could scarcely be overemphasised.

(The reader is invited to re-read Berger's words. The patient, static nature of linear print is ideally suited to recapitulation. Unfortunately we tend to read like automata, across and down, across and down, misled by the uniform size and spacing of print into devoting equal time, thought and attention to each line. We know that the fine grooves on the surface of a gramophone record all look alike, but we also know that what the record player offers to our ear out of these grooves is a vast differential of sound, tone, pace and emphasis. Similarly a musician reading a score or an actor studying a text recognise that as interpreters their task is to decipher a symbolic code — musical notation or print — and then translate it into an expressive code — sound, voice, gesture. But with books there is no obvious translational, interpretive process intervening between the act of writing and the act of reading. Yet this step of interpreting before finally receiving, this unravelling of a deceptively uniform code (print), is necessary. The whole burden lies with the reader; consequently the act of reading, no less than the act of writing, is susceptible to infinite degrees of skill.)

Art, then, is poorly suited to immediate political protest and agitation. Entering too narrow a funnel, it will burn badly. Clearly agitational and political language is designed to close our perceptions, to define the frontiers of right and wrong, to excommunicate the heretic, to crush the enemy to dust. (Cartoon and caricature can also effectively serve these aims.) Political language is dogmatic, assertive, exclusive. It regards language simply as a tool, a tool in the service of a Truth existing in complete independence of the language which expresses it. By contrast, literary language is open, exploratory, tentative, probing ambiguity and multiple levels of meaning, referring back on itself, connoting more than it denotes. When we react to an excessively programmatic novel or play with the complaint, 'But this is not art!', we are perhaps expressing our resentment at seeing the unique potentialities of the artistic matrix squandered and debased. We came expecting coq au vin and had to swallow bangers and mash.

EIGHT

'A good book . . . is a force, a tool or weapon, to make the

dreams of today become the reality of tomorrow.' (Roger
Garaudy.) Now it is true that a novel, no less than a book
like *Silent Spring*, can have an enormous impact on public
opinion. Upton Sinclair's *The Jungle* without doubt speeded
the passage of the pure food laws in the U.S. Congress, and
Galsworthy's play *Justice* is said to have been directly instrumental in bringing about penal reforms. Such achievements are undoubtedly a tribute to the didactic power of
creative writing, and it is quite possible that if Sinclair and
Galsworthy had not conveyed their case in fictional form the
impact would have been less. The recent British television
play, *Cathy, Come Home*, created a nation-wide outcry
against prevailing housing conditions — a documentary
programme might have passed unnoticed. But notice that
these cases deal with issues which are social rather than
political. You will protest, quite rightly, that the state of the
Chicago meat-packing industry, or of the prevailing British
law on strikes, or the cancer of slum landlordism, all have
profoundly political causes and ramifications. True. But
the issues involved are social in the notable sense that the
reader or spectator can be persuaded to respond to them
irrespective of his political commitments. Like negligence in
hospitals, they become in the public consciousness what
is called 'a national disgrace'. In this sense the audience is
potentially 'open'. The more open the sensibilities of the
audience, the more narrowly and directly they can be
appealed to.

But when we turn to what I would call authentically
political issues, the most divisive issues, the issues which
challenge the basic ideological system, what is narrow and
direct inevitably boomerangs. It is sometimes counter-
productive. Consequently I regard Garaudy's euphoric
assertion as mere caber-tossing. Literature is certainly a
form of action, but a form of secondary action, action by
disclosure, a contribution to a more reflective general consciousness. This does not mean that the writer must spread
his wings as wide as the Greek legends, scorning what is

immediate, specific and concrete; it is the *treatment* which is crucial.

Dionys Mascolo has said this: one must choose — to be either a revolutionary, a man of action, or an artist, a writer. 'The artist as a man of action can only be a false artist and a false man of action.'

In pursuit of this,

Take the case of Malraux.

La Condition humaine is one of those 'perfect' novels, dramatic in its development, exquisitely balanced in its structure, deeply committed to its own characters yet procuring for itself the necessary 'distance' by which the creator guarantees mastery of his creations. Four years later, in 1937, Malraux publishes *L'Espoir*, a breathless epic which scorns the conventions of symmetry, a procession of heroism and death which derives its basic form from that of the Spanish Civil War itself. The dilemmas of loyalty, commitment, nationality, hope, violence and torture, and the fictional characters who incarnate these dilemmas, cascade through the book in a series of short, staccato scenes which echo the machine-gun fire outside Madrid. Gone is the delicate bamboo theatre of the East, the spectator's theatre, of *La Condition humaine*. The artist has ceased to observe from the sidelines; now the struggle against fascism is his struggle, he is both combatant and reporter, he is overwhelmed by the field of blood. Malraux has not yet shed the habit of fiction, nor lost the power of his imagination, but 'art' is left behind. The author's own revised sense of priorities is reflected within the novel. Says Vargas: 'This war is going to be a war of mechanized equipment — and we're running it as if noble emotions were all that mattered.' Says Manuel: 'Courage is a thing that has to be *organized*, you've got to keep it in condition, like a rifle.' Malraux sits with a typewriter in his lap and a brace of grenades at his belt; the enemy Junkers are returning to the attack, the air reeks of burnt cordite and diesel fumes. In such circumstances why invent, why fabricate, why indulge the effete and feminine conventions of artistic form? After a decade as committed intellectual and artist, Malraux has discovered his true vocation as a man of action. He will later serve in the doomed French army of 1940, be captured, escape, lead a Resistance unit, and offer his services to de Gaulle. Meanwhile in Spain Hemingway is observing the Civil War with a mixture of involvement and detachment analagous to Malraux's mood ten years earlier in Indo-China. Whereas *L'Espoir* issues from the press while the war still hangs in the balance, Hemingway takes his time, steps back, fashions characters, plot, symmetry and 'art' out of his experiences. When *For Whom the Bell Tolls* finally appears, Franco has held the reins of power unchallenged for two years. In the period ahead Malraux will continue to write, but never fiction *(Les Noyers de l'Altenburg* is essentially autobiography and social philosophy). Fiction here succumbs to Action.

For Sartre, 1952 is a turning point. 'But after ten years of ruminating I had come to the breaking point, and only needed that one straw. In the language of the Church, this was my conversion.' During those ten years Sartre had written, if my calculations are correct, eight plays, three novels and a large number of short stories. Now Sartre lends his full weight to the Communist cause. But this is symptomatic of a more profound sea-change. The masses, the poor, the proletariat, the oppressed, about whom Sartre had written so much, and whose cause he had championed *on paper*, suddenly declare their absolute reality. Their cries, their songs, their stench, their marching feet invade his study; they move towards him accusingly, challenging his right to turn them into figments of his imagination. Art can only mock their desperate predicament. In the seventeen years which ensue, Sartre writes only three plays and no novels. But his literary output remains prodigious. Weighed down by historical crises, convinced that art is both contingent and superfluous at a time of global crisis, Sartre hurls himself into the study of history, economics and sociology. He turns from art to science. In *Les Mots* (1963) he releases a remark which shows how far he has withdrawn from the theory of art-as-social-action expressed so confidently in *Qu'est ce que la littérature?* 'For a long while I treated my pen as a sword; now I realise how helpless we are . . . Culture saves nothing and nobody, nor does it justify.'

Perhaps Chekhov exaggerated about needing twenty years to get a balanced perspective of the Russo-Japanese war. But it cannot be denied that the artistic process requires a certain reduction of pressure, a veil of detachment, a sense of space. Where life is most dangerous, vivid and critical, the inspired reporter tends to supplant the novelist. No society lives so constantly in the burning present as the American. No culture has brought on-the-spot reportage to a more inspired level: John Reed, John Hersey, Norman Mailer . . . One can almost discern — I exaggerate a little — a division of function within American letters, whereby the reporters expropriate the dynamic, and the novelists the static, as the proper provinces of their writing. America is a volcano; the intrepid reporters are gathered round the crater, catching the white-hot lava as its falls. But not the novelists, they are camped further down the slopes, observing the cool, the petrified, the tormented lava below. The American post-war novelists whom we most admire as novelists tell us remarkably little about the history — the diachronic sequence — of their country: Faulkner, Nabokov, Malamud, Bellow (not in order of merit!), Roth, Updike, Purdy, Salinger, Hawkes . . .

Mailer wrote three novels and then he stopped. Here again a writer senses the superfluity and the irrelevance of fiction and contrivance. Mailer turned instead to reportage, social criticism, autobiography, and to minor forays as activist, participant and candidate for mayor. With the Vietnam war and the Pentagon demonstration of 1967, the two Mailers attempt to join forces: *The Armies of the Night* is subtitled *History as a Novel, The Novel as History*. Yet one is not convinced; the impulses of the novelist remain dominated by those of the reporter, the immanent event and the immanent reaction to it kaleidoscope and destroy the

necessary detachment and speculative space of fiction. The
novelists who went to Vietnam, like Mary McCarthy and
Susan Sontag, mostly came away as reporters. I read one
remarkable novel about the war, *The Prisoners of Quai Dong,*
by Victor Kolpacoff, and I had almost reached the end before
it dawned on me that this was fiction, rather than an account
of a real prison camp and a real interrogation of a Vietcong
suspect. When Mailer finally offered a novel, a genuine work
of fiction, on the subject of Vietnam — it was set in Alaska.

There was a time when America had a problem, a running
sore on the body politic. It was called the Negro problem (or
question). Out of it came *Native Son, Raisin in the Sun, If He
Hollers Let Him Go, Go Tell It on the Mountain, Invisible
Man,* and many other novels of formidable stature. Then
America stopped having a Negro problem and a Negro
question, just as Russia in 1917 stopped having a proletarian
problem. Suddenly the Negro was everywhere: the fate of
America and the destiny of the Negro became one and the
same. The black writers did not stop writing; they only
stopped writing fiction. I realise that such fissures of genre
and time are never clean-cut; I know that Le Roi Jones is a
playwright and that some Negroes continue to write novels
and plays. But in terms of social and intellectual impact, for
blacks and whites alike, the *essays* of a Baldwin, a Cleaver,
or a Carmichael today fulfil the same central, perspective-
orienting function as Wright's novels fulfilled thirty years
ago. The tree of fiction withers in the burning city.

NINE

Literature and revolution . . . Why do I not call this book
just that: *Literature and Revolution?* (Admittedly Trotsky
has already stolen the title.) It would certainly improve sales
. . . the ideal, scrumptious chocolate box for the leftist intelligentsia, hard on the surface, soft at the centre, an attrac-
tive reconciliation of our own useless, minority pleasures

and of the heroic dialectic of collective struggle. So we are real and relevant after all! Here I am, curled comfortably in my armchair, armed with spectacles, a glossy pack of filter tips, a mug of hot coffee and the Book . . . and suddenly my hands develop jungle sores, my carpet slippers become ankle-high boots (against snakes, fool), my soft double bed is a spartan hammock slung between trees, each slot on my Dimplex radiator conceals a machine-gun bullet . . .

Don't kid yourself. If you are reading this, you are going precisely nowhere. Be happy about it.

Let us continue to play with ourselves.

The revolution — any revolution, whether viewed as a programme or as event — is monist. It wishes to arrange the world according to a unitary and uniform principle. It is pulled towards Finality, almost as if nostalgic for an inorganic state, for that absolute tranquillity among men which arrives with death. The For-Itself reaches for the security of the In-Itself, attempting to annihilate the gap between Itself and the Other, to throw off the ontological burden of choice, conflict, even freedom.

(Read only the surface of this, and take the meaning from the texture of mental sounds, the echo-pattern of the language itself. Do not attempt to translate the 'content' into a more familiar idiom, and do not try to measure this content against what you 'know' of history and revolution . . .)

Against the triumphant yet inhuman victory song of the Caesarian Revolution, Camus offers us the virtues of revolt, of rebellion, of moderation, of the perennial humanistic refusal. 'But rebellion, in man, is the refusal to be treated as an object and to be reduced to simple historical terms.' The revolutionary is obsessively totalitarian in his thirst for finality, says Camus. In *Les Justes*, the proto-Bolshevik Stepan declares coldly: 'For us who don't believe in God, there is nothing between total justice and utter despair.' Camus offers us Stepan in order that we may abhor him. Man, in Camus' view, cannot possibly conceive history in its totality because he is part of it; therefore it is less the ultimate end of revolt, the programme, which is valuable than the existential quality of life involved. 'The struggle itself towards the summit suffices to fill a man's heart. One must imagine Sisyphus happy.'

Sartre — it is 1952 — disagrees. He quarrels with Camus. He accuses Camus of attempting to stand on the sidelines of a dirty world — a world of mass starvation, exploitation and violent struggle — while proclaiming his own clean hands. Necessity for Camus is one thing; for the Chinese peasant, another. Sartre has already remarked of Baudelaire that the metaphysical rebel really aims to perpetuate the conditions he rebels against so that he may experience his own virtue in perpetuity. Sartre reminds Camus (and Malraux) of this. For the intellectual, the price of absolute purity is absolute irrelevance. No, worse: you give comfort to the oppressors. If you want to influence the revolution, says Sartre, you must first join it.

The controversy between Sartre and Camus is about two things; about politics, and about the intellectual's proper relationship to politics. Variations on this argument or on part of it are numerous (Isaiah Berlin on liberty, Karl Popper on the open society, etc). I do not wish to try and resolve it; that is not what I am on about. But what strikes me as relevant here is that both Camus and Sartre seem to have assumed that what holds good for the revolution must hold good for the writer also. Whatever principles of political action best synthesise realism, morality, efficacity and justice in the theatre of life must therefore be reflected and canvassed in the novel or the drama. This assumption springs almost automatically from a commitment to commitment and from the anxiety of the *écrivain engagé* to merge totally his life as a writer with his life as a citizen. I believe that this assumption is false because it assumes that literature can faithfully reflect and convey an objective truth and an objective morality which exist outside of it. To think in this way is to forget what *writing is and does*.

I have pointed to the dangers of literature committing

itself to too narrow a cause, programme, party or course of
action. If commitment to 'the revolution' — however that
may be interpreted at a particular time — involves these
errors (as in many socialist realist novels it does), then
obviously the same objection holds. But it need not do so,
and the point I am making about 'literature and revolution'
is poised at a different angle. The novelist or playwright
runs no greater risk as an artist in adopting Sartre's theory of
revolution than Camus' theory of revolt. And if he does so
skilfully, his political philosophy will doubtless permeate the
work and penetrate the reader. *But* — and this is my point —
the very nature of his work *as literature* will also generate a
different set of signals on a different wavelength, and these
signals will both complicate and partially offset what he has
to say about the validity of mass revolutionary action. This
is because both the novel and the drama are products of a
culture, or expressive of an aspect of a culture, which is in its
very structure individualistic. The whole continuum of our
artistic culture, of which we are both the beneficiaries and
the prisoners, is impregnated by the tradition of singular
revolt. Art affirms reality only to deny it; the act of art is an
act of revolt. It is the enduring expression of the Promethean
rebellion. I do not refer simply to the preoccupation of the
Greek dramatists with the tragic hero's hopeless struggle
against destiny; nor to the fact that many of Shakespeare's
greatest plays are named after one or two main characters;
nor to the well-known flowering of the novel in the age of
laissez-faire and liberal individualism. Artistic language and
the forms of imaginative literature lend themselves to private, individual explorations of the universe; like oil with
water do they mix with the assertive, closed, schematic and
rhetorical idiom employed by the Revolution. Camus notes
how Rousseau, Saint-Just, the Saint-Simonians and the
Russian nihilists had all revealed a distrust verging on hostility towards the caprices of art. The revolutionary doctrine
is pushing a panacea; the artist is sceptical; he gives form to
values which fly into a perpetual future. The revolutionist

trades in categories, in millions of men. But the 'characters'
who crowd the pages of a novel, even a 'public' novel, or
the boards of a stage, are incapable of representing millions
of men. The act of their conception affirms their singularity.

This is true even of a novelist like Solzhenitsyn, who
clearly aims to paint a general picture of Soviet society in the
Stalin era by presenting us with a panorama of interlocking
individual cases and personal tragedies. At one point the
author remarks: 'Prisoners are generally inclined to exaggerate the number of people "inside"; when the actual prison
population was no more than twelve or fifteen million, for
instance, they were convinced that there were no more men
left outside.' Here we take in the (shattering) kind of statistical knowledge we find in academic works and political his-
tories. But ultimately Solzhenitsyn achieves his over-view
not by means of statistics or generalisations, but by way of the
key structural elements of creative fiction — individual men
and women. In the last resort we weep with rage and grief
not for the 'fifteen millions', but for Ivan Denisovitch,
Nerzhin, Bulator, Sologdin, Nadya and all the other victims
of Stalinism whom Solzhenitsyn brings to life. Somewhere
in *The First Circle* he briefly refers to the desirability of free
elections and a social-democratic government in Russia, but,
whether we agree or not, this is not the kind of programme
that fiction conveys very convincingly. What committed
fiction can do is to convince us that a social system which
treats Solzhenitsyn's Ivan, or Richard Wright's Bigger, or
Zola's Gervaise, or Gorky's Vlassova, in so degrading and
inhuman a way, is an abomination. The novel or play as a
structure, as a genre, tends to *affirm* the individual and deny
the society. That is why the most successful committed
novels are critiques of one social system rather than hymns
of praise to its alternative.

Even an ultra-sociological novelist like Zola singles out
certain characters for special attention. It is true that the
effect can be partially offset by adopting an epic style, introducing large choruses, and by listing characters in terms of

their social typology — 'Second Worker', 'A Priest', 'Armed Peasant', etc. But there are limits. Even the most radical of us is inevitably conditioned by education, convention, the past. However great our goodwill, the style of the Peking ballet, *The East is Red*, causes us to smile.

There was once a genius who died very young. His name was Georg Büchner. In July 1834 he is writing as a revolutionary journalist for a clandestine sheet, *The Hessian Courier*. Freedom for the Hats! he cries. War on the palaces! 'The prince is the head of the leech that creeps across you, the ministers are its teeth, and the officials its tail.' Büchner issues a call to revolution, *and holds up the French Revolution as a model*. 'Germany is now a field of battle, soon it will be a paradise. The German people is a *single* body, you are a member of it.'

A familiar state of mind, a familiar optimism, a familiar rhetoric.

Büchner has to flee the country. He goes to Zürich, he writes three plays. It is for these that we judge him a genius.

One of these plays is called *Danton's Death*. It deals, as its title indicates, with the French Revolution, the same Revolution whose flag he had held aloft in *The Hessian Courier*. But something has happened in the interval. In the play the Revolution is not exalted; on the contrary, it is depicted as relentlessly destroying its own ideals and consuming its own children. Danton, paralysed by a death-wish brought on by chronic disillusionment and boredom, emerges as the passive but stubborn Rebel. His ally Hérault-Séchelles makes the case against the Iron Men of Virtue, Rousseau, Robespierre and Saint-Just. 'The Revolution', he pleads, 'must end and the Republic begin. In our Constitution we must place right above duty, contentment above virtue, and self-preservation above punishment . . . We're all fools, and not one of us has the right to impose his own foolishness on anyone else.' (Thus Camus' case is anticipated by more than a century.) In scene two, we meet the crazed populace. First Citizen: 'Kill a man who reads and writes!' Second Citizen: 'Kill a

man who walks like an aristocrat!' Scene three, the Jacobin
Club. Declares a Jacobin deputy from Lyons: 'You are
murdering the Revolution with your compassion . . . A
coward dies for the Republic, a Jacobin kills for it.' Robespierre calls for Terror in the service of Virtue. 'My conscience', he tells Danton, 'is clear.' Danton is doomed, his
end is tragic.

How are we to account for the transition from Büchner
Mark One to Büchner Mark Two? Only a few months are
involved, so there is no question of the writer growing older,
mellower, more conservative in his senescence. No. What we
encounter here is the passage from journalism to drama,
from political rhetoric to art. I like to imagine, quite without
evidence, that when Büchner began *Danton's Death* he
intended to dramatise the cruel but necessary justice of the
Revolution, as well as the tragic decline into corruption and
idleness of a once-heroic figure, Danton. I like to imagine
that what so profoundly modified his perspective was not a
scholarly reconsideration of the historical evidence, but
rather *the act of writing a play* . . . that Danton became in the
process of writing the hero because he was already 'the
hero'; that the more a dramatist invests his own *creative*
sympathy in a character, the more *moral* sympathy he feels
towards him; that the dramatist becomes hostile towards
mob passion because mob passion bursts the boundaries of
the stage; that the artist finally offers the laurel to the rebel
within history because he, as an artist, is a rebel against
history.

Take another German play, a modern one, Günter Grass's
The Plebeians Rehearse the Uprising. The scene is East Berlin
in 1953, at the time of the workers' rising. 'The Boss' (obviously Brecht) is depicted rehearsing his own Marxist
adaptation of Shakespeare's *Coriolanus* (in fact, as Grass
admits, Brecht was rehearsing a different play at the time,
but the poet's licence is here justified). Brecht, as an eminent
intellectual of international renown, finds himself courted
and pressured from two sides: by the mutinous workers,

representing the socialistic *rebellion within the revolution*, and
by the Party bureaucrat Kozanka, representing the iron
purity of 'the Revolution'. Thus the problem is posed for
Brecht in terms very similar to those of the Sartre-Camus
controversy, always remembering that for this fictional
Brecht the outcome may involve his professional if not his
physical survival. But Grass also extends the dilemma to
the problem of politics and art. Brecht at first takes refuge in
aesthetics; he studies the behaviour of the German workers
at a time of stress in order that his actors may present a more
realistic portrayal of the Roman plebeians in *Coriolanus*.
Thus the urgent human predicament of the German workers
who hurry into his theatre is ignored; they are de-humanised
and exploited as mere models for 'the revolution' on stage.
But Brecht does not intend to incorporate their attitudes,
their cause and their claims into the play, he is concerned
only with the naturalistic details of their behaviour as proto-
types of a certain social class. Grass indicates that in
sacrificing genuine individuality to an abstraction, Brecht
endangers not only his political integrity but also his artistic
integrity. And this is true even if, as seems probable, Grass
is unfair to the real Brecht; the point he makes so skilfully
should therefore be taken in terms of a fictional theatre
director, 'The Boss', rather than as a plausible indictment of
Brecht himself.

In the present century few if any revolutionary or socially
optimistic novels have had the popular impact, emotional,
intellectual and artistic, of Kafka's *The Trial*, Zamyatin's *We*,
Huxley's *Brave New World*, Orwell's *1984*, Koestler's *Darkness at Noon*, and Golding's *Lord of the Flies*. Our mount-
ingly oppressive, *angst*-ridden fears of monoliths made by
man, whether political, scientific or both, no doubt make us
a captive audience for such novelists. But is it not equally
obvious that the very structure of the novel itself is better
adapted to the vision of one flickering torch held defiantly
against a surrounding darkness than to the celebration of a
million feet marching in step towards the promised land? Of

course it is. The content of a novel is partially conditioned
in advance by the form of the genre. At a level deeper than
transitory convention, at a level which excavates our cultural
conditioning deeper than political commitment, we demand
of the novel an absolute affirmation of the value of the individual. To say this is by no means to subscribe to the atomis-
tic and bourgeois view of man advanced by Berlin, Popper
and, in a sense, Camus. Nor is it to forget that whereas the
prosperous English gentleman conceives his individuality
in terms of *solitude*, the exploited Chinese or Cuban peasant
must invest his hopes of individual dignity in *solidarity*.
What I am saying is that literature over the centuries has
been fashioned to represent the singular against the plural,
the unique against the general. The socialist novel is capable
of demonstrating that true individuality can only be achieved
within the collective — so long as it also affirms the claims
of the individual against the collective.

For the ultimate rebellion of the singular man is not
merely social, it is also ontological. It is his perennial and
undeniable revolt against his own mortality, his own limitations, his own imprisonment within a skin and skull he did
not choose. It is his cry of protest that neither the welfare
state nor the public ownership of the means of production
can relieve him from the experience of fear, solitude, doubt,
hope, anxiety. The greatness of Malraux's novels lay in their
juxtaposition of socialistic optimism and a deep, brooding,
Nietzschean pessimism. For Malraux's heroes, solitude burns
in the very heart of solidarity; defeat is the black jewel of
victory; the absurd and the surpassing of the absurd leap-
frog in a perpetual cycle.

I recall (in this connection) a visit to the German Democratic Republic and in particular a series of gruelling failures
to live on the same mental planet and within the same system
of logic as those representatives of the official socialist culture
whom I encountered. It was spring, cool and grey, a semi-
city of Stalinesque apartment blocks, barren spaces, wide,
empty streets, a strangely sedate, sexless, non-city haunted

by the grave, bloodless face of Walter Ulbricht. And the Wall — just like in the photographs. They had erected platforms and podia for May Day. In the Humboldt University I was courteously received by Professor Wilhelm Girnus, formerly a member of the government and now director of literary studies in German socialism's leading university. Three pretty girls, graduate students, sat admiringly around his desk, taking notes. Coffee and cigarettes were courteously served; I declared myself in all sincerity, tremendously impressed by the social achievements of the G.D.R. . . . the kindergartens, the recognition of the Oder-Neisse line . . . Girnus nodded politely and glanced at his watch. So I plunged in. Kafka, I said, what about Kafka? Girnus shrugged and pointed to his bookshelves, to the complete works of Kafka. But, I persisted, Kafka is available neither in the bookshops nor the libraries. 'It will come', said Girnus, 'in time.' I declared myself to be bored and unconvinced by much socialist realist writing. Girnus referred to a new campaign, personally instigated by Walter Ulbricht, to raise the level of novels and plays in the G.D.R. Yes, I said, but really this institutionalised optimism, this world of social heroes and anti-social villains, of positives and negatives — something was missing. 'What?' asked Girnus. And it was here that I mentioned Malraux. But not only Malraux; the names of decadent Western writers gushed from my lips like soft marbles. I was trying to say that a certain sadness or pessimism in the face of the human condition was an invariable element of authentic writing.

'Here we do not have time to be pessimistic,' Girnus said, 'we are too busy building a better world for our people and our children.'

The girls nodded vigorously. The professor's pipe smoke filled the office. I drew breath. Would he not agree that through the ages the greatest writers and poets had been moved by the awful solitude and loneliness of the individual life and the individual death? Had socialists anywhere yet succeeded in building so brave a new world that we could afford to exorcise this dimension of feeling from our literature?

Girnus paused. His posture was calm, scholarly, tranquil.

'For five years', he said, 'I was a prisoner in a Nazi camp. I knew that every day might be my last. But I also knew that my comrades were continuing the struggle and that ultimate victory was assured. I held my own fate to be of little account. I never felt lonely.'

One has to admire such men. But I would rather live with Kafka, Malraux, Camus and Sartre. I would rather read Kazantazakis' remarkable *Toda Raba*, where Geranos says: 'We must love not human beings, but the inhuman flame that devours them. We must fight not for humanity, but for this flame which makes fire out of the damp, crawling, nauseating straw that goes by the name of Humanity.' Geranos is a committed Communist, yet a man 'now emancipated from all hope'. What he finds to be alone worthy of a soul such as his own is 'the red line that pierces and passes through men like a rosary of skulls.' Yes. Imagine, says Camus, Sisyphus happy. Yes. 'But for the present the storm approaches its thunderhead, and it is apparent that the boat drifts ever closer to the shore so the blind will lead the blind, and the deaf shout warnings to one another until their voices are lost.' (Norman Mailer, *Barbary Shore*.) Yes.

CHAPTER TWO

Realism and Reality

ONE

The pursuit of mimesis finds its practical manifestation in two great modern literary traditions, 'naturalism' and 'realism'. 'Realism', of course, is an elusive notion; like 'socialism', practically everyone lays claim to be its true guardian. (Surrealism, which many people would regard as the absolute antithesis of realism, means when translated 'supra-realism'.) However the central realist tradition and its supporting philosophy are not difficult to distinguish, nor is it particularly baffling to learn that Balzac, Dickens, George Eliot, Tolstoy, Ibsen, Gorky and Sholokhov have been widely recognised as realists whereas Mallarmé, Jarry, Breton, Joyce, Kafka, Beckett and Robbe-Grillet have not. I do not intend to dig too exhaustively — literary excavations if painstaking soon share the tedium of other forms of archaeology, and it will serve our purpose here if we penetrate no further than the naturalist movement which rose to prominence during the last half of the nineteenth century.

But first, a few guiding propositions:
— Both naturalism and realism have historically a specific sense and a general sense. On the one hand they describe two coherent and fully articulated philosophies which are not only literary but also social; on the other hand they describe a general tendency, style or mood in works which are hybrids of several traditions.

— Not all naturalists and not all realists share the same socio-political philosophy.

—Naturalism, particularly in its specific sense, contains certain political corollaries which render it unacceptable *in toto* to socialist realists.

— Yet both schools share the mimetic, mirror-of-life, representational philosophy of literature.

— Despite disagreements, socialist realism owes much to naturalism. In fact the naturalists adopted and accentuated certain features of, say, Balzacian realism, and these features in their accentuated form were subsequently fed back into the later realism.

Naturalism was a by-product of a prevailing faith in science. It caught hold of the literary imagination in an era when social philosophers like Saint-Simon, Comte and Durkheim were insisting that sociology and even politics could be put on a basis as rational, inductive, scientific and 'positive' (to use Comte's phrase) as physics or chemistry. Emile Zola, the greatest of the naturalist writers, concluded that literature too could achieve a scientific status. An end to metaphysics! An end to theology, ideology, romanticism and hot-headed dissension! How progressive and modern it all seemed then, the very vanguard of the Enlightenment. (We have come full circle; today the prevailing school of Anglo-American behavioural social scientists look forward to a post-industrial age uncontaminated by the virus of ideology and dissent.) But in fact we can now appreciate to what extent these 'positivists', with their fear of class warfare and ideology, were reacting in bourgeois panic to the upheavals of 1848 and the ensuing conservative-clerical reaction.

According to Zola, literature could and should portray life exactly as it is. A mirror held up to life. Facts, empirical observation, direct experience, documentation — these must be the foundations of naturalism. Zola denounced melodrama, false heroics, outlandish situations, improbabilities, and long, rhetorical declamations. 'It seems impossible,' he wrote, 'that the movement of inquiry and analysis which is precisely the movement of the nineteenth century, can have revolutionised all the sciences and arts and left dramatic art to one side, as if isolated.' Truth, he believed, could afford to walk naked. The truer to life, the greater poetry becomes. The novelist and playwright must convey reader and spectator into the milieu of the mine, the factory, the market, the railway station. 'What we need is detailed reproduction.' Everything must be 'lifelike'; everything must march 'in step along the naturalistic road'. Man must be portrayed as determined by the precise environment that 'produced him'. The incidents in a novel or play should be 'absolutely typical' of the social cycle and the life cycle.

A theory is always purer than its practice. But it must be conceded that Zola's novel, *L'Assommoir*, came very close to fulfilling the naturalist prophecy. As a literary structure, *L'Assommoir* reveals the following characteristics: (a) a distrust of 'artiness'; (b) the use of colloquial speech patterns not only in the dialogue but also in the narrative; (c) a story rather than a plot; (d) an attempt to make the central character or characters as unheroic as possible; (e) a sustained emphasis on the material environment and on the description of *things*; (f) crowd scenes; (g) the world changes slowly, it evolves, and talk of revolutionary panaceas is so much metaphysical balderdash; (h) a pseudo-scientific attempt to depict things as healthy or unhealthy rather than as good or bad; (i) an emphasis on passion, emotion, the id, rather than on reason as the source of human behaviour — hence a good deal of sex (though not in all naturalist writers).

Now Zola was greatly out of sympathy with Marxism, and Marxist critics, notably Lukács, have been proportionately out of sympathy with Zola. Nevertheless naturalism has close affinities to the kind of realism favoured by Marxists, and its impact on left-wing writing has been far-reaching. The positivistic naturalist school and the Marxist realists may differ about social and political reality, but they share in common the assumption that literature can and should reflect that reality. Realism has incorporated from naturalism a preference for colloquial dialogue, detailed descriptions of milieu, and 'dirt in the finger nails'. But realism, particularly in its Marxist form, emphasises man's rationality, his ability to radically change his environment by revolutionary-political means, and it therefore shows more partiality for the heroic 'hero' and for plot. Zola chastised those writers who injected their own utopian visions into their depiction of reality; the Marxist writer, armed with his insights into the historical dialectic, identifies reality with a particular future destiny. Zola wrote to portray the world, the Marxists to change it. Zola distrusted commitment, the Marxists insist on it. It is noteworthy that where Zola's social indignation was most furiously aroused, and where as a consequence he wrote with a view to mobilising public opinion, the naturalistic mode shows signs of disintegration. Compare, in this respect, *Germinal* with *L'Assommoir*. But even more instructive is a comparison of *Germinal* (1885) with Maxim Gorky's *The Mother* (1907), the seminal work of modern socialist realism.

Gorky opens with a depiction of working-class life almost as gloomy and fatalistic as Zola's. 'Life had always been like that. It flowed on in a turbid stream, slowly and evenly, year after year, and everything was bound together by deep-rooted habits of thinking and doing the same thing day after day.' A classic text of naturalism! But this is Gorky, not Zola, and within a few pages the Russian novelist will have discarded the pessimistic determination of milieu for the optimistic determinism of history. Gorky's revolutionaries, courageous, rational and inspired, will break their chains and run up the Red Flag in the heart of the enemy citadel. Here 'character' gives way to 'hero', story to plot (partially), the id to the ego, instinct to intellect, inertia to action, the description of things to the proclamation of ideas, the iron environment to the will of iron. We pass from naturalism to socialist realism.

In the socio-political context of the late nineteenth century naturalism retained its generally progressive political impact. Regimes were on the whole reactionary and the Marxist movement weak and hesitant. When Gerhart Hauptmann's *The Weavers* was staged at the Berlin Deutsches Theater in 1893 it caused a political uproar. To describe an event naturalistically — in this case the Silesian weavers' uprising of 1844 — is always to comment upon it; in the authoritarian climate of Hohenzollern Prussia the description itself was tantamount to insurrection. But set against the emergence in the twentieth century of highly organised workers' parties and, after the First World War, of a Communist International dedicated (at least initially) to revolutionary upheaval, naturalism assumed a political complexion which was increasingly neutral and quietist.

Take for example D. H. Lawrence's three plays about the Nottinghamshire mining communities. In terms of the theatre, *The Daughter-in-Law*, *A Collier's Friday Night* and *The Widowing of Mrs Holroyd* carry naturalism to its limits. Everything that Lawrence offers is 'real', 'typical', a 'slice of life'. Here, it would seem to the audience, is a genuine miner's cottage on a genuine Friday evening; it just so happens that the fourth wall of the room has been removed to enable us to overlook and overhear what passes. But Lawrence's style creates not only total illusion and total empathy, it ultimately leads to total acceptance of the miners' crushing existence. This, the author insists, is what life for them is like; the artist's function is that of a literary camera; let someone else, some political ideologue crammed full of utopian zeal, tell us what the future holds.

Consider another case, somewhat different. Lawrence was not a socialist, whereas Sean O'Casey's radical political commitments were never concealed. Yet as soon as we read or see *The Plough and the Stars* we appreciate how extensively these same commitments were blunted in O'Casey's drama by the naturalist tradition he inherited and adopted (bearing in mind that naturalism involves a view of the relationship between art and reality which has political implications). Compassion and indeed indignation on behalf of the poor and downtrodden, yes; but when it comes to flags, barricades and hot gospelling, the playwright offers a smile which is both sad and bitter. The naturalist writer stands very close to his material; his vocation is not to dream but to observe men's actual behaviour, the discouraging continuity of human nature. Society may be brutal but so is the effort to change it. Spilt blood, O'Casey reminds us, is never tomato ketchup and it usually pours from innocent veins.

That pure naturalism has built-in limitations from a socialist point of view has been recognised by a number of writers within their working lives. Henri Barbusse's novel, *Le Feu*, moulded its massive indictment of war out of the clay (or rather trench mud) of naturalism. At a time (1916) when the official France, the regime, the Church, the ruling class, the *union sacrée*, had made the very word 'war' synonymous with *la gloire, le sacrifice* and *la patrie éternelle*, Barbusse's gruesome and gruelling descriptions of what it was really like to be blown open by shrapnel while crawling through the slimy entrails of one's comrades amounted to an act of mutiny. Even so, Barbusse was leaving nothing to chance; time and again the naturalistic depiction of the confusion of the peasant *poilus* is interrupted by improbably coherent diatribes against the capitalistic causes of the war. Lenin admired *Le Feu*; Barbusse reciprocated by becoming a militant Communist; henceforward his writing rapidly shed its naturalistic tone in favour of didactic exposition. The novel *Clarté* resorts to unceasing rhetoric.

Finally the example of two American novelists.

In the space of a single work, James T. Farrell encompassed the whole journey from ultra-naturalism to a particular form of committed realism. I refer to his great trilogy, *Studs Lonigan*. 'Life had always been like that. It flowed on in a turbid stream . . .' At the outset Farrell transposes Gorky's initial naturalistic mood to the Irish backstreets of

Chicago. 'Studs saw a tin can. He commenced kicking it, and stopped . . . He looked at the tin can. He came back and kicked it.' The undergrown, mal-educated would-be tough-guy Studs is destined to become one of urban America's tin cans. He wanders and struts through the first volume, bewildered, imprisoned by his environment, a non-hero incapable of inspiring literary development or plot. And then, as Farrell's own social attitudes change, fragments of didacticism infiltrate the narrative: 'He had come to America, haven of peace and liberty, and it, too, was joining the slaughter (World War I), fighting for the big capitalists.' Born out of the naturalist womb, Studs, like Zola's Gervaise, is doomed, denied a literary reprieve, destined to die before his time, beaten by a cruel milieu. But, as the novel progresses and as Farrell's own opinions clarify, new, politically enlightened, potentially active characters emerge, speeches are made, crowds gather in protest, and reactionaries fulminate. In the last volume, Farrell's commitment reaches a pitch; the result, in literary terms, is a radical structural transformation. Extensive use is made of techniques rendered famous by John Dos Passos — newspaper headlines, excerpts from newsreels, snatches of radio, typographical variations. The private, hermetically sealed naturalistic environment is burst asunder; throughout *Judgment Day* the private and the public, the local and the national, play literary leap-frog. Zola had been much influenced by the work of scientists such as Claude Bernard; the young Farrell in his time had turned to recent American positivists and behaviourists like G. H. Mead and C. Judson Herrick *(The Brains of Rats and Men.)* Now these influences were set aside; Farrell the writer no longer aspired to be the scientifically impartial observer of human behaviour; the Great Depression brought the ghost of Marx to the battlements of the stock exchange.

Dos Passos' *USA* is a unique hybrid of two traditions (plus some marked innovations). On the one hand a naturalistic insistence on detail, on letting life speak for itself, and a hyper-absence of hero or plot; on the other hand, highly stylised intrusions ('Newsreel', 'The Camera Eye') which have the effect of conveying the author's strongly committed overview of how private lives in America are related to the social system as a whole. Dos Passos' eccentric typography and his sudden breaks of rhythm and subject matter might at first sight appear incompatible with naturalism; and yet, as the history of modern painting shows, naturalism and impressionism are close cousins. (The average citizen's inability to visualise let alone comprehend his total environment is conveyed in the form of a kind of social stream of consciousness, complete with hiatuses and *non sequiturs*. Where the naturalist differs from the modernist is in his insistence that reality is intrinsically coherent and intelligible, granted the proper scientific apparatus of inquiry.) Dos Passos has been called a behaviourist, largely because his characters are portrayed mainly in terms of their actions, but the savage bursts of irony and the pointed juxtapositions that he permits himself in the 'Newsreel' and 'Camera Eye' passages betray and are intended to betray the author's conviction that American capitalism is warlike, exploitative and wasteful of the nation's resources of talent and goodwill.

The techniques employed by Dos Passos and to some extent by Farrell in *Judgment Day* could legitimately be described as alienation techniques (and, as such, intrinsically hostile to naturalism). But they are not alienation techniques in the Brechtian sense, and they do not yield a dialectical perception of the relationship of literature to reality and to itself. The alienation techniques of Dos Passos and Farrell are *internal*; in other words they convey the alienation of the characters alone. (At the level of holistic social description they bear more than a metaphorical relationship to the techniques employed by Joyce in his depiction of the individual.) The novelist is inviting the reader to share his privileged understanding of the world depicted within the book; but he is not drawing attention — except accidentally, except in so far as the critical spirit constantly sabotages empathy and illusion — either to himself, the reader or the book.

TWO

'Write the unvarnished truth!' demands the Soviet critic. And make no mistake, the pursuit of realism, of mimesis, the desire to 'tell it like it is', has an ancient and honourable lineage. 'That painting is most praiseworthy which is most like the thing represented', noted Leonardo da Vinci. In modern times the left-wing writer, the committed writer, the public writer, has pursued realism as if it were the Holy Grail. 'The first demand of art', wrote Chernyshevsky in *What is to be Done?*, 'consists in this, — to so represent objects that the reader may conceive them as they really are.' Elsewhere, in his essay on 'The Aesthetic Relation of Art to Reality,' the same author commented: 'Thus, the first purpose of art is to reproduce nature and life, and this applies to all works of art without exception.' Characters in novels, he maintained, were copies not creations. Marxists took up the cause. 'Literature', wrote Gorky, 'must attain to the level of real life. That is the point.' A French Communist critic, Jean Fréville, added: 'Realism demands that nothing be interposed between the world and its literary representation.' Certain words, often repeated, form the motif of mimesis: 'reproduce', 'reflect', 'mirror'. The contradictions in Tolstoy's novels, said Lenin, 'mirrored' the contradictions within the Russian peasant movement. Here is Mao on the subject: 'Works of literature and art, as ideological forms, are products of the reflection in the human brain of the life of a given society.'

Naturalism and realism share an attachment to mimesis. But we shall discover that mimesis in art is a mirage (except in so far as a clever reproduction can be passed off as an original painting or an artist's style so cunningly imitated that the forgery is not recognised).

We can approach the question of mimesis from several angles.

Feuerbach and Chernyshevsky were both 'mechanical' materialists: they held that sensations, thought and art reflected the experienced effect of things. Marx insisted on the contrary that thought and art were the products of man's *active* relationship with his environment — thus they contained a social as well as a biological dimension. In *The Eighteenth Brumaire of Louis Bonaparte*, he writes: ' . . . a century earlier, Cromwell and the English people had borrowed speech, passions and illusions from the Old Testament for their bourgeois revolution. When the real aim had been achieved, when the bourgeois transformation of English Society had been achieved, Locke supplanted Habakkuk.' Nevertheless when Marx and Engels distinguish between the intellectual and artistic superstructure and the economic infrastructure, a noticeably mechanical element has intruded. The sea and the soil exist independently of and prior to human activity, but this is not the case with spades, ploughs, steam engines and computers. Such objects, consigned by Marx to the economic infrastructure, are of course products of the inter-action of mind and matter; they not only determine thought, they are also determined by it. They are products of human *praxis*. What relevance has this to literature and particularly to the theory of mimesis? Every relevance. Literature, the written or spoken word, the descriptive passage, the total book, enters into that praxis. It is an active element. It not only reflects, describes and imitates the world, it also reshapes the world. In so far as it aims at absolute mimesis it inevitably deceives itself. It enters the general flow of consciousness and culture and becomes the negative which constantly redefines our perception of the positive, of 'reality'. When Lukács comments that although art mirrors reality it always contains an irreducible subjective component, he is providing an entirely misleading formulation. Although we distinguish between mind and matter, we have no way of grasping objectivity except through subjectivity.

Notice that mimesis involves a prescription as well as a description. If some books are 'truer to life, more realistic' than others, then evidently life does not impose itself on consciousness automatically. The picture is only as good as the camera. But I introduce this metaphor only to dismiss it as misleading. Can we say that the camera employed by George Eliot when writing *Middlemarch* was more accurate and of a finer fidelity than the apparatuses which produced *Alice in Wonderland* and *Ubu Roi*? Of course not. What is involved in this contrast is the particular writer's philosophy, his project, his active aim. A Daumier cartoon differs enormously from a Rembrandt portrait; their respective realism-content can be judged not in terms of an absolute human anatomy but only in terms of what we see in a man and what we wish to say about him.

THREE

'Realism, to my mind,' wrote Engels to Margaret Harkness (a lady thereby endowed with enduring fame), 'implies, besides truth of detail, the truthful representation of typical characters under typical circumstances.' According to Lukács, the great realist writer links every element, human and social, to every other element. Thus for example in Tolstoy the exploited Russian peasant is always 'present' even when invisible. 'The poetic starting point in the presentation of each character by Tolstoy was the question: in what way was their life based on the receipt of ground-rents and on the exploitation of the peasants, and what problems did this social basis produce in their lives.' Realism, according to Lukács' definition, rests on three supporting pillars: a reflection of the totality of the age; the location of the action in a precise time and place; and, last but not least, a politically progressive perspective. In order to achieve this triad, the nineteenth-century *Bildungsroman* form is recommended — dramatic-epic form, multiple complex plots, a variety of precise settings, strong political and social contrasts. Lukács speaks of Thomas Mann's mastery of 'the timeless rules of epic narration'.

To expound the theory is to expose it. Marx merely expresses a personal taste when he makes 'strong Rembrandtian colours' an essential attribute of realism. To equate ultimate realism with particular literary conventions evolved in the nineteenth century is simply a narrow provincialism of spirit. The structural elements of the *Bildungsroman* are literary conventions or codes with a limited life-span. And since no novel or play can record everything, Marxists demand that realism concentrates on what is typical. But what is 'typical' apart from the writer's highly subjective and programmatic philosophy? If sociological statistics had been available to Balzac, he would not and could not have established in literary terms the statistical mean of contemporary social attitudes; on the contrary, he would have exaggerated certain features and then concentrated them in a single character. The character of a realist novel or play is less likely to be an average man than a quintessential man — which means, although our semantic tradition resists the usage, that he is more a caricature than a character. This factor becomes even more evident when we come to the idealist-romantic heroes of socialist realism. Gorky's Vlassova was less typical of Russian actuality than symbolic of Marxist ideality.

Take a page of dialogue in any naturalistic novel. Slang, colloquialisms, abound in half-finished sentences. The writer, being a dedicated naturalist or realist, has perhaps taken a tape recorder into a café. But compare the unedited tape with the corresponding page in the novel, and you will discover that changes have been made, and cuts, the number of discrete voices reduced, remarks made in the café by A, B and C all attributed in the novel to B . . .

'I try to give the unspoken, unacted thoughts of people in the way they occur,' said Joyce. Impossible. A non-articulated thought is not simply an articulated thought waiting for

words to convey it into society. The process of verbalisation
modifies the thought. What Joyce succeeded in doing was
not to plant a tape recorder in Leopold Bloom's mind, but
rather to evolve a literary style which could be accepted as a
parallel equivalent to Bloom's inner life. All literature is a
code composed of signs, symbols, images, conventions.
What seems real to one generation strikes the next as absurdly stylised. Artistic unity springs not from 'reality' but
from the transformation which the artist imposes on it. The
great works of realism are full of suicides and murders. But
most readers have never witnessed one. Said Nietzsche:
'Art is not an imitation of nature but its metaphysical
supplement, raised up beside it in order to overcome it.'

This time next year I shall probably be sitting at my desk
as usual, more or less unhappy, more or less wealthy, more
or less in good health . . . But if you put me into your realist
Bildungsroman I can certainly expect within twelve months
to experience an emotional catastrophe, lose my fortune,
undergo a spiritual conversion, hold a decisive, cathartic exchange with my father and lose the use of my right arm.

Behind the apparently real or natural effects of dramatic
realism lie hours of contrivance in the beauty shop called the
well-made play, the *pièce bien faite.* John Russell Taylor
comments: 'With Pinero, as with all those who subscribe
somehow to the theory of the well-made play, the issue is
simply stated: how to convey the appearance, the impression
of real life unmanipulated, while at the same time mani-
pulating it as much as one needs to fit it into a play which
keeps the audience held unquestioningly . . . Audiences have
to be made to suspend disbelief . . .' Indeed, when the convention underlying realism became culturally unacceptable
for serious drama, it was adopted for comedy, with the convention itself, suitably exaggerated, an integral element of the
humour. Lukács praised Ibsen for his dramatic realism, his
strictly concentrated dramatic plots and his trueness to life.
But is life a strictly concentrated dramatic plot? Shaw remarked that Ibsen had changed the basic structural shape of

the drama from 'exposition-situation-unravelling' to 'exposition-situation-discussion'. Fine, a notable development for drama no doubt — but you might be surprised if an old man on his death bed summed up his life experience in terms of 'exposition-situation-discussion'. And even this old man would probably have longer to live than many of Ibsen's youthful characters. I find Lukács' opinions on the proper literary representation of reality considerably less convincing than the following point of view expressed by the avant-garde writer Zamyatin. 'The old, slow, soporific descriptions are no more . . . every word must be super-charged, high-voltage . . . Syntax becomes elliptical, volatile . . . and therefore realism — be it 'socialist' or 'bourgeois' — is unreal; immeasurably closer to reality is projection onto fast-moving curved surfaces — as in the new mathematics and the new art.'

FOUR

Mimesis, then, is a mirage. The best we can say for naturalist pretensions in that direction is that, according to certain cultural conventions, naturalism sets up a series of signs and signals along one code (language) which we recognise as *equivalent to* the signs and signals of a different code (our sense perception of reality). No doubt many thousands of Zola fans have put down *L'Assommoir* with the delighted exclamation, 'how like life!' Naturalism flourishes because it succeeds. But the creaking strains in the hull of didactic realism must be apparent. When the quintessential or typical truth about contemporary society is conceived with reference to a highly partial, partisan and problematical vision of a regenerated future, the novelist's attempt to be a literary camera cannot be sustained. The writer's desire to convey to us a self-contained universe, with a claim to its own mimetic reality, is thwarted by our awareness of the author's manipulations and interventions. My complaint against the

realists is of course not on account of these manipulations
and interventions, which I consider to be necessary and inevitable, but rather on account of the attempted concealment
and the failure to make a dialectical appreciation of the relationship of literature to society. (I shall devote more space
to this question in a later section.)

I shall deal very briefly with three typical forms of structural stress within didactic realism:

              (1) Character and contrivance
              (2) Indirect exposition
              (3) Direct exposition

Character and Contrivance:
Because the realist fictional character is quintessential rather
than statistically average, there is an innate tendency towards
caricature. With socialist realism and revolutionary didactism,
the tendency is hugely magnified. This problem is not a new
one. Joseph Payan, of the Revolutionary Committee of
Public Instruction, complained in 1794 that contemporary
French dramatists were providing caricatures instead of
characters. Such writers, he said, were 'of no use to literature,
to the moral welfare, and to the State'. Study — one hundred
and fifty years later — the rebukes handed out by a Zhdanov
or a Revai to the writers whom they had bullied and panicked
into over-zealous black-and-white writing. Comrades! The
negative features of our society and indeed of our great Party
also demand attention!

Now a different kind of contrivance:

In Barbuss' *Le Feu* we get to know Corporal Bertrand.
The portrait is naturalistic. Bertrand gets on with the job,
tries to stay alive in the trenches, he doesn't waste words.
Then suddenly he exclaims: 'There is one figure who has
raised himself above the war and who will shine for the
beauty and the importance of his courage . . . Liebknecht!'
You may not know who Karl Liebknecht was — rest
assured that 'Corporal Bertrand' knew even less. In the heat
of that war, a war of passionate national hatreds, even the

most radical and mentally mutinous soldier did not take his heroes from the other side.

Upton Sinclair wrote a novel called *The Jungle*. The hero, Jurgis, is a simple, strong, good-hearted Lithuanian hurled into the desperate jungle of industrial Chicago. But Sinclair will ultimately put Jurgis through the most improbable range of adventures, a veritable Cook's tour of the city and the soul, in order to satisfy a realistic convention. The author wishes us to forget his own existence; everything must be seen and explained as an extension of the hero's own experiences. But the contrivance is obvious.

As a satirical commentary on character and contrivance in didactic realism, the Soviet writers Ilf and Petrov published a story called *How the Soviet Robinson was Created*. A Soviet editor hires an author to produce a story about a Soviet Robinson Crusoe. As soon as the editor receives the finished manuscript he begins to take it apart. The mood is too individualistic . . . the desert island provides inadequate indications of the nature of Soviet life . . . The editor suggests to the author that he find a means of including in the story a local trade-union committee, a bottle of ink, a fireproof safe, the General Store Commission, a conference table and the broad strata of the toiling masses. The writer is flabber-. gasted: how can a single wave cast all these items onto a desert island? The editor ponders . . . then he has a brainwave: the writer must cut out (a) the shipwreck, (b) the desert island, and (c) the Soviet Robinson.

The editor is a socialist realist.

Indirect Exposition:
Exposition betrays the author's hand and shatters the illusion. The creator's voice must be obliterated; the reader must not suspect the presence of art, artifact or contrivance. The conjuror guards the tools of his trade like his life — he works entirely for *effects*. For the realist, literary talent, like a camera lens, is a means not an end. Unfortunately, the didactic realist has so much to say, so many points to push across

. . . Determined to disguise his own identity, he labours mightily to plant his own beliefs on the tongues of his fictional characters.

In *Bread and Wine*, Silone — a fine novelist — wishes to tell us more about the past life of his anti-Fascist hero, Pietro Spina. But if Silone himself were to provide the information by means of direct exposition, Spina's absolute reality, his absolute claim to an independent existence, would be in jeopardy. So: 'He stopped writing and thought of the naïve illusions with which he had entered his first Socialist group.' A long, elaborating passage follows, similar in style to exposition but safeguarded by that original 'he stopped writing and thought . . .'

Another case: in *Spartacus*, Howard Fast wishes to describe in retrospect the hero's dreadful experiences of slavery in the Egyptian gold mines. Adhering to the rules of realism, he entrusts the account to one of his characters, the slave-owner Batiatus, who happens to have found a willing audience in the aristocrat Crassus. But here a problem arises; Fast's perspective, which he is reluctant to withhold, is that of an ultra-radical; at the same time his descriptive powers, his command of language, which he is equally loth to withhold, fit oddly into the mouth of a greedy, cynical, *nouveau riche* upstart like Batiatus. Fast desperately attempts to resolve the incongruity: 'He [Batiatus] was the kind of sensualist who combines sadism with an enormous power of self-pity and subjective identification, and his tale of the gold mine had been told with power and colour and pity too . . .'

Very convenient.

In *Native Son*, Richard Wright analyses the racist basis of Chicago's housing system. The voice is clearly that of the author. But the realist mode dictates that exposition always be rescued from itself and disguised; the reference back to a fictional character is obligatory, even when that character is plainly incapable of conceiving, clarifying or expressing the notions which his creator foists upon him. So at the end of a long, expository onslaught on Chicago racism, Wright abruptly tells us: 'In a sullen way Bigger was conscious of this.'

The tension between the conventions of realism and the demands of didacticism assumes a peculiarly acute form in novels which predict the political future, be it dream or nightmare. In *The Iron Heel*, for example, Jack London hammers home his own Marxist critique of capitalist society for page after bloody page. BUT, predictably, the voice belongs not to London himself but to his insatiably loquacious super-hero Ernest Everhard. In two optimistically utopian novels, Morris's *News from Nowhere* and Skinner's *Walden Two*, an identical structural device is brought into operation. Morris's character Hammond and Skinner's character Frazier are invented simply to act as couriers who conduct visitors (conveniently uninformed and thirsty for information) on a guided tour of the utopian paradise, chattering non-stop, speaking entirely for the author, but rendering the conventional sacrifice on the altar of realism.

As for Sinclair Lewis, his normal artisan-like mastery of the naturalist-realist *appareil* goes completely haywire in his nightmarish vision of a fascist America, *It Can't Happen Here*. The hero of the novel is a liberal, small-town newspaper editor named Doremus Jessup. Whatever Lewis as author wants to say about politics and society Jessup must say for him. We come to a passage where ways and means of resisting the dictatorship are pondered. Surely this is Lewis's voice? But no: 'So debated Doremus, like some hundreds of thousands of other craftsmen, teachers, lawyers, what-not, in some dozens of countries under a dictatorship . . .' Well! First we get what is blatantly direct exposition, then a half-hearted attempt to make it indirect (so debated Doremus . . .), and finally a despairing assassination of Doremus' claim to an independent existence, the brutal and abrupt reduction of the flesh and blood hero to a sociological statistic.

Direct Exposition:
The tension of the novel mounts, the dam bursts under the

4*

pressure of didacticism, the author finally hurls himself into the arena . . .

We have already found Sinclair and Fast attempting to hide behind their own shadows. Here is Sinclair at the breaking point: little Stanislas earns three dollars a week in Chicago; Sinclair cannot resist the comment: 'just about his proper share of the total earnings of the million and three-quarters of children who are now engaged in earning their livings in the United States.' The pregnant Ona, wife to Jurgis, suffers acute pains. Again Sinclair must comment: 'The great majority of the women who worked in Packingtown suffered in the same way and from the same cause . . .' Forty or fifty years later the didactic-realist heritage carries Howard Fast to the same breaking point: 'Cicero was one of those young men — present in every age — who are capable of shedding every scruple, every ethic, every confusion of current morality . . . every impulse of mercy or justice which might stand in the way of success.' With four words, 'present in every age', the author shatters a painfully fabricated illusion. But he cannot resist the temptation.

The didactic realist may experience despair when he reaches the climax of his novel and discovers that everything remains to be said. His characters have been conceived as quintessential representatives of irreconcilably antagonistic social forces; his fictional entrepreneurs have sweated with the utmost cynicism for profits and more profits, his fictional workers and their wives have groped bravely towards the light, towards self-emancipation; his scenes, his plot, his action, his narrative, his dialogue have all been painstakingly fashioned to illustrate the dialectic of class conflict — yet everything remains to be said. The novelist's naturalistic impulses have proved immune to the virus of ideology; 'life itself' has intractably refused to yield its historical message. The novelist's ingrained sense of nuance, contradiction and the unpredictable has somehow confused and dispersed his political over-view. Total coherence remains out of reach. The novelist draws a deep breath. He prepares to stage a grand finale. Exposition and indirect exposition will run rampant; to hell with the story, the characters, the illusions of fiction; in the last resort it is not to literature but to real life, the real struggle in the streets and factories, that the novelist owes allegiance.

At the climax of *The Jungle*, Upton Sinclair sends his hero Jurgis into a conference hall. A debate is taking place in which every major socialist faction is represented. Finally a great orator rises to expound remorselessly the author's own point of view. Jurgis listens transfixed: he is getting the word, the light! 'It was a miracle that had been wrought in him . . . in his soul a new man had been born.' The grand finale of Louis Aragon's novel, *Les Cloches de Bâle*, involves an even more startling change of tone and style. The author abruptly jettisons his young heroine Catherine in favour of a real personage, the future (we are in 1913) Communist heroine Clara Zetkin. Aragon is quite explicit about it: 'I can no longer speak of Catherine, hesitant, vacillating Catherine, as she slowly approaches the light', because it is Clara who presages the brave socialist future. Surrendering to direct exposition, Aragon abandons his novel as a lost cause. When Howard Fast brings the curtain down on the drama of Spartacus he cannot resist offering as a bonus the reminder that, 'Tales become legends and legends become symbols, but the war of the oppressed against those who oppressed them went on and on.' (In case we missed the point.)

Personally I have little admiration for either Aragon or Fast as novelists, and Sinclair's limitations are always apparent. Similarly when a second-rate writer like Barbusse attempts to tie up his didactic novel, *Clarté*, with a thick web of jargon like 'The republican idea is the civic translation of morality, that which is anti-republican is immoral' — in such circumstances very little has been lost. But with a novel such as Wright's *Native Son* the effect on the reader of the 'grand finale' impulse is quite deplorable. Wright was a magnificent novelist; if any writer knew how to make his points implicitly, in terms of character, plot and action, if any writer was master of the realist convention, it was he. And yet for some reason, perhaps some failure of nerve, he felt unable to bring *Native Son* to a close without laboriously and extensively spelling out the whole socio-racial proposition again under the guise of court-room dialogue, the cut and thrust of competing attorneys. The unity of the novel, its coherence of mode and mood is shattered by the long, rhetorical terminating monologues which dot every 'i' and cross every 't'.

Realism and naturalism have been responsible for some of the richest and most relevant works of modern fiction and drama. They represented in their time highly progressive elements within the prevailing *Zeitgeist*. It is certainly not my intention to disparage their achievements. But our recognition of Michelangelo's genius does not oblige us to imitate his style or adopt his philosophy of art *in toto*. Zola believed that naturalism expressed the most advanced, scientific and up-to-date tendencies of an enlightened age. But one enlightenment soon yields to another. Yesterday's avant-garde becomes today's arrière-garde. It is not simply that naturalism and realism palpably fail to fulfil their mimetic pretensions; nor is it simply that political commitment and the didactic spirit produce unresolvable tensions within the structural conventions of modern realism. Our understanding of literature and language, and of their dialectical relationship to perception and experience, has hurried forward. The question is this: can writers who claim to represent the most advanced and progressive socio-political movement of their time really afford to be satisfied with a literary style and philosophy which evolved in the age of the steam engine?

CHAPTER THREE

Marxism and Modernism

ONE

The Marxist attachment to realism has as its corollary a
deep distrust of modernism in all its decadent manifestations.
Aeschylus, Dante, Shakespeare, Balzac, Scott, Goethe,
Pushkin, Heine, Dickens — these were the authors Karl
Marx took to bed with him. Engels' literary tastes were
apparently no different. As for Lenin, the modernist avant-
garde left him stone cold; Pushkin, Nekrassov and Tolstoy
excited his admiration. To Clara Zetkin he confided: 'I
however make bold to describe myself a "barbarian". I am
unable to consider the productions of futurism, cubism,
expressionism and other isms, the highest manifestations
of artistic genius. I do not understand them. I experience no
joy from them.' In the poems and public orations of the
Bolshevik-futurist poet Mayakovsky, Lenin perceived only
frantic and incoherent posturings, an aimless bohemianism.
As for Mayakovsky's poem, *150,000,000*, it was 'tricky and
affected'.

TWO

Now I would rather explore modernism than define it. The
scope of the notion is enormous, intimidating. It is inevitable
that I shall fail to draw distinctions where distinctions should
be drawn. No writer and no painter has to my knowledge

proclaimed himself a modernist. The flag of identity is hoisted from without the citadel rather than from within. Kafka does not write like Beckett, nor Mallarmé like Robbe-Grillet: Jarry's style differs from that of Pinter, and Klee's paintings resemble Bacon's not at all — yet all are modernists. We need not expect any two modernist writers to share an identical philosophy, whether ontological, social or political. Nor is modernism necessarily synonymous with 'avant-garde' or 'experimental' writing; naturalism in its day was highly avant-garde and experimental, as indeed were the plays of Ibsen; neither was modernist.

Let us begin with a very broad yet central notion: the anti-Enlightenment. It is essentially a late nineteenth-century phenomenon which one finds in the philosophy of Kierkegaard, Schopenhauer, Nietzsche and Bergson, in the sociological and political theories of Pareto, Mosca, Michels, Spengler and Sorel, and even in the psychoanalytical schools set in motion by Freud, Jung and Adler. And in Dostoyevsky. The anti-Enlightenment is a delayed reaction to the Enlightenment, to that eighteenth-century joyous proclamation of a universal secular knowledge and a universal Reason, whose flagship was the French Encyclopedia (Diderot, d'Alembert, etc.). In the nineteenth century the Enlightenment continues to insist that 'knowledge liberates and absolute knowledge liberates absolutely', but by now the manifestation, the concrete principle, is Science: natural science, biological science, social science, political science, every form of science. Great cities spring up, railways are built, wealth multiplies; everything, evidently, lies within the reach of man.

But something has gone wrong . . . Wars do not abate; poverty and human degradation scar the earth, class struggle becomes the Great Fear of the age. But more than this: somewhere a vital spiritual and metaphysical dimension has been lost: where is the soul, the spirit? God is dead, yes, but what can replace Him? Is man not mad, pitifully blind in his strutting egoism, thus to worship the work of his own clumsy hands? Is all this optimism and utopianism really justified? Are men really any the wiser, any the happier, any the closer to the mysterious sources of life?

The anti-Enlightenment thinks not.

Karl Jaspers described the reaction well: 'Beyond question there is a widespread conviction that human activities are unavailing; everything has become questionable; nothing in human life holds good; that existence is no more than an increasing maelstrom of reciprocal deception and self-deception by ideologies . . . The epochal consciousness has turned a somersault in the void.'

The origins of modernism are to be found in this somersault.

But Marxism is the golden child of the Enlightenment. It gathers together, synthesises and enshrines in a coherent social philosophy the most cherished propositions of scientism and rationalist humanism: an ultimate, verifiable Reason, both as a principle of human conduct and as a principle of understanding that conduct, an inexorably progressive historical process etched with bold, undeniable strokes into the tablet of the human race, and a not-so-distant future where the real and the ideal will once more be united after their unhappy separation during the successive. epochs of class society. Action founded on knowledge and knowledge founded on experience will carry men from the realm of necessity to the realm of freedom. It makes little difference that anarchists, reformists, revisionists, syndicalists, Fabians and Christian socialists have all picked notable quarrels with Marxism — nor, indeed, that Marxists have increasingly quarrelled amongst themselves in a welter of mutual excommunications. The basic assumptions of the Enlightenment permeate the whole socialist movement.

The anti-Enlightenment involves a massive onslaught on these cherished assumptions. Instinct is placed above reason, the will above the mind, the subconscious above the conscious. Knowledge? — mere subjectivity. History? — chaotic, arbitrary, a cycle of recurring spasms. Freedom? — man is

as free as a slave crawling east along the deck of a ship
travelling west. Alienation? — it is ontological, rooted in the
very human condition. The popular masses? — a vile, stupid
herd, destined to put their trust in one leader after another,
one élite after another. For the anti-Enlightenment, the
relationship of the sensitive, artistic or perceptive individual to the demands of mass society could only be one of
insurmountable antagonism.

The Enlightenment visualises the human personality as
advancing in rationality and self-control with the growth of
knowledge and mastery over nature. But Samuel Beckett's
Molloy disagrees: 'The fact is, it seems, that the most you
can hope to be is a little less, in the end, the creature you
were in the beginning, and the middle.' The modernist individual struggles within a perpetual crisis of identity. Molloy
recalls his own name with surprised detachment; his confusion as to where he is is equalled by his bewilderment as
to how he got there. 'Perhaps in an ambulance . . .' As
Lukács says, the non-hero or central consciousness of the
modernist novel operates in an opaque, impenetrable *in-
cognito*. 'What do you expect,' cries Molloy, 'one is what one
is, partially at least.' The realist writer working within the
Enlightenment tradition endows his characters with something called psychology; psychology is supposedly the
mechanism which mediates between the inner and the outer,
between impulse and reason, between the power of instinct
and the demands of society; it is the language or code by
which the 'irrational' can be grasped rationally and so, ultimately, diminished. Modernist novelists regard psychology as
a bogus metaphor. 'The secret source of our existence in what
might be called its nascent state', writes Nathalie Sarraute,
'are tropisms, these movements, of which we are hardly cog-
nizant, which slip through us on the frontiers of consciousness
in the form of indefinable, extremely rapid sensations.'

According to the modernist vision, human existence is
static, solitary. The 'hero' is not explicable in terms of social
or personal history — he is thrown into the world. For the

realist novelist, 'development' implies experience, increasing awareness, growth of personality; whereas for the modernist it means the gradual revelation of an unalterable condition, a sequence of tenuously related experiential fragments.

Marxist critics react sharply. Lukács attributes the modernist angst, the sense of primitive awe in the face of a hostile reality and the obsession with psychopathology, to a blind, despairing attempt to escape from the reality of capitalism. Sidney Finkelstein deplores the despairing introspection of the modernist writer: 'The more the impoverishment of the outer life, as he sees it, drives him inward, the more his inner life contracts.'

The key question for the realist here is 'what should I do?'; for the modernist hero it is 'who am I?' '*Je est un autre*', answered Rimbaud. A Beckett character is liable to change name in mid-stream; Faulkner gives two men in one novel the same name; the central character in both of Kafka's novels, *The Trial* and *The Castle*, is called simply K. On the first page of Sarraute's *The Planetarium* the reader is plunged into the consciousness of an unidentified someone: 'No, really, try as you might, you could find nothing to say against it, it's perfect . . .' In Marguerite Duras' *The Square* the narrative shifts without formal transition from character to character; the contrapuntal deployment of descriptive passages alternating with dialogue replaces analysis, motivation and a logical sequence of events. Sarraute herself has remarked that successive disappointments have taught us that there is no final basis to reality, only bases which multiply indefinitely. The typical odyssey of a Beckett novel runs: apparent self — arbitrary self — inessential self. These very real provocations have angered the smallest Marxist mice to bite furiously at the toes of the biggest modernist cats. Marcel Proust, declared Ralph Fox, 'has not mastered life with sufficient intensity to make his people live a complete life of their own, a life in which you can ask them any question and force an answer.'

The provocation is real, the legitimacy of the Marxist

reaction unarguable. Beckett offers a portrait of the human condition as an indefinable nothingness within, conscious of a possible relation with an equally indefinable nothingness without, yet somehow invalidating the potential relationship by the very act of consciousness. Here is our friend Molloy again: 'And perhaps it was A one day at one place, then C another at another, then a third the rock and I, and so on for the other components, the cows, the sky, the sea, the mountains. I can't believe it. No, I will not lie, I can easily conceive it. No matter, no matter, let us go on, as if all arose from one and the same weariness, on and on heaping up . . .' Speaking at Leningrad in 1953, the Czech Communist writer Jiri Hajek remarked: 'One can talk about the crisis in the novel only when literature becomes charged with radical scepticism, the conviction that it is impossible to know reality and that human existence on earth has no meaning at all.' The Russian novelist Leonid Leonov made the same point with the down-to-earth peremptoriness favoured by Soviet writers: 'Original thinkers, originators of ideas, do not waste the strength that has been granted them in cogitations which . . . are sterile; what is life, what is the sun, what is man made for? They haven't the time to waste.'

THREE

The realists and Marxists insist that the literary depiction of a coherent outer reality requires a logical sequence of time, plot, action, development, *dénouement*. Not so the modernists. 'The superficial dramatic action constituted by plot', writes Nathalie Sarraute, 'is nothing but a conventional code we apply to life.' Clock time is also jettisoned (and with it history). Just as the impressionist painters dissolved the accepted components of pictorial space, so Proust, Joyce and their successors disintegrated the traditional elements of literary time. The moment shatters continuity; the structure of time becomes private, subjective and circular;

the past is constantly re-created in terms of the present. In the flux of relativity time and space merge, flow apart, integrate. The second part of Kafka's *The Metamorphosis* sees the gradual erosion of clock time. Twilight fills the room; measurable units of time surrender to indefinite adverbs. In *The Trial* we join a Ferris wheel of motion without origin or aim, an indefinite cycle whose separate chapters could be reordered almost indefinitely. Once again, the Marxist reaction is hostile. The critic Paul Reiman describes Kafka's K as 'a mouse who happens to walk into a trap and, looking for an escape, helplessly runs to and fro, and finally exhausted, collapses.'

Aragon's *Le Paysan de Paris*, a product of the surrealist phase which preceded his conversion to Communism, is ultra-modernist in its spasmodic structure, its abrupt changes of theme, its abandonment to dream, its elevation of the image over the concept. True consciousness, seized at the moment of birth by 'spontaneous' or 'automatic' writing, is held to be both free from and superior to logical reflection. Fantasy alone can unearth the latent content of the age; the latent content is the real content. The surrealist mode revives, slightly modified but full of vitality, in the plays of Ionesco, where logic succumbs to anti-logic, *non-sequiturs* pursue one another in a dense dance, language chases its own tail and false syllogisms collide like homeless meteorites. Traditional norms of logic and causality are stripped away — they are arbitrary. Heidegger remarked that the first condition of man is *to be there*; for the modernist playwright it is apparently both the first and last condition . . . or *not to be there* . . . same thing (Godot).

FOUR

Without doubt Marxists are justified in rejecting large sectors of the *Weltanschauung* of modernism and the anti-Enlightenment. The political implications of this philosophy

tend to be quietist when they do not provide positive comfort to reaction. Ionesco may be correct that death, boredom
and absurdity will be waiting for man in utopia — but the
main task is to reach utopia. What is the use of paying high
taxes for schools and pensions if life is really absurd?, ask the
bejewelled ladies as they stream out of the theatres of Paris,
Berlin, London and New York. The hungry and the starving
are not unduly worried about the Absurd — they will come
to that when their stomachs are full. But the modernist
writer is frequently (not always) irritated by the stupidity,
the *bêtise*, of the ordinary man and woman; his literature is
virtually an act of disassociation. There is a world of difference between the ridicule of a Molière and the ridicule of
a Ionesco; I know of no former concentration camp inmate
who has permitted himself the abuse of his own species with
which Monsieur Ionesco fills the gilded auditorium of the
Comédie Française. Beckett's brilliant demolition job on
causality prompts the hostile question: does the author, or
his cook, bother to light the gas before frying an egg? And
when the narrator of *Le Paysan de Paris* tells us, '*le hasard,
voilà toute mon expérience*', we can legitimately wonder
whether it is *le hasard* alone which leads him into a bank
whenever he is short of cash. The narrator of Alexander
Trocchi's *Cain's Book* dwells in a blind, Beckett-like depression: 'Thus I must go on from day to day accumulating,
blindly following this or that train of thought . . . No beginning, no middle, and no end.' Well, drugs do have that effect.
But the drugged modernist will not rest until he has convinced us that his own condition is no different from that of
the whole species. Man, evidently, is a paranoic psychopath.

A lot of modernist writing seems to have been conceived
during a vast yawn of boredom. Recently I read a very excellent and sensitive novel by a British exponent of the
nouveau roman, Christine Brooke-Rose. It is called *Between*.
The heroine 'thinks' (and it is her thoughts which fill the
greater part of the novel) in short, fragmentary, recurring formations, similar to Sarraute's tropisms. There is justification

in the fact that she is a simultaneous interpreter whose life has become a cycle of airplane flights, hotel bedrooms, congresses and garbled speeches. Phrases from a speech at a demographers' conference mingle in her mind with chunks of Romanian travel propaganda. This is convincingly done. But it is not by accident that a novelist chooses her theme, her milieu, her central character. The perpetual airplane journey, or the recurring park bench, or the dustbin, or the drug-soaked needle are presented to us by many modernists as valid metaphors for the total human condition.

Of course the Marxists and socialists, the heirs of the Enlightenment, have become frightfully rhetorical Man-mongers. Ultra-humanism reeks of sententious piety: the dignity of man, the will of the people . . . the working man . . . the new Soviet man . . . one can afford an occasional smile at all that jazz without joining the CIA payroll. Never-theless the socialists, Marxists and humanists have done well to hold the anthropological line under massive attack. The most recent assault — conducted by Robbe-Grillet and the proponents of the *nouveau roman* — has created confusion by proclaiming its own rationality, realism and indeed humanism. The argument, briefly, runs like this: 'The world is neither significant nor absurd. It *is*, quite simply.' Notions of signi-ficance and absurdity, argues Robbe-Grillet, emanate from the anthropological fallacy, the ancient myth that the material universe is an extension of human feeling and pur-pose. Sense, meaning, significance — what can we really be sure of? Very little, except what we see. Hence, according to Robbe-Grillet, the need in literature to renounce the visceral, analogical style for the descriptive, measuring, optical style. Man is banished. But is he? The optical and the descriptive, as Robbe-Grillet has conceded, have a human reference point; man stubbornly resists ejection; a detailed description of a table top or a landscape is inevitably the result of human perception, human categories, a human vocabulary. And this perception, these categories, this vocabulary are intimately linked to purpose, project, fear, desire, emotion, pleasure.

Robbe-Grillet's theories amount to a new form of positivism, but, as with the Comtean positivism which inspired the nineteenth-century naturalists, the scientific pretensions turn out to be spurious. Yet the naturalist writers were at least intensely humanistic and intensely preoccupied by people; whereas the cool, detached surface of Robbe-Grillet's novels fails to conceal a supercilious boredom, an élitist withdrawal, a cultivated disdain for the passions, hopes, confusions, ideas and triumphs of men.

FIVE

This having been said, the virulence of the Marxist attitude towards modernism remains remarkable. Lukács has gone so far as to equate realism and modernism in the post-war world with the forces of peace and war. According to this analysis, the great 'bourgeois critical realists', Anatole France, Romain Rolland, Bernard Shaw, Theodore Dreiser, and Heinrich and Thomas Mann, contributed effectively to a progressive rearguard action against the dominant forces of imperialism and war. Whereas the modernists, by depriving us of our capacity to comprehend or resist imperialism (whether advertently or inadvertently), have given positive encouragement to the dogs of war. Even more extreme in its depiction of the politically noxious effects of modernism is the current East German critique of Franz Kafka. (Poor K.) At a ceremony held in Weimar early in September 1968, Dr Klaus Gysi, the East German Minister of Culture hit out at revisionist critics like Eduard Goldstücker and Ernst Fischer who had attempted to rehabilitate Kafka. 'Such reverence for Kafka', said Dr Gysi, had been 'the ideological origin of all the theories and tendencies of the "third way to socialism" in Czechoslovakia, especially the non-recognition of the power of the working class and its leading role.' To foster admiration for this decadent writer was, Dr Gysi firmly believed, 'a kind of spiritual rape' which had been the 'mental preparation for those events which have plunged our neighbour-nation into the deep crisis exploited by counter-revolution.'

To anyone familiar with Kafka's work, all this may seem rather curious. His view of alienation is as much social as ontological; he examines the existential predicament of man in terms of social situations. In *The Trial*, K. shows himself perfectly capable of explaining each situation quite lucidly. Bewilderment stems less from incomprehension or inward fragmentation than from comprehension followed by powerlessness. A rational mind confronted by an irrational world. Kafka offers many indications that he attributes this irrationality to the nature of the prevailing social system. He never dissolves the outer world; he never abandons the struggle for rationality; he never abandons man to the id, to instinct, to chaos. Logic continues its unequal struggle against the illogical.

Now it is true that Kafka was not a revolutionary. He indicates no way out of the impasse. Indignation, yes, protest, yes, but never revolt. He neither surrenders to absurdity nor attempts to overthrow it. From a Marxist point of view this is all no doubt reprehensible. Yet there are many non-revolutionary authors for whom Marxists have expressed the keenest admiration — Balzac and Dickens, for example. So if we are to locate Kafka's inborn criminality, we shall have to search elsewhere. Nor need we look far. For the bureaucratic society described metaphorically in *The Trial* and *The Castle* must evoke discomforting feelings among the official ruling élite of the Communist one-party states. And this is precisely the reason why liberal Communists in Eastern Europe have recently found Kafka — undeniably a modernist — a uniquely relevant writer; not because they wish to restore capitalism, but because they wish to restore the value of the individual in the face of political and bureaucratic tyranny. So, unless we subscribe to the official East German mumbo-jumbo about counter-revolution, the leading role of the working class, etc., we have here at least one instance of modernist literature fulfilling a politically progressive function.

The modernist movement has made a deep exploration of the Subjunctive. Can the socialist writer, the committed writer, afford always to lean on the Indicative? Can he afford, indeed, to dismiss the whole modernist movement as a manifestation of capitalist decadence? I confess to being a little sceptical about capitalist decadence. In the Marxist canon capitalist imperialism is always to be found in its last stage, or the last stage of the last stage, or the last stage of the last stage of the last stage . . . but someone somewhere is notably reluctant to give up the ghost.

But there are further objections to the thesis that modernism is simply a manifestation of capitalist decadence. The factors which determine a cultural climate are both many and varied; reference back to a single genetical factor, the prevailing mode of production and its class structure, is always futile. Joyce and Wells were contemporaries; Sartre and Beckett have both lived in the same city and shared, I suppose, a roughly comparable standard of life. The modernist tradition is weaker in Britain than in France or Germany, but monopoly capitalism is no less strongly entrenched. Lukács heaps odium on the modernists for their *wilful perversity* in adopting the obscurantist *Weltanschauung* of the anti-Enlightenment, and gives out prizes to Shaw, Rolland and Mann for their *wilful virtue* in upholding critical realism. But can both groups have been equally 'determined' by the environment of a decadent capitalism? Cultural history and economic history do not dovetail neatly: they overlap, and the ragged edges can span centuries. Modernism is neither anchored to capitalism nor is it intrinsically decadent.

Artistic decadence is something else. It is the shadow without the substance. It involves extravagant imitation of a style which has lost its original dynamism and sense of purpose. Thus — to switch back to the social plane — the modern West African bourgeoisie is decadent at the moment of its birth, parodying the tastes and habits of a European class which remains productive as well as parasitical. But the modernist movement has embarked on ceaseless explorations, energetic innovations, renovations, renewals. Occasionally, it is true, the obsessive quest for novelty at all costs has assumed a decadent colouring; but no movement should be judged by its epigones and camp followers. Wishing to offend no one, I must nevertheless suggest that Soviet neo-classical sculpture is nothing if not decadent — the repetitious and slavish imitation of a dead formula. The same holds good in the field of literature. All but a few of the novels and plays produced in the Stalin era clung nervously to formulas which shed their freshness and became over the years stale stereotypes. And *that* is decadence.

The fact is, modernism is *the* authentic artistic movement of our century; by and large it has failed to flourish only where it has been censored out of existence. It has enormously extended the horizons of art and literature; even at its most private, withdrawn and obscure, it indicates a sharp, contemporary reaction to the nature of the age. We are witnesses, I think, to a kind of tragedy: the most progressive political tendency and the most adventurous artistic tendency of our time have glowered at one another in mutual fear and suspicion. But I am not concerned here to persuade. modernists to accept facets of socialism; I have the immodest ambition of persuading socialists to accept facets of modernism. Consequently I shall pursue a little further the folly of the Left.

SIX

The Treaty of Brest-Litovsk was signed in 1918. The new Bolshevik government, recognising its physical inability to defend Western Russia against superior German military forces, decided to cut its losses, ceded vast territories and made peace. In the 1960s many Marxist literary critics, shattered by official Soviet revelations of Stalinist crimes, and recognising that in the battle for public appreciation the old socialist realism was in perpetual retreat before the modernist tanks, decided to cut their losses and cede vast territories. Some examples: *Les Lettres Françaises*, a cultural weekly sponsored by the French Communist Party and edited by Louis Aragon, was, in the post-war era, a terrible blunt instrument of Zhdanovist vituperation. In its pages the latest philistine banality of Zhdanov, Fadeyev or Stalin himself jostled for prominence with shabby reproductions of Ukrainian collective farmers frozen into stone. Camus? A neo-fascist. Sartre? 'A servile executor of a mission confided to him by Wall Street.' (In those days, naïve materialist theory insisted that the CIA must be financed by Wall Street; it occurred to no one that Wall Street is a front organisation for the CIA.) Typical of the literary jewels which glittered in the old-style *Les Lettres Françaises* is this gem by Stalin Prize-winning novelist André Stil:

'It is true, they think, it is well known that everyone has a little of STALIN at the bottom of him, which watches us from inside, smiling and serious, giving confidence. It is our own consciences as Communists, this internal presence of STALIN.' (Stil's capitals.)

Yet today *Les Lettres Françaises* is the most entertaining and instructive journal of its kind in France. Read all about yesterday's demons! German expressionists, French surrealists, Jarry, Joyce, Henry Moore, Cocteau, Beckett, Virginia Woolf, Georges Bataille, Faulkner, Kafka, Eliot, Robbe-Grillet, Butor, the new novel, the theatre of the absurd, the new structuralist criticism, Godard, the new cinema. You name then, we buy them. Long may it continue.

But the basic strategy of the new Marxist criticism leaves much to be desired. By a curious paradox the revisionists have applied to modernism the same analytical system that Lukács, the doyen of the old guard, put to work on the nineteenth-century bourgeois realists. I shall call this 'objectification'. According to Lukács, the avowed, subjective social philosophies of a Balzac, an Ibsen or a Tolstoy are quite irrelevant to the social perspective which *emerges* from their novels and plays. Thus the genius of their art transcends the limitations of their bourgeois ideology; it is through the alchemy of this genius that the great, dialectical, realist vision of society in transition emerges. But when Lukács arrives at the detested modernists, his working hypothesis mysteriously changes: the vice of these writers is their conscious adoption of a retrograde *Weltanschauung* which is consciously reflected in their work. The new school of Marxist critics have quite simply declared irrelevant the *Weltanschauung* and favourably re-objectified the social content *yielded* by the work. Thus, however aberrantly Joyce, Kafka, Beckett and Faulkner may have understood the social process, their genius — so the argument runs — gave birth to novels and plays which, when read objectively, expose the inhumanity of modern capitalism. In the opinion of Ernst Fischer, the *œuvre* of Beckett constitutes a revolutionary critique of Western society.

The dead are even more suitable for body-snatching than the living. Poor Kafka's permanent post-mortem in the Marxist morgue continues. Kafka's Gregor changed from man to vermin; the same happened to Kafka, but now he is man again. When he died in 1924, Czech Communists were lavish in their praises: S. K. Neumann described him as a 'sensitive mind . . . who loved the exploited and inexorably punished the rich in an extremely complex yet moving fashion.' Then the Inquisition arrived to reverse this provincial naïvety. Condemnation, burial. In 1958, *The Trial* was republished in Prague; by 1963 the Czech Travel Agency was organising Kafka tours for foreign visitors. The corpse, now embalmed, is wrapped in a clean red shroud. Says Ernst Fischer: 'Kafka has created total negation, but in it there is also hidden the negation of the negation, the breakthrough from alienation to a decision which bestows upon existence a sudden meaning, and the sense of belonging.' According to Roger Garaudy, Kafka, although ignorant of the true causes of his own alienation and although incapable of proposing remedial action, nevertheless succeeded in creating a mythical world whose identity or refracted identity with the actual world implies the need for a *dépassement* of that world.

Note the key phrases of the new Marxist criticism: 'negation of the negation', 'hidden', 'objectively'. To master this trick you only have to discard the writer in question and choose the kings, queens and aces of the Marxist pack. Everything is turned upside down; the old criteria of criticism are abandoned wholesale and realism, according to Garaudy, emerges as a literary territory 'without boundaries' *(sans rivages)*. The new Marxists handle the great modernists in the same way that the old Marxists handled the great realists — the author's known intentions or philosophy are discarded as irrelevant to what emerges from his books. The Marxists have declared themselves losers in the war against modernism but at the same time have taken the modernists prisoner! This may bring in petty dividends at a narrow, tactical level, but as general cultural strategy it shows little or no advance in perception and sensibility. That crude tactics are involved can be readily gathered from the following statement by Ernst Fischer, one of the most enlightened Marxists (and recently expelled from the Austrian C.P.): 'We ought not to abandon Proust, nor Joyce, nor Beckett and even less Kafka to the bourgeois world. If we do not permit it, these writers will not help the bourgeois world, they will help us.' The new Marxist critics ignore what modernism *is*; they persist in ascribing alienation to a single genetic factor — the capitalist mode of production — and thus ignore the manifold sources and types of alienation which modernists have depicted with such pain and brilliance. Once again the worker-as-artist is denied all cerebral or conceptual powers — he is the mindless magician who works wondrous miracles but knoweth not how. Once again Marxist literary critics display more concern for Marxism than for literature.

Ghost-like, an ageing warrior emerges on the battlements

of my conscience. He is a compound figure, stuck together out of people I have known, militants, fellow-travellers, Party intellectuals whose faces are creased with integrity and the imprint of hard times, and whose voices, even when pitched in repose, seem permanently primed to the urgencies of large conference halls. Speaking his mind, this old man dresses me down, reprimanding me for scoring points at the expense of comrades whose situation remains difficult. Of course Ernst Fischer could put certain things differently if the opponents of the liberal view within the socialist movement did not remain powerful and determined . . .

Enough. I have listened, I have absorbed all these tactical arguments, these special pleas for (permanently) extenuating circumstances, but I refuse to hear. Old man, you should have learned that the writer or critic who delivers himself up to tactical manœuvres eventually loses his voice.

SEVEN

A few paragraphs back I suggested that I had in mind to offer socialists a more favourable perspective on modernism, rather than to lure modernists to the barricades. But now I have second thoughts. A modernist or avant-garde writer is not necessarily a man consciously or tenaciously wedded to the basic pessimistic tenets of the anti-Enlightenment. Chances are, he has never heard of the anti-Enlightenment. He may simply wish to pursue his art, his craft. And what is likely to reinforce his political blankness or neutrality may have less to do with Marxist aesthetic theory than with his knowledge (precise or blurred) of how revolutionary regimes in practice have dealt with his unfortunate colleagues; not only with avant-garde artists and modernists, but with any writer or intellectual who pursues his own muse or fails to satisfy the diligences of the regime in power. (When a Picasso joins the Party it reacts like a nauseated boa-constrictor, uncertain whether to swallow down or vomit up this enormous prize.)

The revolutionary impulse is always to place virtue above freedom; or, rather, to equate 'true freedom' with virtue. The English Puritans closed the playhouses altogether, the French Jacobins attempted to harness the theatre to their own cause. On 2 August 1793, the Committee of Public Safety, 'desiring to mould further the sentiments and character of the French into a truer form of republicanism', proposed a 'regulation of dramatic performances'. The Convention adopted the proposal and suggested productions of republican tragedies such as *Brutus*, *Guillaume Tell*, *Caius Gracchus*, etc. In June of the following year the Committee of Public Instruction headed by Joseph Payan, published a circular on the subject of *Spectacles*, complaining that the theatres remained clogged with the rubbish of the old regime. 'We must clear the stage, and allow reason to enter and speak the language of liberty, throw flowers on the graves of martyrs, sing of heroism and virtue, and inspire love of law and the *Patrie*.' *Le Cid* was adapted to erase traces of the old regime. The only permissible new plays were those in which republican virtue triumphed; this was a didactic, agitational, empathetic form of theatre which caused the enthused *citoyens* to leap on to the stage, embrace the heroine and pummel the unfortunate actor playing the villainous aristocrat.

But the Jacobin dictatorship did not last long. The guillotine was turned against its exponents. The short cutters were cut short.

The Bolsheviks had little to learn from the Jacobins . . .

At first the omens were good, Lenin told Clara Zetkin: 'Every artist, everyone who considers himself such, has the right to create freely according to his own ideal, independently of everything.' It is true that in his much-quoted *Party Organization and Party Literature* (1905) he referred to literature as 'a cog and a screw of one great Social-Democratic mechanism . . .', but he may very well not have been referring to 'artistic' literature or belles-lettres. In any case, he then went on: 'There is no question that literature is least of all subject to mechanical adjustment or levelling, or by the rule of the majority over the minority. There is no question, either, that in this field greater scope must undoubtedly be allowed for personal initiative, individual inclination, thought and fantasy, form and content.' Bravo Lenin! Trotsky's inclinations were no different: 'The Party has not,' he wrote in 1923, 'and cannot have, ready-made decisions on versification, on the evolution of the theatre, on the renovation of the literary language . . . Our Marxist conception of the objective dependence and social utility of art, when translated into the language of politics, does not at all mean a desire to dominate art by means of decrees and orders.' The Party, he believed, must to some extent remain *uncertain* about matters of art and science. 'No one is going to prescribe themes to a poet or intends to prescribe them.'

Unfortunately things were turning out rather differently . . .

Boris Pilnyak (1923): 'Our state power has installed in these recent years incubators for Party literature.'

Nine years later socialist realism becomes *the* official art-form; its doctrine is inscribed in the statutes of the newly created Soviet Union of Writers: 'Socialist realism, the basic method of Soviet belles-lettres and literary criticism, demands of the artist truthful, historically concrete representation of reality in its revolutionary development.' (Echoes of the French Committee of Public Instruction.) The magazine *Red Virgin Soil* now demands 'a classical, strictly constructed rhythm, a classical development of the subject.' The whole weight of state propaganda and state power is hurled against modernism. In 1934 Karl Radek, addressing the first congress of the Soviet Union of Writers, describes Joyce's *Ulysses* as 'spiderwebs of allegories and mythological reminiscences . . . a dung heap, swarming with worms, photographed by a movie camera through a microscope.'

The message is taken up elsewhere. Mao, speaking at the Yenan Forum in 1942, warns the writers that they must undergo a long and painful process of tempering. Time passes and new empires emerge. In April 1953 *Neues*

Deutschland (East Berlin) declares: 'The Soviet theatre is the most highly developed form of theatre in history.' And in case any recalcitrant writers fail to grasp the point, the Party creates the State Commissions for the Arts. Brecht comments: '. . . a great ideology was not put before the artists as a tempting offering, but forced on them like sour beer. The unfortunate ways of the Commissions, their dictates, with their poverty of argument . . . repelled the artists.' Brecht had admired the work of the great Soviet theatre director Meyerhold; but Meyerhold had been deprived of his theatre, arrested, never heard of again . . . 'The campaign against the formalism of decaying bourgeois art was turned into a campaign against the sense of form . . . *It is only boots that can be made to measure.*' (Brecht.)

Even when the Communists do not enjoy state power they extend their campaign of edicts and intimidation, alienating large segments of the sympathetic intelligentsia. Laurent Casanova, the French Communist Party's spokesman on cultural matters, reminded the comrades in 1947 that any deviation from the artistic rules laid down by Zhdanov and Fadeyev constituted a political attack on the Party. This brought murmurs and protests. Louis Aragon, Party Writer Number One, hurried to the rescue, urging comrades to grasp the hand (Zhdanov's) generously held out to them, a hand which would help them escape from their own petty-bourgeois contradictions, which would enable them to place a foot on the ladder of the new world, a ladder built — believe it or not — by 'the persuasive and melodious engineers of singing tomorrows'.

Cut to 1963: can this be the same Aragon who now writes: 'It is time to finish with dogmatic practices in history, science, literary criticism, the argument from authority, the reference to the sacred books which close one's mouth and render discussion impossible.' Yes, the same Aragon.

But for many writers it was too late; rehabilitations do not bring the bones from their coffins. Zamyatin, framed and forced into exile; Essenin, suicide; Mayakovsky, suicide;

Pilnyak, a bad end; Tretiakov, shot; Babel, having an-
nounced his mastery of a new genre, silence, is nevertheless
liquidated. In 1937 Ilya Ehrenburg returns from abroad
and visits the offices of *Izvestia*. The purge is at its height. 'I
was well received but I could not see a single familiar face.'
Later, after the war, there is the case of Zoshchenko who
ranks, alongside Ilf and Petrov, as the funniest writer of the
Soviet era. His *Adventures of a Monkey* brings down on him
the wrath of A. A. Zhdanov of the Politbureau: 'The venom
of bestial enmity towards the Soviet order . . . only the scum
of the literary world could write such "works", and only the
blind, the apolitical, could allow them to appear.' The
offending journal, *Leningrad*, is promptly closed down. As
for Zoshchenko, he is lucky; his ration card is simply withdrawn. Comments Zhdanov: 'Let him change; and if he will
not, let him get out of Soviet literature . . .' But getting out is
not easy . . . In *The First Circle*, Solzhenitsyn's fictional
prisoners play an ironical game during which they invent
Article 20, Section A, of the Criminal Code, which sentences an enemy of the people to be expelled from the USSR
so that he can rot in the West.

In the post-war period Zhdanov turns on a fine and sensitive lyric poet, Anna Akhmatova. 'What has her poetry in
common with the interests of our state and people? Nothing
whatever.' Eisenstein has already been censored, silenced;
Prokofiev and Shostakovich are persecuted for attempting to
gratify 'the individualistic emotions of a small group of
selected aesthetes'. In Zhdanov's opinion Tchaikovsky
should be the model for the Soviet musician.

The Yiddish writers liquidated. And later,

Pasternak silenced, disgraced.

In Communist Hungary, Jozsef Revai, Minister of Culture, assumes Zhdanov's role with enthusiasm. 'When Revai
appeared at the first performance of a play, the critics
watched his expression, not the stage.' (Aczel and Meray —
The Revolt of the Mind.) 'He determined how many films,
both historical and current, should be produced this year

and next year, or what poems should be left out of the poet's next volume. *He* decided whether the role of the Party Secretary was positive, or whether the role of the kulak was negative enough, in a new play . . . then suddenly he, Jozsef Revai, began to protest against exaggerations . . .'

Back to the Soviet Union. Despite the thaw, despite de-Stalinisation, Andrei Sinyavsky and Yuri Daniel are put on trial:

Prosecutor: 'What do you think, Daniel: is it ethical for a Soviet citizen to send abroad through a foreigner things that, to use your own expression, have a political tinge?'

Judge: 'What have Zoshchenko and Akhmatova got to do with it? Those were different times, but you still go on hiding things.'

The literary critic Vasilyev testifies that Sinyavsky had received 'two jackets, two sweaters, a nylon shirt and something else' from his French friends.

For a while the Judge rebukes the Prosecutor for his unfair comments. But soon the Judge becomes the Prosecutor.

Daniel: 'Our literature and press are silent about the things on which I write. But literature is entitled to deal with any period and any question. I feel that there should be no prohibited subjects in the life of society.'

Judge: 'You write about thought-readers and filters under toilets . . . That is the sort of thing covered by Article 70 — slander. Doesn't this malign our people, our society, our system?'

Sinyavsky is attracted by modernism; he has ridiculed socialist realism. He gets seven years' hard labour; Daniel gets a mere five.

Brodsky, Ginsberg and Litvinov go to prison . . .

Yevtushenko and Voznesensky permanently in trouble . . . Solzhenitsyn silenced.

In May 1968 the young men and women of Prague are eagerly reading *Literarni Listy* on the trams and in the cafés. I visit the Writer's Union and find a buoyant atmosphere of confidence, hope, new oxygen . . . wave after wave of creativity and invention. The Russians answer with tanks, *Literarni Listy* is no more. A microphone falls through the ceiling of the playwright Václav Havel; soon they take away his passport. I no longer hear from my Czech friends, and I fear the consequences for them if I write. Socialism has shed its 'human face'.

These were different times, said the Soviet Judge. But not for Alexander Solzhenitsyn:

Surkov (ancient literary bureaucrat) to Solzhenitsyn: 'You must declare that you renounce your role as leader of the political opposition, the role that has been ascribed to you in the West.'

Solzhenitsyn: 'My book, *One Day in the Life of Ivan Denisovich*, is being suppressed, the campaign of slander against me is continuing and expanding. You are the only ones who can put a stop to this.'

Fedin (novelist and literary bureaucrat): 'No. The order of events is incorrect. First of all, you must make your declaration and it must be published.

Literaturnaya Gazeta (26 June 1968): 'The writer A. Solzhenitsyn could have given his literary abilities to his country, instead of to the "evil breathers".'

Solzhenitsyn: 'A writer's task is to choose more universal and lasting themes, the secrets of the human heart and conscience, meetings of life with death, how to overcome pain of the soul, the laws of humanity in history, born in the unattainable depth of millennia, which will disappear only when the sun is extinguished.'

I wish that I had expressed the point so well when talking with Professor Girnus in the Humboldt University.

I recall an incident during a conference of novelists held in the vast McEwan Hall, Edinburgh. It was 1961 or 1962. Mary McCarthy, mentally and physically rather muscular, standing before the microphone and giving the ratings, the top ten, on the current American literary scene . . . Mailer, good-humoured in a tweed three-piece suit, giving a fair

imitation of a baby bear stampeded into maturity . . . J. R.
Ackerley, pale and silent, inscrutably watching and listen-
ing . . . William Burroughs raising his hat to my wife on the
bus to the airport . . . But the incident I have in mind concerned Lawrence Durrell, a short, pudgy man in an angry
mood. Two invited Soviet guests, one of them the same
Alexei Surkov who had joined in the persecution of Solzhenitsyn, had failed to turn up for the Conference. The sponsoring
organisers were proposing to send a telegram of regret and
goodwill to them in Russia. But Durrell was adamant; he
could not possibly regret the absence of a man like Surkov.
I can't remember what solution was reached, but I do recall
reacting with youthful, leftist indignation to Durrell's attitude. Perpetuating the cold war! What about capitalist
crimes? . . . etcetera. But of course Durrell was right. Building bridges, fostering mutual understanding, what can such
admirable concepts mean for men of Surkov's detestable
breed? Some of us used to believe that Soviet censorship and
bullying were a reaction — understandable if not legitimate
— to capitalist encirclement. In fact they turn out to be an ingrained way of life. And total ostracism is the only valid
response available to us.

Today, as I write this, Anatoly Kuznetsov has explained
in London his reasons for defecting. 'If Stalin is on top then
praise Stalin. If they order people to plant maize, then write
about maize. If they decide to expose Stalin's crimes, then
expose Stalin. And when they stop criticising him, you stop
too . . . Oh, the number of holes I have dug in the ground to
conceal my jam jars full of "dangerous" and "doubtful"
manuscripts.'

It is all very well to assure modernists that they can reconcile their art, or aspects of their art, with socialism so long
as they are living in capitalist-democratic states. But little
comfort can be drawn from that unless, as socialists, we are
secretly in love with perpetual opposition, with perpetual
protest, with being perpetually in a minority. The artist,
whether modernist, avant-garde or anything else, is entitled

to ask the socialist: 'What will happen when you come to power, my friend? Freedom, you say? In that case it will be the first time.' But that is not quite true; remember what Lenin said and what Trotsky said about creative freedom; remember, also, what Castro said in 1961: 'What principles of expression should the artist follow in his effort to reach the people? What should the people demand from the artist? Can we make a general statement about this? No. It would be over-simplified.'

I cling to that 'No' as to a raft.

EIGHT

The political and artistic avant-gardes — are they doomed to mutual antagonism? What, in any case, is the avant-garde?

In the space of a century the notion has undergone a radical transformation. Before 1848 it was used exclusively in connection with a writer's political views — indeed if you are at all interested in the history of small-circulation French newspapers, broadsheets and periodicals, you will find that to this very day there has always been one, often more, calling itself *Avant-Garde*. In 1845 the Fourierist writer Laverdant claimed that the true avant-garde artist was he 'who lays bare with a brutal brush all the brutalities, all the filth, which are at the base of our society.' Most of us think of Baudelaire as a distinctly avant-garde figure — but only according to modern usage. In fact Baudelaire's notebook of 1862–44 employs the phrase '*les littérateurs d'avant-garde*' in order to ridicule those writers obsessed by political radicalism.

Only after 1870 did the notion assume a primarily cultural or aesthetic connotation. And for this there is an obvious sociological explanation. During the first half of the nineteenth century, the deeply reactionary era of the revived *anciens régimes* and the Holy Alliance, political radicalism was driven underground. It had no mass following. Its exponents

belonged to small sects and clandestine lodges. Men like
Mazzini or Garibaldi or Bakunin or Blanqui spent the
greater part of their lives in prison or exile. By the 1880s,
however, the general European scene was changing rapidly.
Industrialisation had struck the Continent like a tidal wave.
The population of Germany doubled between 1870 and 1914.
Political radicalism attached itself to massive political parties
and trade unions: it became, in the true sense of the word,
vulgar. The great engine of science had brought in its wake
(or so it seemed) smoke, squalor, slums. The smug bourgeois
had his foot on the throat of the starved worker. A section of
the artistic intelligentsia recoiled in horror from the whole
set up. It washed its hands of social problems, preferring
the ivory tower of cultivated sensibility. It rejected both the
past and the present. It very deliberately cut itself and its
supporters, its *appassionati*, off from the philistine majority.
Tolstoy fulminated against its 'insanities', its lack of morality,
its utter meaninglessness to the people, its obscurity, its
affectations, its cultivated obscenity. The old Russian turned
his blazing pen against Baudelaire, Maeterlinck, Mallarmé
and Verlaine, whom he accused of profligacy, moral impotence and Catholic idolatory. From a Marxist point of view,
the new avant-garde assaults on the bourgeoisie amounted
to nothing more than a harmless, purely symbolic bohemianism. The bourgeoisie for its part tolerated these wild
animals because it knew they were domesticated at heart.

One point must, however, be made abundantly clear. The
avant-garde is not a sociological category: its matrix of definition arises purely within the cultural-aesthetic context. Nor
is its life-style invariably bohemian. It possesses no built-in
political posture and its only consistent social demand is
freedom of creativity. Baudelaire may have been contemp-
tuous of democratic politics but Zola, equally an experimental writer breaking with tradition, was not. Many of Ibsen's
plays, whether viewed stylistically or in terms of their content, had an impact no less innovatory and scandalous than
Rimbaud's poetry. Signac and Picasso are avant-garde

painters by any criteria; yet both chose to join the Communist Party. Marinetti and Mayakovsky both contributed to the futurist movement, but the one subscribed to Fascism while the other threw in his lot with the Bolsheviks. The potential relationship of the literary avant-garde to left-wing political movements therefore remains an open question; the neutral or conservative political posture adopted by the late nineteenth-century avant-garde was a tendency rather than a rule, and it represented chronologically only one phase among many. Deep and wide as the influence of the anti-Enlightenment has no doubt been on the avant-garde, it has been by no means all-pervasive. Daumier, Courbet, the Pissarros, Signac and Luce continued the radical tradition of Delacroix; Courbet, a friend of Proudhon, was a leading Communard. Jean Grave, a prominent French anarchist, conducted a sympathetic correspondence with the neo-Impressionists and published a regular avant-garde literary supplement to his journal, *Le Révolte*. Mirabeau and the young Valéry regarded themselves as revolutionaries, while the radical current within the symbolist movement was a strong one.

In the long-term retrospective the anarchist movement appears, of course, entirely untypical. Its structure, scale, life-style and philosophy corresponded more closely to those of the early nineteenth-century secret societies than to the mass social-democratic parties of the modern era. The anarchists who threw bombs and tossed burning mice into bourgeois barns were absolutists, purists, intransigents and individualists. The attraction for the avant-garde artist is obvious.

Nevertheless we cannot conclude from this that the avant-garde artist's political radicalism stops short at the futile and romantic gesture of *tabula rasa*. The immediate aftermath of the Bolshevik Revolution in Russia witnessed a formidable explosion of avant-garde creativity. Malevich, Lissitsky, Kandinsky, Tatlin, Pevsner and Rodchenko all fervently believed that experimental art could exercise a

profoundly beneficial influence on social development. The
Revolution encouraged the notion of the artist-engineer and
inspired a wave of experimental typography, new formats for
books and posters, and pioneering stage designs. The great
Soviet film directors employed expressionistic forms to sym-
bolise mass agitation and the disintegration of the old order
(who can forget the trembling crystal chandelier, symbolising
the shattered power of the bourgeoisie, at the close of
Pudovkin's *The End of St Petersburg*?). Despite criticisms
from Trotsky, Bukharin and Lunacharsky, the formalist
school of writers and critics continued in the Petrograd
Institute of Art History and elsewhere to pursue their enthusiastic synthesis of the two revolutions. El Lissitsky,
fascinated by constructivism and the new techniques of
communication, produced fabulous posters such as 'Beat the
Whites with the Red Wedge'. It was he who pioneered the
integration of the word and the image in poster and book
design. The arts flowed together as never before: Rodchenko,
for example, collaborated with Mayakovsky in uniting
literature and photo-montage, while Meyerhold made his
theatre famous throughout Europe for its inspired integration of political commitment and aesthetic innovation.
Zamyatin, engineer, artist and writer, epitomised the new
breed. Of course such men are never content with political
formulas alone; they deny the Secretary-General of the
Party the comic historical grandeur which he appropriates
to himself. 'Revolution', wrote Zamyatin, 'is everywhere
and in all things; it is infinite, there is no final revolution, no
end to the sequence of integers . . . The new people who are
right now coming into life are naked and fearless as children,
and they too, like children, like Schopenhauer, Dostoevsky,
Nietzsche, are asking their "whys", and "what nexts".' The
bureaucratic mind, petrified into a 'for us or against us' mould
by years of tribal warfare, will at once perceive that Zamyatin
has given himself away. Schopenhauer, Dostoyevsky,
Nietzsche — what is this? Paying tribute to the arch-
demons of the anti-Enlightenment? It is useless to argue.

The spirit which has been clenched like a fist is not easily prised open. You say that all this experimentation was irrelevant to the popular masses, to a nation where illiteracy remained not the exception but the rule? Well . . . when the apple first fell on Newton's head it was immediately relevant only to Newton's head. Judge all art by the yardstick of the lowest common denominator and you invent your own Stone Age. And it was ultimately to the spirit clenched like a fist that the Russian avant-garde succumbed.

Leopold Kolakowski has written: 'Twentieth-century avant-garde arts (painting, poetry, literature, theatre) have chiefly, though obviously not entirely, a clearly leftist orientation. This was true of futurism, expressionism and cubism. ("Cubism — Bolshevik art", Hitler wrote in *Mein Kampf*.) Quite possibly, one of these trends that the official doctrine so brutally repudiated bore the seeds of a future culture.'

The poet Essenin wrote:

> *By what odd chance did I go shouting in my song*
> *That I am a friend of the people?*
> *My poems are no longer needed here.*
> *And I too — by your leave — I am no longer needed.*

Essenin committed suicide. In 1930, Vladimir Mayakovsky, greatest of all left-wing, avant-garde writers, declared bitterly:

> *In all conscience,*
> *   I need nothing*
> *except*
> *   a freshly laundered shirt.*
> *When I appear*
> *before the CCC (Central Control Commission)*
> *   of the coming*
> *   bright years,*
> *by way of my Bolshevik party card,*
> *   I'll raise*

> *above the heads of a gang of self-seeking*
> > > *poets and rogues*
> *all the hundred volumes*
> > *of my*
> > > *communist-committed books.*

The same year Mayakovsky also became committed to suicide.

NINE

So we deplore *le poing brandi*, the political fist clenched menacingly in the face of explorative or experimental art. How, then, can the political left learn to relax its fears, let the guillotine rest, and offer *la main tendue*? The answer cannot be contained in a single sentence — indeed the question is one which I shall pursue from a number of perspectives throughout this book. But clearly there is one factor indispensable to such a change of attitude; I mean a recognition of *what art is and can be*, a recognition of its own particular languages and modes of communication, as displayed for example in Jean-Paul Sartre's discussion of the painter Lapoujade and how the two revolutions, political and aesthetic, can merge: 'This is what characterises the new painter of crowds: he can incarnate their presence only by refusing to represent them through figures . . . A man, he refuses to be excluded by virtue of his privileged position and to contemplate his species from the outside . . . His crowd is real, surging, uneasy. He is *exposed* to it and following the gradual annihilation of detail, there remains the meaning of the mass rally . . . Action, the multiple link between men, moulds splotches of colour and matter into a coherent structure and brings to perfection the painter's project: to use the visible splendours of non-figurative art to incarnate that which cannot be expressed through figures.'

Pursuing the analogy of painting, I offer an analysis of my

own, an attempt to interpret art politically but *nevertheless in terms of art*. Consider Picasso's *Guernica*. Communists and Marxists are normally less enthusiastic about the painting itself than what they know about it — namely that it is an eloquent expression of protest against fascist barbarism. But if you study the painting at a literal or representational level, there is no absolute confirmation of its political orientation. The prime symbols of the work are ones which Picasso had been developing for years — the bull, symbol of darkness and violence, the horse, symbol of innocence and goodness, the women witnesses, a sort of chorus. Behind *Guernica* are a host of small canvases, none of them in any way political, depicting minotaurs, horses, bullfighters and bloody deaths. The painter, then, was imposing an intensely private vision on a public event; the effect is tangential; alienated, highly personal. In point of fact, judging the painting in purely representational terms, it might equally signify outrage at news of some anarchist atrocity in a hitherto Nationalist town. But the meaning of the painting resides in the work as a whole, its total movement, design, metaphor, symbolism and spirit. The painting is nourished by life not only vertically, as plants spring out of the soil, but also horizontally, as cloud formations indicate the presence of mountains bordering on the sea. The radical meaning of the painting resides less in its representational aspects than in its aesthetic categories, its ferment within space, its optical statement, its pictorial self-consciousness.

But this, of course, is all very speculative, and in practice, under the pressures of an actual environment or an immediate sequence of events, such high-class marriages between the revolutionary husband and the avant-garde wife prove difficult to consummate. Separation, divorce, is more common. It frequently occurs that a political conversion generates in the artist a stylistic conversion. He may, quite simply, wish to reach the greatest number of people with the greatest simplicity and immediacy. Such transformations are often accompanied by a confessional *mea culpa*. The sheltered private sensibility is suddenly exposed to the ultra-violet of public catastrophe; what ensues is a complete burn-out and a hasty acceptance of 'highbrow' or experimental writing as reactionary or escapist. This happened to Aragon, to Eluard, to Brecht, to Rafael Alberti and to Pablo Neruda. Neruda's early poetry had dispensed with rhyme and consistent metre, staging a struggle at the heart of language — an implosion of symbols, images and metaphors partly inspired by theories of automatic and auto-hypnotic writing. But in 1939 he wrote: 'The world has changed and so has my poetry.' Now he wanted his poems to be:

> *useful and usable*
> *like metal and cereal*
> *that waits for the plowshare*
> *tools for the hand*

And elsewhere he wrote:

> *Simplicity,*
> *be with me, assist in my birth,*
> *teach me again how to sing,*
> *a floodtide of virtue and truth,*
> *a crystalline victory.*

Perhaps the most tortuous and tormented of attempted marriages between the political Left and the literary avant-garde concerned the relationship of French Communists and surrealists in the late 1920s and early 1930s. Here a number of crucial problems were fully exposed: does the 'revolution' begin in the 'mind' or 'spirit' or in the tangible world of social relations? Does art have a radical potential in its own terms or merely as an adjunct and ally of ideology? In the event the alliance was too mutually intolerant and short-tempered to do more than exacerbate traditional suspicions and enmities.

Before 1925 the life-style of the Parisian surrealists was clearly that of nihilistic bohemianism. The surrealists indicated their contempt for all political activity and insisted that the true revolution had to come within the sphere of '*l'ésprit*':

the first task was to liberate language and rejuvenate the creative impulse. Aragon described the Bolshevik Revolution as having no more intellectual significance than a ministerial crisis. But in 1925 the war of the Riff in Morocco precipitated the surrealists into the public arena and brought on something approaching a mass conversion to Marxist Communism. In 1927 Breton, Aragon and Eluard all joined the Party. But the Party was in no mood to compromise; Breton was summoned five times before its Control Commission (echoes of Mayakovsky's 'freshly laundered shirt') and asked to explain why he still called himself a surrealist. When instructed to make a factual report on the state of the gas industry in Fascist Italy, he declined. He and Eluard soon fell away from the Party; Aragon resolved the dilemma by renouncing the surrealist heritage entirely and by eagerly embracing the new emerging aesthetic of socialist realism.

Most of the surrealists could not stomach socialist realism. Alquiné spoke of a wind of cretinisation sweeping the USSR. Breton continued to insist that art could not successfully express the manifest content of the age, only the latent content. Only in the realm of the emotions, of the interior, of the subconscious, only on the frontiers of the fantastic could art and literature thrive. The surrealist attitude towards realism and classicism was unashamedly iconoclastic. Lautréamont, Rimbaud, Mallarmé and Apollinaire — these were the authentic modern liberators of the spirit. Until a genuine revolution in mental attitudes was achieved, a genuine stripping away of myth, convention and sterile logic, until the id burst through the fetters of the super-ego and the whole human being, not simply the repressed dummy, was given scope for self-expression — until this superstructural revolution came about, political and economic changes, however 'revolutionary' in appearance, could only result in the replacement of one collective repression by another.

The surrealist avant-garde attributed to itself a politically revolutionary role. Nor did it repudiate organised political violence. 'I believe, however,' declared Antonin Artaud,

'that our present social state is iniquitous and should be destroyed. If this is a fact for the theatre to be preoccupied
with, it is even more a matter for machine-guns.' But here
the surrealist view separates itself sharply from that of the
Marxist realists. Artaud did not want the theatre to try and
resolve social conflicts, he wanted it to unravel and express
certain secret truths, the metaphysical dimension of man,
his true animal impulses, his buried soul. Ionesco perpetu-
ates the tradition: 'The avant-garde writer is, as it were, an
enemy in the very heart of the city — a city which he is
fighting to destroy, against which he is in active revolt.' And
the true revolution, he adds, is 'a revolution which is a
change in mentality'. Writers who adopt the Sartrean view of
commitment are accordingly dismissed as committee men.

The closest contemporary counterpart to the old, left-
wing surrealist movement is to be found in the cohesive
nest of writers grouped round the magazine *Tel Quel*. The
similarity may not be apparent at first glance, for whereas the
spirit of surrealism was intensely romantic, the *Tel Quel*
writers adopt a style which is ostentatiously dry, analytical
and 'scientific'. A passion for numbers replaces a passion for
dreams; instinct gives way to cerebration. But the resem-
blances are nevertheless striking. Both groups pay respect to
Marx and Lenin, and both groups insist that the authentic
contribution of literature to the social revolution consists not
in exhorting the reader to the barricades, but in operating
subversively within the domain of thought, language and
culture. The *Tel Quel* group have no more patience for
orthodox realism than the surrealists had, and they too em-
phasise the intransitive, non-representational nature of
literature. But the *Tel Quel* group go even further by adopting literary creation as the authentic subject of literary creation. The Surrealists admired Sade because he had released
the damned from their chains; the *Tel Quel* group admire
him because he demonstrated that it is possible to *say* anything. The surrealists visualised Sade as releasing Eros, but
the *Tel Quel* writers transpose the significance of this by

treating Eros as a literary sign — it is the sign which contains subversive powers. The surrealists maintained if not
one foot at least a few toes in the instrumental, representational universe; in other words they believed that writing
expressed something other than itself. But the *Tel Quel*
writers tend to treat the Book as an *En-Soi*, an absolute
milieu. Thus a *littérature de dire* gives way to a *littérature
de faire*.

If I had to make a judgment or state a preference, it would
be this: the surrealist emphasis on the subconscious, on
latent consciousness and on the virtues of unreflective thinking was a fashion which has not stood the test of time. The
influence of the anti-Enlightenment is too strong here for
my taste. Similarly, the spokesmen of the *Tel Quel* group
spoil a good case by exaggerating it; what is in fact a tendency, one possible dimension of literature among many, is
elevated into an absolute. This having been said, the balance
of my sympathies lies with the surrealists, with Artaud and
Ionesco, and with the *Tel Quel* group against the Marxist
socialist realists for the reasons I have set down in the last
chapter and for others I will propose in the next.

TEN

In France and Germany the post-war era has unfortunately
tended to juxtapose politically committed writing and experimental writing as alternatives. When the French intelligentsia grew tired of politics (Sartre, Camus, de Beauvoir,
etc.) they turned to experimental writers who rejected political themes or implications. Robbe-Grillet is among the
most articulate: 'The socialist revolution distrusts revolutionary art, and, what is more, it is not evident that it is
wrong to do so.' As for commitment, he will have none of it.
'Literature is not a means which the writer puts at the service of some cause . . . the novel is not a tool . . . The writer
by definition does not know where he is going . . . I write to

understand why I feel the desire to write.' In Germany the writers of the left-wing Gruppe 47 betrayed a growing fatigue about didactic literature and gradually hived off into forms of experimental writing where the political stance was diffuse or ambiguous. Enzensberger is the most notable exception. Günter Grass chooses to keep separate his roles as citizen and writer (or court jester, as he puts it). As for England, the famous Angry Young Men of a decade ago have not only failed to develop arresting art forms, they have also jettisoned their radical pretensions. Kingsley Amis, for example, backs the American position in Vietnam and joins the Tory party. Now take a look at this: 'I don't know any students, and I certainly wouldn't like to see a Negro minority taking over this country. A lot of nice bus conductors running the Government isn't my idea of a sensible way out. And student power is a very factitious thing. It always seems to me that "What am I?" is a much more interesting question than "What are we?", but now they're all "we-ing" all over the place . . . What happened at the Sorbonne seemed more animal than human to me . . . the prospect of rule by instant rabble doesn't appeal to me either.' (John Osborne inter-viewed by Kenneth Tynan, *The Observer*, 7 July 1968.)

. . . And yet there are grounds for optimism (perhaps more in the theatre than in the novel), evidences of fresh thinking, fresh feeling, new patterns of language, the banish-ing of old cobwebs and fixed literary routines. This is par-ticularly true in America. But what catches light there soon burns throughout Europe and beyond.

CHAPTER FOUR

Form, Content, Meaning

ONE

In what senses and by what means can literature become a valid expression of overt socio-political commitment? In the present chapter I shall approach this question in terms of the nature and structure of literature — form, content, meaning, language.

The reader should by now be aware that a war is being conducted on two fronts: against the assumptions of traditional Marxist criticism, and against the claims of the ultra-modernists. The one represents the extrinsic fallacy, the other the intrinsic fallacy. It is not a matter of keeping the peace between two factions, of playing the professional mediator, or of becoming a kind of literary Count Bernadotte or Dag Hammarskjöld (their fate is sufficient to deter). The point is this: the real potentialities and limitations of literature as an expression of socio-political commitment can be achieved only if the writer and the reader alike understand *what writing is*. And it seems to me that neither the traditional Marxists nor the ultra-modernists have got to grips with the problem in an entirely convincing way.

On the one hand the Marxist materialists have presented thought, language and literature as reflections of 'life'. These reflections are more or less accurate according to the ideological position (or, alternatively, 'genius') of the author. The world (society) is primary, literature, viewed as a mirror, secondary. Within literature *content* is primary, both in terms of genesis, of inspiration if you like, and in terms of the normative value of the novel, poem or play. Form exists to facilitate content. It is a vessel, a medium, a conveyor belt, *a means to an end.*

The opposite point of view is expressed by the ultra-structuralists who emerge as the critical phalanx of latter-day modernism. Here all the priorities are reversed. Form is given primacy over content, or, alternatively, the form-content dichotomy is declared misleading since 'meaning' is held to reside in form itself. Literary and linguistic structures are regarded as autonomous, as shaped by their own internal laws and principles; they preside over and pre-determine the efforts of the writers and readers who inherit them. They generate meaning intrinsically, in terms of their own specialised codes.

I shall first take issue with the ultra-structuralists (I say 'ultra' because, as we shall see, structuralism has made an impressive contribution to our understanding of literature).

TWO

Northrop Frye insists that 'the work of art must be its own object: it cannot be ultimately descriptive of something, and can never be ultimately related to any other system of phenomena, standards, values or final causes.' Robbe-Grillet asserts that 'content resides in form' and claims that the only valid commitment for the writer is to problems of language and their resolution 'from inside'. The true writer, he argues, 'has nothing to say, only a manner of saying it'. The leading exponent of the French school of literary structuralists is Roland Barthes. According to Barthes 'the word [*la parole*] is neither an instrument nor a vehicle, it is a structure'. He aims ultimately to remove from the reading of a text the emotional and ideological preconceptions that both writer and reader bring to it, so that it exists solely as a book, essay

or play. This reading is symbolic; it deals in the internal logic
of the language, the phrases and the plot structure. So we
now find that literature is akin to music in so far as its meaning lies entirely in the internal interrelationship of notes and
signs. (An obvious instance which justifies this approach:
compare 'she is here' with 'here she is'.)

But now compare these three: 'she is here', 'here she is',
'there she is'. The shift of meaning between the first and
second phrases is achieved purely formally, but this is not
the case between the second and third phrases. Words in fact
differ from musical notes; they are not only elements in a
structured system, they also have individual significative
reference points in the outer world. That is why dictionaries
are possible. It is not possible to say that a combination of
musical notes is 'wrong' except in terms of musical grammar
and tonal convention: but words and phrases are susceptible
to both internal grammatical objections ('here am I' or 'here
I am', *but not* 'am here I') and also to extrinsic objections
('no, you are not here, you are there!'). But all this is so
obvious that it need not be laboured.

Structuralists make a useful distinction between diachronic and synchronic analysis. The diachronic order is
one in which each literary 'moment' is understood in relationship to those that precede and follow it. The synchronic
order is one in which each element is understood in relationship to others contiguous to it. Good. But literature is not
chess; its components always retain an extrinsic reference
point. Imagine that two men have been playing chess; you,
as spectator, arrive on the scene after the fifteenth move. You
can make an absolutely sufficient intrinsic synchronic analysis.
The total system is the board and its latitudes and longi-
tudes of possibilities; the elements are the pieces which
have no meaning outside of the rules and powers of the
game. But this is never the case with literature. A purely
internal synchronic analysis is never possible. For what is
the proper unit for synchronic examination. A single page?
That would be unduly arbitrary and involve us in cutting

short the analysis in mid-sentence. What then? A phrase, a clause, a sentence, a paragraph? These are certainly established grammatical units, but a grammatical unit also contains a semantic dimension. Compare these: 'If I give', and 'If I fall'. The first of these sentences appears grammatically less sound because the verb is transitive, but to put it that way is only to find a general grammatical expression for the fact that such a statement is semantically incomplete. You want to know, 'If I give *what or whom?*'

To make such elementary points is certainly gruelling, but the justification lies in the widespread prevalence of a certain mystification. The ultra-structuralists insist that a proper reading of a book ignores everything but the book itself. It disregards questions of genesis and environment — how, when, where and why the book was written, and what the author had been recently writing or experiencing. Forget his notebooks, stick to the text. Very well . . .

In the 1830s and 1840s, British and French novelists often published their novels in serialised *feuilleton* form. The reader would have to wait two weeks or a month before the next episode arrived. Knowing this, the novelist naturally tended to climax each episode with fascinating tensions and question marks: what will happen to her next, will she get married, be murdered by the villain or whatever? Today, when these same novels are bound together in a single volume, it is surely wise to recall the conditions of their original publication and the sociological climate which fostered the *feuilleton* form. The regime of Louis Bonaparte (the Second Empire) manipulated the tax system to make the *feuilleton* an uneconomic proposition and so put literature out of reach of the popular masses. The impact of this on the form, style, mood and content of the French novel was considerable; but how can you properly investigate this change of form and style without paying attention to its extrinsic causes? Towards the end of the century, the three-volume novel was a widely accepted form in England. In 1894, 184 three-volume novels were published. But in the same year

the big lending libraries turned against them, the result being
that in 1897 only four three-volume novels were published.
Now no one needs to be told how such a shift in publishing
fashion will affect the form and content of the novel. The
point is obvious but demands reiteration: no book can be
understood in isolation. Any practising playwright is liable
to be told that he must cut his text because the audience
won't tolerate more than two-and-a-half hours. He finds
that he must cut half a scene here, a whole scene there; the
internal form, the balance, the total meaning of the play is
thereby modified. To fully understand the final text you
must also bear in mind that audiences won't tolerate more
than two-and-a-half hours. If the critic ignores what is
known about an author's life and environment, he is amputat-
ing a vital critical limb.

Pierre Macherey argues that the *necessity* of a work of
literature manifests itself in the fact that one cannot change
a word of the text. The language instituted by the act of the
writer is irreducible. Well! Of how many books could that
be said? On the contrary, all experience indicates that the
final text is a purely arbitrary moment in a long process of
amendment and revision. The author returns the corrected
proofs to the printer when he is mentally exhausted or runs
out of time. Macherey, although a Marxist and a disciple of
Louis Althusser, is so overwhelmed by the prevalent ultra-
structuralism that he is able to suggest that only 'degraded
literature' goes outside of itself in search of tradition,
morality and ideology. He claims that even realist literature
is capable of resisting this corruption. What we have here is
simply a mystified fetishism of art.

Macherey refers to the 'humanistic fallacy'. What is it? It
apparently occurs when you pay attention to the role of the
author, his choices, intentions and decisions. Now we can
agree, indeed insist, that a writer's freedom is limited or defined by the literary structures available to him. We can also
agree with Macherey that a book develops a logic of its own
in the course of the writing. But there are limits. The logic of

the book may modify the author, but so equally can the author wrench and push by acts of will the logic of the book. As I sit and write this, as the typed pages pile up on my desk, I may be creating a formless, meaningless heap, but I am not Frankenstein. The French structuralists are engaged in a massive onslaught on the concept of authorship; for them books are born not conceived. The attraction of this approach for the new-school Marxists structuralists has to be understood in terms of a reaction to a reaction. The emphasis of the first phase of Marxist philosophy (Marx, Engels) was on socio-economic determinism, minimising the role of the individual. But the second phase (Lenin, Stalin), which accompanied the birth and growth of international Communism, was by contrast voluntaristic: Party leaders, Stakhanovite workers, inspired socialist realist novelists, they were all heroes thrusting socialism on the world by dint of their iron love of justice. The abuses of Stalinism and of the cult of personality have discredited this tendency, with the result that a new, somewhat heterodox breed of Marxists, inspired by Louis Althusser, have attempted to purge the historical process of its idiosyncratic and individual causal elements. Not even Marx himself has escaped their epistemological ruthlessness. Marx, they argue, is to be understood not in terms of what he thought he was saying but in terms of what he actually 'said'. And this 'said' is yielded through an objective structural 'reading'. Macherey now extends the same system to artistic literature with the result that the real dialectical relationship of society, the writer and his book is petrified by the ice-cold lava of ultra-structuralism.

It is one of the merits of Lucien Goldmann's 'genetic structuralism' that he discards the notion of literary structures as autonomous entities which imprison writer and reader alike. As Goldmann points out, these structures were created by men, by human praxis, and they are constantly modified and advanced by that praxis.

THREE

Susan Sontag wishes to raise the general level of aesthetic appreciation of the American public. She wishes that they would pay less attention to the content of a work; she wishes they would discard the crude dichotomy of form and content; she wishes they would understand that the meaning of a work of art resides primarily in its form.

It seems not beyond the bounds of possibility that she has confused 'content' with 'subject'. This is a fairly common confusion. I paint your portrait; the 'subject' of my painting is your face, neck and shoulders; the 'content' of my painting is this subject mediating and mediated by the artistic form I employ. If Picasso were to undertake the same portrait the form would be different and with it the content. The Anzin miners' strike of 1884 is the subject of Zola's novel *Germinal*; the content of the novel is what emerges through Zola's literary treatment of this subject. It is not therefore, as Miss Sontag apparently assumes, a matter of choosing between form and content because every work of art, however 'abstract', however formalistic, has a content. Content always refers to the world (material, mental, associative or whatever) *outside* the work of art mediated and re-shaped by artistic form. This fact is grasped once we cease to identify content with the mimetic representation of a subject or theme. However 'formal' a concrete poem may seem, however 'purely' it deals in sequence, harmony, rhythm, discord, dissonance, it always engenders a chain of associations which are extrinsic to the poem. This is the content. Literature is not mathematics, or music, or chess.

What we encounter is a general phenomenon with several compartments. Art for art's sake, ultra-structuralist criticism, the insistence that art is primarily form — all these positions belong to the same syndrome. If we accept the syndrome we accept that literature and socio-political commitment are generally incompatible. But what is involved here is not only a misunderstanding of art, it is once again a mystified fetishism of ART.

We call Trotsky's *History of the Russian Revolution*, or Isaac Deutscher's biography of Trotsky, works of art. We don't know where 'art' begins or ends and I daresay we never will, since the word and the category are perpetually chasing their own mutual tail. (Of that, more later.) Within the sphere of literature and of writing, many of the formal, selective, shaping, emphasising, harmonising principles employed by novelists are also used by biographers, historians, journalists and publicists. But, so far as I know, none of the ultra-structuralist critics has dared to propose that Deutscher's authorship of the life of Trotsky is irrelevant to our appreciation of the book, or that Deutscher inherited certain literary structures which took control of the work, or that the biography is an autonomous entity in which not a word can be changed and whose meaning is purely intrinsic, purely structural. The biographers and historians have not been victims of this mumbo-jumbo. And why? Because there exists a strange fetish of 'creative' or 'artistic' literature as something not merely different but also completely distinct, completely *sui generis*. This is what I mean by the mystified fetishism of ART. Of course it's rubbish. Any writer who has worked in several genres, and any intelligent reader who has read in several genres, will recognise the crudity of the fallacy.

It makes no difference whether the novel in question was conceived as an attempt at representational realism or, alternatively, in the phenomenological tradition of the *nouveau roman* (as an exploration of consciousness, how consciousness relates to objects and how consciousness can be transmitted). In both cases the writer will regard the novel form as having special creative potentialities of its own. But in neither case does it make sense to say that the content corresponds exactly to the form and the form to the content.

FOUR

The structuralists argue that the meaning of a book or play resides in and emanates from its *form alone*. They are suspicious of the notion of content, regarding it as dangerously symptomatic of the extrinsic fallacy. The Marxists on the contrary raise content on to a pedestal and then equate it with the *subject matter interpreted*. They in their turn are suspicious of undue attention to form, regarding it as dangerously symptomatic of a separation of art from life. For them form, properly used, is simply the correct vehicle for conveying the subject matter correctly interpreted. The right words are found to transmit the right message.

The critic who ignores the role of form and structure in literature dies two deaths. All literary structures have a symbolic element (first death); and one of the distinguishing features of 'creative' or 'artistic' literature is its deliberate exploitation of this symbolic element. Failing to recognise this, Marxists have inevitably failed to offer interesting contributions to aesthetic theory: second death. (In fact it is harsh but not entirely unfair to say that most Marxist literary critics give little impression of being interested in literature.) The complete lack of sympathy or understanding displayed· by these critics towards modernist writing is, as we have said, partly to do with its gravitation towards the *Weltanschauung* of the anti-Enlightenment, but it is also to do with the modernist movement's unique preoccupation with literature, what it is, how it works, how it modifies our perception of reality, how it deals with itself. Faced with such deviant pursuits, the Marxist critic — Walter Benjamin was an exception — becomes rather homespun and commonsensical; Balzac and Dickens, he says, did not worry themselves with such introspective nonsense, they got on with the job, and a damned fine job too . . .

Ralph Fox wrote: 'Form is produced by content, is identical and one with it, and, though the primacy is on the side of content, form reacts on content and never remains passive.'

This statement is typical of the old, rough Marxism. Once again content and subject matter are confused. But if, as I have maintained, content is the result of the inter-penetration of form and subject or theme, it obviously cannot 'produce' form or be primary to it. (I said earlier that an abstract painting or concrete poem need not necessarily have a subject: how, then, can it have a content? The answer lies in a distinction between concrete subjects selected in advance and ghost subjects which emerge amorphously from the work of art; between subjects to which we can attach a name and identity (a tree) and subjects which are nebulous, synthetic and associative. In the case of 'non-representational' or abstract art the embryonic representational element or ghost subject emanates from the work as one pole of the content.)

Another Marxist critic, Ernst Fischer, offers a different formula. Form, he says, is a state of equilibrium, content a state of movement or change. Content constantly explodes form. This also is incorrect. We are back again at the old question, what is the best jar into which to pour the hot jam? In fact formal developments (printing, cheap books, film, radio, television, etc.) encourage and demand new treatments of subjects. When the producer tells the writer, 'That is not a suitable subject for television', he means that the interaction of the medium and the subject will produce an awkward or bastardised content. When a playwright begins to mould a theme or subject into an expressive content he does so precisely through the formal medium of the theatre, its limitations and possibilities. The interesting dialogue I overhear in a pub will emerge differently depending whether I am writing a novel, a film script or a play. Technology is promiscuous; innovations originally pioneered in relation to one medium, such as lithography, the etching and the linocut, embark on independent journeys of their own, offering new possibilities in another medium.

Every formal variation within a novel modifies the content. First person narrative, third person narrative, disembodied narrative, author's narrative . . . Present tense, past tense . . . Conscious symbolisation, unconscious symbolisation . . . If the narrator speaks in the present tense we derive a sense of open-ended uncertainty, the feeling that he is groping in the dark, that he is no wiser than the reader. This effect is achieved in French by the (rare) use of the past indefinite, as in Camus' *L'Etranger*. But no direct equivalent exists in English. Camus' *Marie a parlé* has to be translated as 'Marie spoke', because 'Marie has spoken' would be too tedious an idiom to employ throughout. What we therefore receive in English is a direct translation of an idiom Camus avoided using — '*Marie parla*'. The meaning and the content are thereby substantially altered.

Recently I read a Free Theatre (Roundhouse, London) catalogue which boldly announces: 'Now a revolution is needed to destroy, finally and completely, the form of the proscenium theatre and the social habits that go with it. To restore impact to the theatre, it must be liberated from the tyranny of any form.' It is true that we can usefully distinguish between major forms or genres (theatre, the novel, poetry) and the subsidiary forms and conventions which coexist as alternatives within these genres. But to speak of liberating the theatre from the tyranny of any form is meaningless; the theatre itself is a highly exacting and limiting form without which writers, actors and directors would find themselves adrift and impotent. When the actors of the Living Theatre angrily or joyously spill off the stage into the auditorium, and then into the street outside, their actions, their rebellion, derives its meaning precisely from the formal limitations of the theatre. Without the super-ego, the id falls into a hopeless abyss. Indeed without the super-ego, the id cannot exist.

The most promising Marxist (or neo-Marxist) attempt to integrate the formal and sociological dimensions of literature is that of Lucien Goldmann (*The Hidden God* and *Pour une sociologie du roman*). Goldmann contends that the socio-political meaning of a novel is to be understood in terms of its form rather than its content. But the curious feature of

Goldmann's epistemology is that he attributes the word 'form' to what clearly involves content. A possible *formal* definition of the novel might be 'a continuous, fictional, non-dramatic narrative, usually in prose'. But Goldmann defines the novel *formally* as 'the transposition on the literary plane of daily life in the individualistic society born from production for the market'. The true (as a genre) novel is, he says, characterised by an insurmountable rupture between a problematical hero and his world. The hero and the action in which he becomes involved are symptomatic of the existence in capitalist society of generally recognised values (liberty, tolerance, political equality) which are to varying degrees denied in practice. The novel as such, continues Goldmann, begins to disintegrate with the onset of monopoly capitalism and the extinction of these liberal values. The writer loses all faith in the coherence of the outer world and of the human personality. The disintegration becomes complete in post-war, neo-Keynesian, state-capitalist, managerial society where, apparently, absolute de-humanisation prevails.

To this thesis one can pose many objections. Goldmann's causal links between infrastructure and literary superstructure are not only schematic, are not only based on chronological phases too neatly delineated, they also ignore a host of mediating factors, particularly the irregular and fluctuating impact of local politics. When Goldmann attempts to impose the whole system of analysis on Malraux's development as a novelist between 1927 and 1942, the thesis burns up in a glare of schematic sodium. But what is particularly relevant in the context of the present discussion is Goldmann's curious definition of literary form. What he in fact does is to take the *content* of the typical nineteenth-century bourgeois-realist novel and then call it the authentic *form* of the novel as such. Consequently when the content (as well as the form) of the novel changes, as it does in the transition from realism to modernism, Goldmann feels logically compelled to announce the death of the novel as a form, of the novel as such. We see here that Goldmann's Marxist inclinations affect his structural analysis in both a negative and a positive way. Negative because, like other Marxists, he makes *content* primary in literature (while claiming not to) and because he regards a literary form simply as a reflection of the dominant socio-economic external reality. Thus like other Marxists he ignores the extent to which the form and content of the novel change because writers consistently adopt new approaches towards language and symbol, towards the possible relationship of the writer, society and the book. But Goldmann's Marxism has a positive value in that, unlike the ultra-structuralists, he recognises that literary and linguistic structures are created and constantly re-created by human projects and human praxis. Unfortunately he pays insufficient attention to the extent that social projects and praxis are influenced by literary structures viewed as components of the general culture and ideology.

FIVE

Problems of literature are inseparable from those of language.

In a sense the Marxists and modernists represent the contemporary combatants in the ancient war between the partisans of 'nature' and the partisans of 'convention'.

The dispute is as old as Greece. But we must skip to modern Europe. In the sixteenth century language was regarded not as an arbitrary system, as an ensemble of independent signs, but as a natural emanation of the world linked to the world by resemblance and its component notions: *convenienta, aemulatio*, analogy and sympathy. One opened a book to discover nature; language resided amongst plants, stones, animals, things. No hiatus was recognised between perception and description.

In the course of the seventeenth and eighteenth centuries this marriage was dissolved. Language took on the shape of an architecture of signs. But this architecture was not immediately regarded as arbitrary or conventional. On the contrary, it was a fundamental assumption of the Enlightenment that language was an outgrowth of logic and reason which in turn resided naturally amongst plants, stones, animals . . . Such was the view of the *Grammaire générale et raisonnée* issued from Port Royal in 1660. The logic of Port Royal included a binary theory of the sign. The sign enclosed two ideas, one being the thing which represents, the other the thing represented. The nature of the sign was to excite the first by the second. We therefore have a theory of representation, a system which revealed language as man's method of regrouping the singularity of his discrete perceptions and of cutting short the continuous movement of his thoughts.

In this approach there is already a nominalist element which later linguists were to develop to the point where de Saussure postulated the complete independence of language from what it expresses (except for a psychological link between the thing and the image). This theory has important implications. If signs are independent then words must be viewed as moving one by one, gap by gap, along a linear order, and this renders them incapable of representing reality or the mental reflection of reality in its totality. The relationship of language to reality becomes rather like that of algebra to geometry. Secondly, the theory implies that the psychological link between the thing and the word, the concept and the image, must be a two-way process; the conventional code of communication is injected into the process of conceptualisation.

It is no coincidence that the rise of this critical theory of language was roughly contemporaneous with the rise of the modernist movement in literature. While the academics were celebrating the utterly arbitrary and conventional nature of language, the writers were mounting an unprecedented assault on everyday significative discourse, enclosing themselves in the hermetic universe of the sign, creating a kind of literary space which (they claimed) contained no point of departure in the outer world and no point of termination. The modernist avant-garde revelled in the notion that men's thoughts are inescapably lodged in verbal forms whose historical dimensions escape them, revelled in the tyranny of language, revelled in the paradox whereby men believe themselves masters of a medium of which they are in fact the slaves. This avant-garde closed itself in on a radical intransitivity, curving on a perpetual return to itself, rejecting the old values (taste, pleasure, truth, progress) which fostered writing and reading in earlier ages, and treating literature as the only object of literature, language as the only valid object of language.

A curious and undesirable situation resulted. Language remained the primary tool of communication used, whether verbally or in writing, by the entire population. And yet, in the hands of certain academic linguists and avant-garde writers, it had parted company with the mundane, everyday, utilitarian world, and gone into a self-contained orbit in a distant, rarefied stratosphere of its own.

SIX

. . . Meanwhile the Marxists adhered, broadly speaking, to the linguistic assumptions of the Enlightenment. They gazed at rhyme, symbol, image, myth, metre, stanzaic patterns, the repetition of sounds, and concluded that they represented a rational expression of a coherent outer reality. They continued to assume that the writer first perceives reality, then conceptualises it, and finally finds the appropriate words to convey its meaning. They mistakenly accepted recognition and designation as two distinct processes in a linear sequence. They failed to realise how powerfully perception and recognition are influenced by the inherited national language *(langue)* and by the prevailing semantic code *(langage)*.

We need not, however, feel compelled to follow uncriti-
cally the school of linguistics which insists on the totally
conventional nature of language. There are enough onoma-
topoeic words in our vocabulary to remind us that, historically, the spoken language precedes the written language and
that the spoken language tends to imitate nature (or the
manner in which our sensory organs receive nature). Nor,
indeed, is language uninfluenced by the physiology of the
mouth and throat. But suppose we forget such factors
(which become decreasingly relevant in the higher or culturally more elaborated languages). Even if we accept language as a conventional code of signs, we are not justified in
concluding that meaning emanates from the internal structure of the code alone. Barthes, for example, would have us
believe that *la parole* is a succession of 'empty' signs of
which the movement alone is significant. This is wrong. The
cry, 'Fire!' is perfectly meaningful on its own. Nor need we
subscribe to the extremist conclusion that an idea or concept
and its verbal image are one and the same thing. (One distinctive feature of certain states of dream is that people,
things and situations appear to exist in a verbal vacuum, just
as the sight of a submarine travelling underwater surprises
us by the absence of accompanying sound.) Animals clearly
reveal the presence of 'thoughts' for which they have no
verbal expression. So do infants. Similarly, when Barthes
insists that language is not the predicate of its subject matter,
but *is* its own subject, the thesis is too radical. When the
Spaniards discovered Peru, a civilisation without any known
contact or common cultural heritage with that of Europe,
they found a new *langue* but not an entirely unfamiliar
langage. The Russian vocabulary of colour may draw its
boundaries at different points on the colour scale from the
English vocabulary, but the semantically isomorphic elements of the known human languages are more regular than
exceptional. The more so, the more common the historical,
social, and cultural experience of the peoples concerned. There
exists no pure architecture of language: the significative

dimension is always apparent and usually paramount. The ontological truth of language is being-for-the-other.

Men despair of language like they despair of improving society. 'The most certain form of dumbness', wrote Kierkegaard, 'is not to be silent, but to speak.' Thomas Mann's Felix Krull adds: 'And the truth is that the word, as used to describe or characterise a deed, is no better than one of those wire fly-swatters that always miss the fly.' However, Kierkegaard evidently believed that the truth of what he said (above) was better conveyed by saying it than by not saying it; as for Mann, he kept on fly-swatting, and to no mean effect. We can sympathise profoundly with the agony of Beckett's Molloy: 'Not to want to say, not to know what you want to say, not to be able to say what you want to say, and never to stop saying, or hardly ever, that is the thing to keep in mind, even in the heat of composition.' But we can sympathise with Molloy precisely because Beckett has succeeded in communicating to us a common experience or predicament.

But what the modernists have understood (although exaggerated) and the Marxists generally ignored, is the nature of the language code, the way it breaks up, rearranges and distorts pre-reflective awareness. Short of jumping into the other fellow's skin (a feat of science as yet unachieved) we possess no means of precisely receiving or transmitting the experience of another. The language code is of necessity negative as well as positive. The word 'I' also means 'not you, not she, not them' etc. Suppose I cry out suddenly while mending a broken fuse. You hear my cry and want to know what happened. I tell you: 'I felt a shock.' But this is only a distorted, codified version of my original, spontaneous experience. Obviously at the time of the horrible pain the last thing that was true for me was that it was 'I' (not she, not them, etc) who was suffering it. At that moment I was the whole universe. Similarly I did not 'feel' it; there was no break down of the experience into subject-predicate-object. I *was* the shock. But the shock was not a shock at the

time: the word 'shock' I attribute to the experience by convention retrospectively, first to convey that the unpleasant
sensation arrived rapidly and unexpectedly, and secondly
because I know that this kind of pain caused by electricity
is called 'a shock'. In objectifying my experience I am compelled to lose much of it. The truest expression of my initial
experience was the cry it spontaneously evoked, but of course
the cry itself in terms of communication is only indicative,
not significative. One of the most fertile features of modernist
writing has been its attempt to capture by means of language
the red-hot moment of pre-verbal experience, the moment
before the 'I' is aware of itself as the subject of perception
or feeling. Naturally we are no more capable of ultimate
success than Sisyphus was capable of bringing the boulder
to the summit of the hill. But, by developing a code within a
code, we can move closer to the communication of pre-verbal
experience by analogy and by parallel. The suspicious reaction of Marxist critics and writers to such attempts has left
them third-class passengers stranded in a nineteenth-century
literary station.

If our modern state of knowledge about the nature of
language and literature destroys some optimistic assumptions of the Enlightenment, then we have no viable alternative to thinking, acting and creating within the most
advanced knowledge available to us. Optimistic rhetoric
and brave gestures are of no avail if you are knee-deep in
fundamentalist clay. The socialist writer has to come to terms
with the nature of his medium. He can no longer assume that
language is part of a superstructure which simply reflects the
socio-economic infrastructure; that concepts derive from
reality and are then translated into mirror-like words; that it
is possible to eliminate the hiatus between the signifier and
what he signifies. He can no longer accept Caudwell's distinction between prose and poetry, the one being congruent
with outer reality, the other with inner reality. Nor can he do
other than discard Sartre's central proposition that whereas
in poetry language is an end in itself, metamorphosising

its material by means of its internal structures, prose is, or can be, purely utilitarian, descriptive and representational. The qualities Sartre attributes to poetry alone are in fact present in all language; more pronounced in the language of art; and more than ever pronounced in lyric or symbolist poetry. But the difference is one of degree not of kind.

The partial dualism of language and the world is therefore a hard fact which the writer must face up to. If he is to make a virtue out of necessity, he must, it seems to me, evolve a greater degree of literary self-consciousness than is common among the realists. He must integrate into his writing an awareness of the dialectical subject-object relationship at every level; language-perception-language; structure-reality-structure; literature-writer-literature; subject-form-content; action-description-action.

Of course he will be Sisyphus again. He will never get there. But he must travel. In what direction and by what guidelines I hope to indicate in the chapters which follow. In other words I shall try to sketch the broad contours of a committed literature which is in honest communion with both radical consciousness and with the act of writing fiction.

CHAPTER FIVE

Two Types of Alienation

ONE

Consider two types of alienation, the one a noxious disease, the other an antidote, a vaccine to the virus . . .

But I should not say 'two types of alienation', I should say 'two widely separated semantic variations of the same English word'. English because in Germany there are — at least since Brecht — two words: (1) *Entfremdung* — noxious and disabling, social and economic, political and psychological alienation; (2) *Verfremdung* — a philosophy and technique of literature, particularly drama, primarily associated with Brecht and involving detachment, non-empathy and disillusion. Art recognising itself as art. Alienated art.

But there is no doubt about it, the phrase 'alienated art', imposed on us by the limitations of our national metaphysical vocabulary, is an unfortunate one. It is semantically confusing; it is liable to suggest a mystified, unhappy, distorted art, an emanation of false consciousness, a deformity. In France they speak of '*distantiation*', but the English equivalent lacks definition, power and self-confidence; it is too grey, too recessive.

In any case, what I have in mind is more than *Verfremdung*, which is simply a component, albeit the most formative one, of dialectical art. But of this, more later.

TWO

The notion of alienation has become a central proposition of contemporary social thought, just as enlightened self-interest was two generations ago. It means a loss of contact with some necessary, stabilising essence or sense of harmony. It conveys some basic discord or contradiction in man's ontological or social existence. It involves a painfully acute disparity between 'is' and 'ought'. It is present when man's consciousness of reality is distorted or mystified. But this, of course, is a question of opinion, an opinion extending from a particular ideological set of suppositions. When a French worker declares that 'de Gaulle was the man to save the nation', his political attitude may be alienated in the eyes of his Communist colleagues but not in his own. And in certain cases the reverse occurs; a sensitive spirit discerns an element of alienation in himself where the man in the street sees none. Camus pointed to the contingent (Absurd) nature of human action and beliefs, a contingency (Absurdity) either unrecognised by the majority of people or accepted implicitly as one of the facts of an imperfect life. There are other sources of disagreement. We hear of economic, industrial, psychological and political alienation; of sexual and ontological alienation; of pathological alienation. It would be relaxing to assume that all these varieties peacefully coexist, each content with its own plot in the garden of unhappiness. But the varieties depend on their interpreters who in turn claim to have discovered the great, paternal tree of grief from which all other branches grow.

This jostling is reflected throughout literature. The alienation of man is a constant theme of literature. The private writer unravels private alienation not as a particular manifestation of a socio-economic dislocation, but as a misfortune either universal to the species (ontological) or unique to the individual (psychological). The public writer tends, by contrast, to present the individual predicament as an example of a social dislocation capable of remedy. He searches

for ultimate alienating sources in the prevailing socio-economic system, in class struggle, in exploitation and the profit
motive, and in the hierarchical psycho-political structures
which reflect and reinforce these dislocations. For whereas
the public writer (I am trading only in tendencies here, but
marked tendencies) regards the singular man as an extension
of general man, the private writer regards general man as a
composite identikit portrait of the eternal singular(s).

This tendency in public writing is one which, I believe,
the socialist writer must preserve, while relaxing something
of its traditional dogmatic rigour. A genuine form of alienation occurs (Brecht points out) when your stepfather arrives
in your life, forcing you to see your mother as a wife, wrench-
ing her from her previous essence-for-you. Neither acts of
parliament nor guerrilla warfare will protect the next generation of children from such experiences. The brash, insen-
sitive, wait-for-the-Day, optimism which permeates so much
committed literature invariably renders it indigestible if not
odious to young readers who demand authenticity. To insist
that all forms of alienation can be banished by social action,
that human beings will not continue to rebel against their
mortal essence, and against their imprisonment in their own
skin ('I shall be there', says Sartre's Rocquentin, 'I shall
weigh on the floor. I am.') is to set up the literary equivalent
of a May Day parade. We are social animals locked painfully
in our own singularity. Genuine alienation occurs every time
(a hundred times a day) my action for me passes to my
action for you. As Sarraute writes in *The Planetarium*, 'Complete fusion exists with no one, those are tales that we read
in novels — we all know that the greatest intimacy is constantly being traversed by silent flashes of cold clear-
sightedness, of loneliness . . .'

In the present century sex has become a symbol and even
the source of disagreement between public and private
writers. If human alienation is sexual in origin, then no
amount of enlightenment, de-repression, sex education,
contraception, legitimised abortions and equality between

the sexes will eradicate a fundamental source of alienation which is both biological and ontological. The private writer knows this, emphasises it and sometimes celebrates the fact. But — and here I am offering a very broad, thick-edged generalisation — the public writer committed to socialism tends to adopt the same dismissive, commonsensical, don't-take-it-up attitude towards sex that our man-in-the-street adopts towards the facets of human existence which Albert Camus found alienating and absurd. The public writer says: sex is a form of hunger and not a form of alienation; men will always want food and women and they will always experience physical pain when injured — this has nothing to do with alienation. The influence of Marx is strong here, but these assumptions, this insistence that alienation is by definition social and never ontological, affects the whole reformist, revolutionary and progressive movement of the nineteenth and twentieth centuries. The fact that many Freudians have turned the entire cause-and-effect sequence inside out, arguing that economic exploitation, social aggression and political authoritarianism are particular manifestations of an eternal sexual tension, has naturally exacerbated the cold war, evoking in many Marxists a hostile reflex towards any discussion of sex. Like sociology and linguistics, sex as a. category became a bourgeois deviation.

For the writer, the novelist and playwright, the problem is an inescapable one. And for two reasons. First, as soon as a character, a fictional human being, enters the pages of a novel or the boards of a stage, he brings with him a gender and a potentially very active set of genital organs. It is true, of course, that he also brings with him a stomach and a defecatory mechanism . . . but we don't feel obliged to record every meal or visit to the lavatory. (Some writers do.) But the demands of sexuality are different in kind to those of the stomach. They are less easily and less readily satisfied; they are less localised in that they ramify throughout the entire personality and pattern of behaviour. We also need to know: how the social, economic and political predicament of a particular person relates to his sexual predicament. John Osborne's dramatic portrayal of Luther introduced, pace Erikson, a strong anal motif; whether the solution is justified or not, the kind of question posed is inescapable in the light of our present knowledge. Lindsay Anderson's brilliant committed film *If* . . . depicts the sexual behaviour of boys in a British public school as a refraction of their political system, and then links this political system to the norms and aspirations of the dominant socio-political élite in the wider society. Fine. But the very clarity and sincerity of the film inevitably leads us to consider whether these causal priorities should not be modified and realigned, whether the sexual factor, the appalling jungle of puberty, does not impose itself on socio-political formation to a greater extent than Anderson suggested.

I can offer no solutions. Yet is it not abundantly clear that philosophers like Reich, Fromm, Erikson, Brown and Marcuse, by attempting to synthesise the socio-economic and psychoanalytical matrices of investigation, have posed questions amongst the most significant confronting that segment of the human race no longer threatened by imminent starvation? One notices how the contemporary New Left, particularly its American vanguard and more particularly its theatrical wing, regards social and sexual emancipation as inseparable. This, at a more elaborate and sophisticated level, is the case argued by Herbert Marcuse in his *Eros and Civilization*. Marcuse distinguishes between the basic phylogenetic restriction of the instincts which marks the development of man from animal to *homo sapiens*, on the one hand, and what he calls 'surplus repression' induced by a particular social system, on the other. Marcuse incorporates Freudian insights into a Marxist teleological perspective by denying that the 'reality principle' fashioned out of anthropological sexual repression is of the anti-social, alienating variety. He equates alienation with the restraints and diversions imposed on Eros by the 'performance principle', which is the specific, noxious form of the reality principle induced by modern socio-economic structures. The main task of social action is therefore clear: to do away with surplus repression and the system which produces it.

Marcuse fails to unbend certain question marks in my mind. As he himself acknowledges, the wonderful release of Eros, of the pleasure principle, into the realm of creative freedom requires at the very least the elimination of material scarcity and the reduction of necessary labour to the point where it no longer dominates the muscular and mental life of the individual and of society. Marcuse attributes material scarcity to specific forms of social organisation. This is true but it is not the whole truth. There is, for instance, the problem of the ratio of global resources to the total population of the planet. Scarcity, moreover, is relative as well as absolute. What represents scarcity for an American worker represents abundance for an Indian peasant. Whatever the level of abundance we are observing, the drive for greater material affluence is always a significant factor. Hence the perpetual extension of the 'performance principle' from pre-industrial to industrial and post-industrial society, involving a perpetually intensified manipulation and distortion of sexual drives. Leaving aside the problem of the inheritance of acquired characteristics at the biological level, experience indicates overwhelmingly that a force or entity (sex) subjected to protracted and sustained environmental pressures undergoes a qualitative transformation. Marcuse, like Rousseau, Marx, Morris and other utopians before him, would have us believe in a pure, uncorrupted human essence which will re-emerge like the golden stone of old Oxford colleges once the centuries of grime have been washed away. But the grime is liable to eat into the stone, to become part of it. Marcuse's vision is that of an idyllic South Seas harmony of man, woman, nature and the cosmos, miraculously unravelled in a world of factories, computers and instant communication. But does not the 'performance principle', itself no sudden acquisition but the product of centuries of socio-economic development, not eat into the fabric of the human stone? In any case, it is by no means self-evident that the basic reality principle, the basic anthropological sexual repression, is a non-alienating force. Marcuse's liberated Eros evokes an impression of innocent, pre-genital, child-like sensuality. The strip-in eroticism of our contemporary left-wing sexual libertarians looks very different. You may say: but this is not what Marcuse had in mind, these liber-tarians have jumped the gun, vulgarised the notion, and parodied the social norms they claim to reject. Well . . . many Marxists have experienced the same reaction to the actual shape taken by Communist regimes. Real men never prove worthy in the event of the Philosopher Kings.

I am not convinced. I am not convinced that the aggressive manifestations of sexuality are not symptomatic of some characteristic of *homo sapiens* — call it generic — which is inherently warlike. About human nature Thomas Hobbes was not so utterly misguided; perhaps he was less mis-guided than Rousseau or William Morris. Or Marx.

THREE

According to Marx, the roots of alienation lie in class society and, most acutely, in capitalism. The solution resides not in adapting man to society but in adapting society to man. This requires, says Marx, a socio-political revolution. Only after such a revolution and after a period of proletarian reconstruction will classes disappear, human nature re-emerge in its true, rational form, and the oppressive political, legal and military superstructure wither away. Men will no longer struggle against each other, but join forces to master nature. Greed and the profit motive will become things of the past, of 'pre-history', in a Communist society regulated according to the principle of 'from each according to his abilities, to each according to his needs'.

Taking Marx's writings as a whole, and leaving aside the reformulations which took place after 1845, the general

Marxian analysis of alienation under capitalism yields the following component elements:

(1) The worker is alienated from his own labour or labour power by being compelled to sell it on the market. Consequently he is alienated from his own activity, from himself. 'The labourer therefore constantly produces material, objective wealth, but in the form of capital, of an alien power that dominates and exploits him.'

(2) The relationship between members of different social classes is necessarily one of extreme alienation. They are bound to regard each other as objects, as sources of or resources for exploitation. The 'de-humanisation' of human relations becomes general.

(3) Wealth, property and the means of exchange (money) assume an alien power. 'Money is the alienated essence of man's work and existence; this essence dominates him and he worships it.'

(4) In the later writings of Marx, elements (2) and (3) are expressed by the terms 'reification' and 'the fetishism of commodities'.

(5) An alienated superstructure arises. The state power (political, legal and military), representing in fact the rule of the dominant economic class, the class which owns the means of production, presents itself to the population as the guardian of morality, order and civilisation. In so far as men accept this projection they, like the institutions of state power, are alienated. The prevailing ideology, which formulates and transmits this projection, includes religion, philosophy, political ideas and literature. All ideologies except the revolutionary proletarian one (scientific socialism) are manifestations of false consciousness, i.e., of alienation.

The history of the last hundred-odd years both validates Marx's general analysis and imposes a number of reservations to it. The system of material incentives and social stratification developed in the Soviet Union demonstrates that he was too optimistic in regarding capitalism as the last historical system under which alienation would prevail. (The

Trotskyist description of the Soviet system as 'state capitalism' is a form of political sophistry; the Soviet system is basically 'state socialism'.) We see also that the proletariat, far from being the 'universal' class whose dictatorship would prelude genuine communism, takes its place, (like an American national minority) among the social groups whose standard of living and status gradually improve until its own ideological attitudes broadly coincide with those of the privileged and conservative classes in general. To make this point is automatically to suggest another: that Marx's vision of communism, of a society where human nature would be truly social, harmonious and generous, has lost its coherence and its claim to be scientific.

Without such a vision, alienation loses much of its meaning. Marx saw man as alienated in class society from his own essence; but that essence would be achieved only in the future. Remove the future and you remove the essence. It then becomes possible to question whether there is any essence from which man can legitimately be said to be alienated. The answer, I would strongly suggest, is to insist that this essence is *ethical*, a religious postulate rather than a scientific one, something which can be claimed existentially rather than biologically. In point of fact the 'scientific' bit in 'scientific socialism' was always under sentence of death. Marx, perhaps more than any other philosopher, mistook his dreams for future realities. Even so the dreams are good ones and the struggle to achieve that conversion (dream-reality) remains the finest available to man. This having been said, one must therefore regard alienation both as an empirical reality and, simultaneously, as fulfilling in modern ideology the same function as the Fall in Christian mythology.

What is more, new forms of alienation arise more rapidly than the old ones are destroyed. Man, making himself less and less the slave of nature, becomes the slave of counter-nature, which springs from the applied science of nature. Scientific and technological innovations outpace our capacity to absorb and humanise them, with the terrible result that man is becoming increasingly alienated from his most distinctive faculty, his intelligence. At the same time the products of this intelligence, knowledge and skill, drive him to fragment his personality, to narrow specialisation, to the imitation of automata, to worship efficiency and pay the price in soul-destroying boredom, to educate himself highly while increasingly delegating to élites his participatory role in collective decision-making.

FOUR

The concept of alienation, when modified and brought up to date, is a sound one. Its ideological virtues become more than ever apparent when we examine its alternative. This counter-concept, called anomie, was first advanced by the nineteenth-century positivists, notably Durkheim, and has subsequently been perpetuated under other names (or none) by behavioural social scientists and the apologists of political technocracy. They, like Comte and Durkheim, persistently announce 'the end of ideology' and with it, of class struggle. Durkheim reacted to the revolutionary political solutions of Marx with distaste and disdain; for Durkheim, man's maladjustment in modern society was 'anomic', the result of human incapacity to adapt rapidly to economic progress and its social requirements. The solution to this maladjustment lay not in retrograde metaphysical chatter about overthrowing the system, but rather in evolutionary adaptation and scientific social engineering. According to Durkheim the call to class struggle was simply a desperate, obscurantist cry of defiance against the inevitable.

The normative tendency of this doctrine is everywhere prevalent today. It accounts for most Freudian psychiatry *in practice* — you are unhappy? then adjust, come to terms with the performance principle. It is grotesquely evident in the belief of Western politicians, generals and social scientists that revolution in the Third World is some kind of alien plague provoked by 'agitators', a plague which can be checked by the compilation of the relevant data and by timely prophylactic measures. Its spirit informs the whole of a recent best-seller, Jean-Jacques Servan-Schreiber's *The American Challenge*, with its reverence for efficiency, higher profit margins, automation and managerial élitism. These things are inevitable, says Servan-Schreiber, tomorrow is already here, and therefore the prime task of politicians and educators is to convince the population of this inevitability and to adapt their attitudes and behaviour to its Leviathan-like demands. Refracted elements of the same positivism occur in the sociological writings of men like Parsons, Shils and Lipset, all of whom define 'intellectuals' in the same way that Comte defined his 'Savants' — as the whole community engaged in science, scholarship and the transmission of culture. Such a definition quietly detaches the intellectual from his special normative and ideological role as general critic of the prevailing social system. (It is no coincidence that the Moscow Dictionary of Philosophy arrives at a similar definition of Soviet intellectuals; the Russians may contest 'the end of ideology' in the capitalist West, but they are equally determined to root ideology out of their own garden.)

Until recently the black girl wanted to have straight hair like the white girl. She wanted to imitate a physical attribute of the ruling culture. And the magazines directed at coloured girls said to her: 'You are suffering from anomie, therefore straighten your hair.' But now they say to her: 'Recognise and rejoice in your own essence; the desire to straighten your hair is an acute form of alienation.'

Everywhere you turn, in newspapers, magazines, TV, radio, films, you are being offered tips as to how to get your teeth into the creamy part of the cake. We live, horribly, in the manipulative society. In the nineteenth-century authoritarian regimes you were lashed on the back if you forgot your place; in the twentieth-century totalitarian regimes you are convinced day and night that your place (or two places up the queue) is the one you have chosen for yourself. The commercial advertisement as a total, cumulative phenomenon projects an utterly cynical view of human relationships. All it can see or feel about man is the money in his pocket. It represents a violent form of reification. The ruling elements in both the capitalist and Communist states generate their own aims and then mobilise vast communicative resources to make those aims not only accepted but actively desired by the population. False needs are stimulated while politically harmless outlets for frustration and surplus energy are proposed. Social domination is tirelessly justified in terms of the rapid cycle of production and consumption, production and consumption. Where manipulated consent fails, naked coercion intervenes. In Russia it intervenes more rapidly than in the West. In the West freedom of critical theory is encouraged among a small minority so that this very freedom can be advertised to prove that the system is not what it is. At this moment somewhere in California a team of behaviourists is calculating on a computer what proportion of its youth America can surrender to radicalism before an extra turn of the screw becomes necessary.

FIVE

I exaggerate? Reason yielding to rhetoric? Well, perhaps... Reading the passage through again, I get the impression that I have bulldozed my way through my own doubts. Is this what I believe, or what I believe I ought to believe? Having pleaded and persuaded young radical students not to exaggerate, I find myself echoing and endorsing their composite ideology. And maybe they, names but not faces now forgotten to me, are somewhere projecting fragments of my own scepticism... Yet that is how we conduct dialogues. We try not to yield ground on the field of battle; it is only after the tents have been struck that mutual retreats take place. But there is also another factor to consider: if you are basically in

sympathy with the social system you have inherited, if your
vision of desirable reform extends no further than parliamentary amendments, then you can afford discretion, a fine
balance in your summing up. But to change the world a little
you have to want to change it a lot. The natural tendency of
man is inertia; society, any society, evolves a fine, constrain-
ing mesh of subtle restraints. Radical ideology, like recupera-
tive medicine, works by overkill. That is why the New Left
has more practical achievements to its credit in five years
than the old Left had in forty. What inhibits me is not the
fear that my analysis is wrong but that it may be unreason-
able to expect anything better of men when they are crowded
shoulder to shoulder on one small carpet. But Che was not
reasonable. To liken Guevara to Christ reverberates with
mysticism; to liken Christ to Che seems more sensible. The
flame is there; to grasp it you have to leap and if you don't
leap you are not bad but simply the sort of person who took
Pilate's point of view.

SIX

If there are two types of alienation, it remains to demonstrate
their connection. If life is absurd, then so is art. But art provides man with the opportunity to maintain or revive his
higher consciousness, to set a form to his hopes and pros-
pective adventures. It is absurdity set in motion against itself.
A critical and progressive art is one which sets man's existence against his essence, or the essences he attributes to himself. Creative literature, by its very freedom of scope and
movement, is uniquely placed to restore to man a sense of his
general coherence and of his capacity for constructive social
action. In short, to contribute to his de-alienation.

This brings me to the notion — central to the present
work — of dialectical writing. Here I must warn the reader
not only that I shall employ the word 'dialectical' in its post-
Hegelian rather than its classical sense, but also that I shall

employ it freely and without the respect no doubt due to its ancestry. Furthermore I shall not hesitate to blur the boundaries between description and prescription, between a literature which already exists and one which I would like to see evolve. As will emerge more clearly later, the foundations of theatrical dialectics have already been securely laid by hands of genius; it will therefore be possible to discuss the theory in terms of specific playwrights and their works. But as for the novel — the committed novel — the absence of corresponding geniuses compels us to shoot in the dark. I would only add that the propositions offered in these pages have not been fashioned out of theoretical speculation alone; they have been considerably influenced by the experience of writing the play and the novel which form the companion volumes to this book.

Naturally dialectical art shares with all art an escapist dimension. Form itself provides a refuge from the chaotic flux of experience. Even the art which opposes reality also reconciles us to it, for the act of literary opposition tends to serve as a substitute for real opposition. But this tendency increases with empathy and illusion. The reader goes to bed somehow acquitted of responsibility; it has been enough to say 'yes', and to be in the know.

The struggle against social alienation *(Entfremdung)* and false consciousness requires an alienated *(Verfremdung)*, anti-magical art, a dialectical literature which recognises its own nature and which is self-conscious, anti-mimetic and self-critical. It never aspires to completion. It knits, unravels, knits . . . It is a process as well as a product. This process is both synchronic and diachronic, both genetic and structural. Its social commitment does not blind it to the fact that its meaning (content) results from the interaction of subject and form. Dialectical literature avoids the 'still-life' effect, the finished picture. It lays bare its own techniques and tools, although it must use other techniques and tools to do this, just as it must set language against language and symbol against symbol. Being literature, it can never escape from itself. But it can approach the door. It can communicate its own communicative nature. It knows that it is not only written but also read. It is no longer a question, as with the Marxist old guard, of the novelist capturing the dialectic of society, like an elusive butterfly, and then placing it on display in the transparent glass jar of realism. Literature itself works *within* the social dialectic. It is part of it. Dialectical literature is both transitive and intransitive: what it says and what it is are inseparable. It interprets the world through signs, and the world interprets itself through it. It vigorously rejects both the extreme intrinsic fallacy of the structuralists and ultra-modernists, and the extreme extrinsic fallacy of the Marxists, naturalists and realists. The replacement of a *littérature de dire* by a *littérature de faire* is a suggestive tendency but not a complete possibility. Dialectical literature does not claim autonomy nor does it wish to cut itself off from everyday language and speech. It takes no delight in obscurity. If it turns out in the present cultural climate to be an élitist literature, it has no wish to be. Dialectical literature strives to do what it cannot do; it attempts representation while discarding the myth of representation; it attempts to transcend its own limitations as a text while never forgetting that these limitations cannot be transcended; it makes a primary virtue of honesty and yet proves its virtue by means of cunning tricks. Like Sisyphus, it goes on trying.

SEVEN

Ernst Fischer writes: 'But art is also necessary by virtue of the magic inherent in it.' According to Lukács, art provides the humanistic alternative to the claims of revelation. The fetish of art as magic has many adherents outside the realist camp. It is more influential than that. 'The artist,' writes James Joyce, 'like the God of creation, remains within or behind or beyond or above his handiwork, invisible, refined out of existence, indifferent, paring his fingernails.' The puppets move fluently, wonderfully life-like, and no string is visible. No thought, remark or action can intrude which does not belong to the characters themselves. The illusion is complete. Nathalie Sarraute reacts against this tradition (although apparently more in theory than in practice). We have entered, she says, the age of suspicion, an epoch when the reader has become suspicious of the author's claims to revelation and has begun to recognise fictional invention for what it is. But Sarraute is too optimistic. The technique or philosophy expounded by Joyce (and, very influentially, by Henry James) is today almost universally accepted in the creative writing schools as an eternal law of literary art. Not surprisingly, the majority of readers also take the same view. They do not see it for what it is, a relatively recent development, an outgrowth of the nineteenth-century fetish of scientific certainty and its corollary — the desire to escape from a distressing but real world into a consoling but equally real illusion.

The most formidable opponent of illusionism is Brecht. Noting that many writers try to give the impression that everything in their work happens of its own accord, like an image forming in a plain, inert mirror, he comments: 'Of course this is a swindle, and apparently the idea is that if it comes off it will increase the spectator's pleasure. In fact it does not. What the spectator, anyway the experienced spectator, enjoys about art is the making of art, the active creative element.' The impact of Brecht on both theatre and cinema has been immense, fostering a movement which, while often indulging in excesses, is evolving its own philosophy within the terms of a given medium. (Sound track of Godard's *Made in USA*: 'And already fiction carries away reality. Already there is blood and mystery in the air, and already I seem to be plunged into a film by Walt Disney, but played by Humphrey Bogart — and therefore a political film.') Nor is this movement confined to the West. More controlled and mature than any Godard movie is Wajda's *Everything for Sale*, a brilliant film about the process of conceiving and making films, and about the adaptation of reality to this process and of the process to reality.

What vanished almost without trace in the age of Darwin, the railway and the electric light bulb was epistemological doubt. Knowledge would liberate and absolute knowledge would liberate absolutely. Between man and knowledge only one space intervened — that of a transitory, constantly diminishing ignorance. Even the modernists, the writers sceptical about human progress, were affected by certain literary consequences of the doctrine. A literature was born which brazenly and bogusly affected to reproduce or re-create reality: in effect a literature was born which masked its own essence; the history of literature became the history of bad faith. The lie was easier to perpetrate in the theatre than in the novel because the theatrical medium itself — live actors, costume, greasepaint, stage props, life-like effects directed at the senses — offers illusionist advantages which are unavailable to the novelist. He, heir to the story-spinner and epic poet, has had to labour mightily and manicure his craft in order to exclude his own voice and his own presence from his own artifact. To become, in short, a magician. As Koestler says, 'The real tears shed over Anna Karenina or Emma Bovary are the ultimate triumph of sympathetic magic.'

But you may well object that this 'fetishism of art', this 'sympathetic magic' of which I complain, has been responsible for some of the greatest art known to man. Balzac? Tolstoy? Flaubert? Proust? Joyce? And what of the Greek potter at work on his perfect vase, Michelangelo at work on 'David', Beethoven at work on the Ninth Symphony — were they not all concerned with the end-product, the finished self-contained illusion? There are several ways of answering this objection. A young writer today may understand why Homer is a greater writer than Graham Greene; nevertheless he is more likely to take Greene as a model. A modern sculptor may stand in awe before Michelangelo's 'David', and then return to his studio to produce a human figure which is abstract and non-representational. There is no contradiction in this. We can never escape contemporary influences and uniquely modern perspectives on art and its materials, even if the traditional aspects of our sensibility respond admiringly to the vision of earlier generations.

The fetish of art (art as magic) becomes more apparent when we compare the spirit of modern fiction and drama to that of other forms of writing. Philosophers, historians, critics and political theorists do not rely on mere assertion. They recognise the obligation to lay bare their reasoning, to offer evidence, to consider objections, to reveal the process of their exposition. Even Nietzsche, an essentially 'artistic' philosopher who traded in imaginative assertions, devoted many pages to justifying them. Yet when we turn to the novel and the drama the code is reversed; all visible brush strokes are removed from the canvas. Like the Holy Ghost, art must reveal no navel. I am not suggesting that novels and plays should be peppered with footnotes and references to learned works. Awareness of the process of literature need not involve leaving ink stains, erasures and fragments from early drafts scattered about the page. Such practice is not only lazy and slipshod but also dishonest. I am suggesting that it should show the same self-awareness as other forms of writing in its own terms. When we are children we delight in the conjuror's ability to mesmerise and deceive us, to make fantasy real. Later we turn to novels for the same experience. It may well be the case that for many children the delight of the conjuring act lies in a delicate balance between illusion and non-illusion, between the miraculous effects and the simultaneous knowledge that hocus-pocus is going on behind the screen. Koestler has suggested that the value of empathetic art lies precisely in the maintenance of this balance between two planes or matrices. It is this precarious suspension, he says, which brings on the flux of emotion and catharsis. This may be true. But catharsis is what we want to avoid. Catharsis is escape, a relief, an evasion, a substitute gratification, a way of coming to terms with the world as it is.

The audience which goes in search of catharsis is looking for a night out, a holiday from life, a turkish bath. Committed writing must aim to send the reader or spectator back into the world with his ideological and emotional tensions unrelieved.

Illusion and empathy in literature involve an element of bad faith and with it, guilt. The sound of a prompter's voice or a sudden, unplanned crash behind the scenes evokes nervous titters from a theatre audience. The matrix of reality collides with the matrix of illusion in a way which the audience cannot accommodate. The laughter of the audience is not only directed at the performers' professional ineptitude but also at the audience itself — at the sudden exposure of its own illusionist make-believe.

Stripped of its clothes, empathy appears rather childish. But of course complete empathy is most unlikely. Even the most self-contained, magical, illusionist drama — even *The Three Sisters* or *Madame Bovary* — cannot induce it. In the audience's response there is always an *active* component, which breaks free of the illusion and pursues its own speculations and associations. For illusionist, empathetic art this active component is a threat — the threat of loss of concentration, loss of attention, the glazed eyes which no longer see the actors or read the lines but which indicate abandonment to private reverie and daydream. An alienated literature, on the other hand, not only encourages this active, personal response, it also creates space for it within the fictional or dramatic action. A working-class woman, moved by the tale of Vlassova in Gorky's realist novel, *The Mother*, must lay aside the novel if she wishes to dream and conjecture what she would or should have done had she been in Vlassova's place. Gorky presents a self-contained world: either empathise or stay out. But in Brecht's dramatised version of the same novel the action is constantly distanced from itself, the text from the text. Consequently the personal, active responses of the working-class woman spectator are both stimulated and incorporated into the drama.

It would be quite wrong, however, to equate illusionist literature with the implicit (folded-in) and dialectical literature with the explicit. The value of the implicit is beyond question. It encourages an active, interpretative working relationship with the content, whether by intrapolation (filling in gaps) or extrapolation (completing hints and suggestions). Literary alienation need not and should not involve the dotting of every 'i' and the crossing of every 't'. Form, metaphor, image, symbol, analogy and allegory are not purged from the text but rather set to work at a secondary level as commentaries on themselves, as ways of exposing the crystalline spatial dimensions of the text. Dialectical writing does not mean chunks of illusion interspersed with heavy-handed chorus-commentaries on the illusion. It is writing exploring its own ontology as book or play, as something incorporating both creation and criticism, both experience and expression. The suspension of disbelief is itself suspended then unsuspended at a higher level of awareness.

EIGHT

The mood and temper of a book depends on its author. In this respect dialectical writing is no exception. It nevertheless seems clear that in tendency dialectical writing is cool, lucid, detached, cerebral, rational, theoretical . . . rather than hot, passionate, involved, imaginative, emotive, intuitive. I cannot over-emphasise the words '*in tendency*', I would put them in double italics if such a typographical phenomenon existed.

Nevertheless it has to be admitted frankly that dialectical writing involves properties and approaches which some of the best brains of our culture have regarded as incompatible with art. According to Hegel, for example, religion apprehends truth by assertion and faith, philosophy through knowledge, and art — by intuition. According to the Russian Marxist Plekhanov, 'Usefulness is perceived by reason,

beauty by the contemplative faculty. The sphere of the first
is calculation, the sphere of the second is instinct.' According
to Tolstoy (unlike the others himself an artist), 'Art is differentiated from activity of the understanding, which demands preparation and a certain sequence of knowledge . . .
by the fact that it acts on people independently of their share
of development and education.' (A ridiculous proposition
and incidentally one refuted by his own arguments in *What
is Art?*) Tolstoy is in no doubt that science enables men to
perceive truth and knowledge while 'Art transmits these
truths from the region of emotion'. The English Marxist
critic Caudwell comes close to this position: 'Art is the expression of man's freedom in the world of feeling, just as
science is the expression of man's freedom in the world of
sensory perception.' Elsewhere he added: 'Man's instincts
are pressed in art against the altered mould of reality, and by
a specific organisation of the emotions thus generated, there
is a new attitude, an adaptation.' Freud regarded the creative
or artistic writer (as distinct from others) as a person who
turned away from reality, allowed his fantasy life to build
up and then, with specific artistic gifts, shaped fantasy into
a new and acceptable kind of reality. Harold Laski complained about Shaw's plays: 'He has sacrificed emotion to
intellect, intuition to the syllogism . . .', the implication being
that Shaw had sacrificed the essential attributes of dramatic
art. More recently Lucien Goldmann has written: '. . . it is
the *imaginary* transposition . . . of the mental structures of
these privileged groups . . . which constitutes the essence of
great artistic and literary creations, just as the *conceptual*
translation of these mental structures constitutes the great
philosophical systems.' (My emphases.) According to Goldmann a work of art is a transcendence on a *non-conceptual*
level of the tension between extreme unity and extreme
complexity. By this theory, the artistic *imagination* has kinship with dream and delusion, but contains an inner principle of order which provokes understanding rather than
sublimation.

Consider, in summary, the key words which these distinguished commentators associate with art: intuition, instinct, feeling, emotion, fantasy, the imagination. Conversely, art is regarded as alien to: knowledge, calculation, intellect, empirical observation (perception), the conceptual, reason.

So apparently we have two clearly differentiated families, poles apart, irreconcilable, subject to an eternal apartheid. And if dialectical writing is at all as I have described it, then it must be a monstrous deformity, an ugly bastard disowned by both families.

However . . .

Take the family of art. According to the philosophers the central essence, the term which embraces and subsumes the others, is *imagination*. Not all products of the imagination are art, but all art is a product of the imagination. Now take the family of non-artistic or scientific literature. Here the central and essential notion is *reason*. (Based on its subsidiary attendants, knowledge and concept.)

We will find, I suggest, that the absolute, generic distinction between imagination and reason is untenable. And with the collapse of that absolute distinction, so the total segregation of artistic and non-artistic writing also collapses.

What is art?

Consider four typical uses of the word, each representing a note on a semantic scale which moves from the specific to the general.

(A) *The Royal College of Art*. Here art refers to the fine arts, primarily painting and sculpture. (B) *The Arts Council*. Here we have the notion of 'the arts', i.e., certain types of literature, the fine arts, music, theatre, opera, ballet — in short, 'culture' in the narrow sense of the word, as distinct from the ensemble of values, beliefs and customs to which anthropologists apply the word. (C) *An Arts Degree. (B.A.)* This use of the word in the universities originates in a binary system which distinguishes between the sciences and the humanities (arts). (Historically and broadly, the word 'philosophy' serves the same sense: you become a Bachelor of Arts and then a Doctor of Philosophy without ever leaving, for example, the field of history or Chinese literature.) (D) *The art of war (or love)*. Here the word signifies something more intangible than technique. It suggests some intuitive skill, a fine practical sensibility which can be partly but never wholly taught.

(D) is crucial, seminal. It contains the general notion which is present in every application of the word 'art'. Consider now (A) and (B). In neither case does there seem any likelihood that the word 'art' has been misapplied. In other words the central notion of (D) is extremely relevant to the spheres of activity associated with (A) and (B). But when we turn to (C), an *Arts Degree*, we are conscious of discomfort, of an idea which has been perpetuated terminologically as a result of institutional inertia and reverence for tradition but which has become increasingly anachronistic with the passage of time. When a new university is founded certain academic disciplines nominally categorised as 'arts' in the old universities are hived off as social sciences (sociology, economics, psychology, statistics, demography, anthropology, politics, etc.) The linguists, too, may wish to indicate that the nineteenth century did not pass them by.

Historically, then, 'science' enjoys an imperialistic relationship to 'the arts'. It constantly extends its territory. A subject once held to be a 'mystery' or art, is later seen to be susceptible to specialised forms of investigation and analysis. New methods of collecting and correlating data are found and with them new methods of logical deduction. The number of 'arts' faculties contracts accordingly.

A parallel development occurs within the field of philosophy. The central, historical notion of 'art' is of course different from that of philosophy, but there is a significant connection. Philosophy concerns itself with the most general causes of (usually) the most general phenomena, and with the most general principles of conduct. But what is considered an appropriate area for general study depends largely on how much is known about it at a particular time. Thus

even physics was once regarded as a part of philosophy. Today the idea seems ridiculous. Just as the arts have had to
surrender large territories, so also philosophy has had to grant
self-rule to history, astronomy, sociology, anthropology and
other usurping provinces.

Now I appreciate that this analysis is schematic and in
need of qualification and refinement. But I am not going to
waste time demonstrating my appreciation. The habitual
nervous disease of writers who have passed as many years in
academies as I is to be forever glancing over their own
shoulders. (As the reader may have gathered.) We are so
busy countering possible objections to our opinions that in
the end we have no opinions to offer — just a series of highly
fortified defensive positions encompassing an empty space.
My point is this: the proper sphere of art, like that of philosophy, at any given time is decided in negative terms, in
terms of the absence or comparative absence from that
sphere of sufficient data, sufficient verifiable information and
sufficiently inductive methods of reasoning to qualify it as a
science or social science. But this is precisely where the trap
lies. Just as the medieval world slothfully retained too many
of its mental holdings in the limited company of the arts, so
the contemporary culture too rashly and precipitously transfers its stock to an equity called science. And this equity,
particularly its social science subsidiary, has the fragile
contours of a bubble. The spectacle of a modern sociologist
calling himself a scientist is no less comic than that of a
medieval astronomer pursuing his art. Neither art nor philosophy submit easily to the usurpations and break-aways of
their provinces. The skills, leaps, intuitive connections and
formalistic resources of the novel and the drama remain
much in evidence in modern historiography, sociology,
political theory and documentary reportage. I refer to more
than the art of writing; I am talking about the problematical
nature of the material, about the problematical nature of its
mode of expression (language), and about the peculiarly acute
way the expression shapes the material.

But the converse tendency also applies. Undoubtedly historiography, sociology, political theory, etc., *are* better informed, more rigorously analysed, more scientific than they once were. *But so also are novels and plays!* Art in its narrow sense ([A] and [B]) does not exist in a watertight compartment, sealed against the discoveries of the Encyclopaedia. Not only do novelists and playwrights avidly absorb historical, sociological, economic and political information, they also pay attention (some of them do) to researches in the field of literature and language.

In conclusion; art and non-art in literature can be separated but never segregated. This being so, any absolute fetish of art is foolish. The same proves to be true of reason and the imagination. Here again the area of overlap is enormous. Without this overlap, dialectical art would be a contradiction in terms. In practice, the overlap becomes a central proposition of dialectical writing.

Compare the following:

(A) 'My imagination is full of formless fears.' (B) 'He has a brilliant mathematical imagination.'

In (A) imagining and the imagination denote a type of consciousness which is divorced from reality. But in (B) they denote a particular mental process by which the discrete details of reality can be ordered and resolved (formal, logic or reason being inadequate to the task).

We appreciate that the imaginative mathematician or architect is mentally ordering and resolving data which are real: cement, steel, stresses, numbers, axiomatic propositions and so forth. But logic and reason also deal in similar materials; whatever the divergence, there is common ground. The student of mathematics or architecture acknowledges this without discomfort, but our philosophers of aesthetics tend to insist on absolute segregation, incorporating the notion contained in (A) into that contained in (B), thus linking the imagination to a refracted perception of reality having kinship with dream and fantasy.

In his book *L'Imaginaire*, Sartre presents image, concept

and perception as three quite distinct types of consciousness. We can agree with Sartre in so far as (*a*) only a chair which is *there* can be perceived, (*b*) the chair which appears in an image is by definition not there, even if its exact replica is there, and (*c*) I can conceive of a chair without having any particular chair in mind, whereas perception and image produce a specific chair, even if blurred in the case of some images. But the 'imagination' is very much more than the process of forming images (the 'image' being defined by Sartre as an act which aims at analogical representation of an object). A snapshot taken at random or by accident produces a materialised image of a man no less than a portrait in oils or a caricature. Yet obviously the 'imaginative' content of the snapshot is nil and that of the portrait or caricature much greater. The imagination involves a process of substitution, re-creation, speculation and depiction; it is a construct or process with a varying cerebral and conscious content and mainly distinguished from the mental process called 'reason' because:

Although there are many forms of 'reason' (analytical, dialectical, inductive, deductive, metaphysical, pragmatic, positivistic, etc) what distinguishes each form is a recognisable set of principles and premises which are axiomatic and semi-axiomatic, as well a vocabulary which serves these principles. The argument that I am conducting on this page, whether right or wrong, is clearly a 'rational' one. The imagination relies less on defined principles and premises than on speculative leaps, tentative 'shots in the dark', the visualisation of ultimate effects. Reason is like a train, it must keep its wheels on the ground for every inch of the journey; the imagination is like a helicopter which rises, spurts, descends, rises again, searching for a suitable termination. But reason and the imagination are not poles apart. Both the train and the helicopter are regulated in their journeys by concrete material factors. It is true that the imagination may, willingly or unwillingly, approach the condition of dream or trance, but this is not always so and

the *conscious controls* of the creative imagination have much
in common with those of reason. A biography of Mr Gladstone and a novel about a statesman like Gladstone both
have resort to reason and the imagination. G. R. Elton very
properly notes: 'Imagination, controlled by learning and
scholarship, learning and scholarship rendered meaningful by
imagination — these are the tools of enquiry possessed by
the historian.' The interplay of reason and the imagination
is most vividly revealed in phenomenological philosophy
(Husserl, Sartre), the philosophy which makes its first point
of inquiry: 'What are things like?' But phenomenology
bears the same relationship to philosophy in general that
symbolist poetry bears to poetry in general — the detection
of an ever-present factor and then the elevation (or exaggeration) of that factor to a position of primacy.

The analytical tendency which attempts to segregate
artistic and non-artistic literature, as well as reason and
imagination, also likes to attribute emotion exclusively to the
sphere of art and the imagination. 'Art transmits these truths
from the region of perception to the region of emotion', says
Tolstoy. Here again a blundering apartheid is imposed on a
multi-racial community. (Remember Apollo and Dionysus.)
As Brecht said, each social class had its own emotion and its
own reason: the two are intimately joined. What in any case
is meant by the 'region of emotion'? Does it mean the description of emotion or its evocation? Interpreted either way,
art holds no exclusive sovereignty over the region. A novel is
likely to describe human emotion, but so also is a work of
clinical psychiatry. The power to evoke emotion (emotion-
for-others) is inherently contained in nothing or everything;
the subjective response is decisive. I know people for whom
War and Peace generates less emotion that Wittgenstein's
reflections on the nature of language. Reason operating
through knowledge can achieve a symmetry which is both
beautiful and emotive. A novel by Robbe-Grillet may strike
most readers as 'cooler', less emotive, than Deutscher's biography of Trotsky, a great labour of scholarship.

As Koestler puts it, 'The equation of science with logic and reason, of art with intuition and emotion, is a blatant popular fallacy.' Max Planck, the father of quantum theory, wrote in his autobiography that a pioneering scientist must have 'a vivid intuitive imagination for new ideas not generated by deduction, but by artistically creative imagination.' Poincaré stressed the links between mathematics and aesthetics. In both art and non-art there is a time and place for specific codes, axioms and matrices of logic, and a time also for the release of these controls and constraints which are liable to impede the vital creative leap. What we find are differences of degree rather than of kind. The Cartesian legacy unhappily equates reason with conscious, deliberate thinking, and the imagination with a kind of dream-like, semi-conscious, sleepwalking state waiting passively for intuitive revelation. The absolute dichotomy is unreal. Concepts, abstractions and rational codes develop historically out of image-building forms of thought. The connection is never severed whether for the individual or for the species.

Planck spoke of the scientist's need of an artistically creative imagination. For their part, artists and writers have always displayed a profound fascination with knowledge and speculative thought. Scientific and pseudo-scientific theories — the golden section, the secrets of perspective and proportion — have obsessed painters and sculptors through time. (Consider the cubists, or the interest of futurists in machines.) The history of artistic literature and of philosophy in France and Germany are inseparable, likewise the history of literature and politics in Russia. I find it hard to think of Goethe, or Schiller, or Lamartine, or Tolstoy, or Shaw, or Rolland, or Thomas Mann, or Brecht, or Sartre, or Camus, as inspired, intuitive, magical witchdoctors of art, divorced from reason, philosophy and logic. Nor did they write in a sleepwalking trance. The Surrealist Manifesto of 1924 insisted that they ought to have done, which only reinforces the point that they didn't.

At no stage have I suggested that all distinctions between

art and non-art are meaningless. What artistic writing can do is to move with a special freedom, creating new spaces of awareness, associating and juxtaposing features of reality, of consciousness, of myth, of aspiration and of belief in patterns and structures which could not be justified by academic or scientific criteria. Like philosophy, it has a special mission to operate in the empty space between the known and the unknown, the verifiable and the speculative. And, like philosophy again, it enjoys a special exploratory relationship with man's most extensively employed means of communication, language. It can demonstrate implicitly what would otherwise have to be expounded explicitly. Itself an act of creation, it enjoys a unique armoury to penetrate phenomenologically the act of creation. The academic disciplines are like table lamps; their plugs are visibly planted in skirting or wall. Art can hang like a chandelier invisibly suspended, posing the first, enchanting question: how am I here?

NINE

Well now: this artist fellow, this inspired magician, this genius of mindless voodoo — do not expect him to know what he is doing or why. And if he does come up with some pretentious theoretical chatter about his art, you can be certain that his creative work will inevitably explode his pretensions.

As I have already indicated, both Marxist and structural critics prefer to minimise and often eliminate the conscious, cerebral and controlled element from art. Genius or talent makes it happen; the critic exists to say *what* happened. Marxists arrived at this conclusion out of their profound distrust of the individual and out of their obsessive preoccupation with social formations. They abandon the writer to the irresistible power of a wider group consciousness which he inhales automatically like oxygen and which overpowers the carbon monoxide lodged in his conscious mind. (How, then, can literary commitment, conscious commitment, be possible? But pass on.) Engels set up the proposition very clearly, declaring that the contradiction between the subjective political opinions of the writer and what ultimately emerged in his work was one of the most important heuristic principles of the sociology of art. Once launched, the tradition of objectification never looked back. Here, for example, is Arnold Hauser discussing Dostoyevsky: 'The fact that the class character of his figures makes itself felt all the same . . . is part of the triumph of realism which makes Dostoyevsky a materialist in spite of himself.' The same writer takes Balzac in hand: 'Balzac is a revolutionary writer without wanting to be and without knowing that he is.' Leo Lowenthal reaches further back in time for his body-snatching: 'The theatre of Corneille is an exercise in political behaviour accepting conditions of absolute monarchy. The tragedies of Racine are an exercise in middle-class behaviour expressing intellectual and emotional resistance to the same institution — the monarchy.'

Goodbye Corneille; farewell Racine.

But at this great game, George Lukács has remained for many seasons undisputed champion. 'The characters created by the great realists', he declares, 'once conceived in the vision of their creator, live an independent life of their own . . .' (A kind of sorcery?) But here a curious value judgment intrudes on an analytical proposition. Those writers who actually succeed 'in bringing their own *Weltanschauung* into "harmony" with reality', says Lukács, are the 'second-raters'. This broadside is mainly directed against those modernists who were influenced by the anti-Enlightenment. Does it apply to socialist realists as well? Are they too 'second-raters' if they not only accept Marxist perspectives but also succeed in illustrating them in their novels? Lukács ducks this question. But the proposition is clear: art, or rather great art, operates indirectly, subconsciously through the alchemy of genius. Pity the great writer. Pity Tolstoy on the Lukácsean operating table. Tolstoy had confided to

Gorky that in his opinion the worst tragedy of his life was, always had been, and always would be that of the bedroom. Lukács knows better. What *Anna Karenina* really demonstrates, he maintains, is the specifically bourgeois hideousness of love, marriage and the exploitation of women under capitalism. Therefore the finished Tolstoyan product 'burst through' the author's 'abstract-dogmatic frame'. And why? Because, says Lukács, the great realist has an 'unconscious possession of a perspective independent of, and reaching beyond, his understanding of the contemporary scene.'

Curious as it may seem in avowed materialists, these old guard Marxist critics invariably fill the space between general historical sociology and the actual, specific literary work under review with a mixture of mysticism and magic. Phrases like 'once conceived in the vision of their creator' and 'unconscious possession' are employed as if they were precision instruments. But in the long run the critic lays one huge sacrificial gift at the foot of the totem-pole of art: the writer himself.

In this respect Marxists and structuralists remind me of the Russian and Anglo-American armies converging on Germany in 1944–45. They didn't like one another but they had a common enemy. The structuralist critic sacrifices the writer's consciousness, his rationality, not to general sociological forces but to the demon boa constrictor of language and literature. Thus Northrop Frye makes his own the old adage that the creative writer is not heard but overheard (presumably like a sleepwalker warbling on the battlements). But other kinds of writing, says Frye, derive from the conscious mind. Therefore, he can safely conclude, criticism is to art what history is to action and philosophy is to wisdom.

This is bunk. One can sympathise with the student of literature's anxiety to prove his indispensability. Consider the two hundred million graduate students labouring at this very hour on Eng. Lit. or Comparative Lit. theses . . . many of them because they are capable of nothing else. But Frye is not of their number. He is a highly intelligent critic who has made a howling mistake. The past exists independently of historians, but *history* does not. I do not mean that we would know nothing about events beyond living memory had not chroniclers and historians set it down. I mean that history is more than the past recorded, it is the past recorded and given shape. History *is* historiography. Similarly, while the discrete elements of 'society' exist independently of sociology, the concept of 'society' itself and anything meaningful we may say about it is synonymous with sociology. (Not necessarily academic sociology — it can be your own sociological ruminations.) Likewise with philosophy and wisdom. There is no wisdom outside of philosophy (again remembering that the man-in-the-street is a kind of philosopher). Wisdom does not flutter around like a butterfly waiting for some philosopher to catch it in his net and say what it is. History, society and wisdom are themselves concepts not things. But a particular work of literature or art already exists as a thing before the critic arrives on the scene. The primary work of ordering and shaping and thinking and imagining has been done by the writer or artist. The sixty-five thousand graduates now writing theses about *1984* are like a swarm of flies dancing on a single piece of meat. (One or two eggs may hatch.) It is Orwell who killed the cow.

But such logic is not palatable to most critics, least of all structuralists. It is not surprising that Lucien Goldmann, who has attempted to reconcile certain Marxist principles with a number of structuralist ones, brings the art of body-snatching live victims as well as dead to a high point. Goldmann, even more aggressive in this respect than Frye, likens the relationship of the literary sociologist and the writer to that of the physiologist and the athlete whose performance and physique he is studying. The athlete can run fast but only the physiologist knows why (or, presumably, where!). Goldmann calls his working method 'genetic structuralism'. Its basic principles are as follows:

(1) 'On the socio-historical plane, of which literary criticism is part, the principle discoveries of genetic structuralism are those of the *transindividual* (or collective) subject and of the *structured* character of all intellectual, affective or practical activity by this subject.'

(2) '. . . the consciousness of the transindividual subject has no reality of its own and exists only in the individual consciousness involved in a complex of structured relationships.'

(3) As regards individual consciousness, three levels must be distinguished:

(*a*) 'the unconscious . . . constituted by the desired aspirations which social life cannot accept and which have had to be repressed . . .'

(*b*) 'the individual consciousness, constituting an area of varying importance, but one area only, that of activity and of its objective significance.'

(*c*) 'the non-conscious, constituted by the intellectual, affective, imaginary and practical *structures* of individual consciousness. The non-conscious is the creation of transindividual subjects and has, on the psychical plane, a status analogous to nervous or muscular structures on the physiological plane.' It can be brought to light only by scientific analysis.

What are we to make of this?

I want to limit the discussion to one question only, the extent to which the creative writer can consciously plan and control his artistic activity. This brings us to (3), above. According to Goldmann, that area of the writer's mind which is conscious, controlled and particular to the individual, is merely one area out of three. Large areas of his mind are dominated by unconscious, repressed desires of which he is unaware. Even greater areas are dominated by pre-structured patterns of thought, derived from the wider social group, operating automatically beyond the writer's consciousness or control.

If this be so, it is no longer a matter of an author writing a book. He is scarcely less an agent of the writing than his pen. The book is written.

If you turn again to (1) and (3c), above, you will notice something curious. On the face of it, Goldmann makes no distinction between artistic activity and intellectual activity in general. The non-conscious, emanating from the *transindividual* (collective) subject operates equally in both spheres. And if this be the case, there is no reason to conclude that a literary sociologist enjoys a more privileged perspective on the meaning or source of a book than its author. But this is not what Goldmann means. Like all theorists who have discovered determinisms operating on and in the human mind, he regards himself as relatively free from those same determinisms. Somewhere is the implicit assumption that scientific knowledge allows a man to escape from the glass jar. In the name of consistency, Goldmann's theory of the transindividual pre-structuring of the individual's non-conscious must *itself*, as a theory, be subject to the same forces it describes. But in order to make any sense at all the theorist must arrogate to himself a certain autonomy and freedom of mental manœuvre. This is perfectly legitimate. But is it equally legitimate to make the assumption that only the 'literary sociologist' enjoys this freedom and never the creative artist? Certainly such an assumption cannot be logically deduced from Goldmann's general phenomenology of mind.

So we are back once again with our old friend, the fetishism of art. Applied, as so often, to art's disadvantage. The artist remains swimming inside the bowl. He may be a beautiful, prized, multi-coloured goldfish, but he has no clue where he is or what he is doing.

The system now chooses its victims. Malraux, for example. Goldmann describes and explains Malraux' literary progress as a novelist (1927–42) in terms of transindividual, non-conscious conditioning structures of which the writer himself was naturally not aware. Malraux is depicted as reacting on the imaginative level to general societal ideological forces generated in turn by the passage of Western Europe from one phase of capitalism to the next — from laissez-faire individualism to monopoly capitalism. But a third socio-economic phase, says Goldmann, followed and has remained with us. This is characterised as neo-Keynesian, state-inter-ventionalist, managerial capitalism. Goldmann grasps this huge net and looks about him with predatory gaze: soon some innocent writer is going to walk too close. It is Alain Robbe-Grillet. The net descends, the victim is captured and held up for inspection; his work, his novels will turn out to be per-fect, but non-conscious, reflections of the total de-humanisa-tion prevailing in this third phase of capitalism.

Now I myself am not much in sympathy with Robbe-Grillet (although I admire *Jalousie*). I feel entitled to quarrel with some of his theories and beliefs, but who am I to tell him that his beliefs are not what they seem to him, that they are *really* products of forces which I discern but to which he is blind, that he is *really* expressing a petit-bourgeois panic in the face of . . . Who am I to say 'really' so repeatedly? (I exaggerate, of course; we are not obliged to accept every statement in the way its author intended, and the notion of false consciousness would be meaningless if we did.) But Goldmann suffers from no such inhibitions. Quite irrelevant to him are Robbe-Grillet's published opinions on philo-sophical, scientific and literary matters; the possibility that Robbe-Grillet is making a coherent contribution is ruled out of court. As for his modest hope that some of his theories have found literary translation in his novels, this is as laugh-able as if an athlete attributed his prowess in the high jump to the colour of his eyes. No, says Goldmann, Robbe-Grillet is a sensitive geiger-counter exposed to third-phase capitalist dehumanisation. He no more understands this than the geiger-counter knows why it clicks. It is however an interest-ing fact that all undamaged geiger-counters click when ex-posed to the same impulses, whereas Robbe-Grillet and his friends remain heavily outnumbered by realist novelists and others who for some reason never did pick up the signals of total dehumanisation. Goldmann fails to account for this. He also fails to account for Robbe-Grillet. One gets the impression that the sheer variety, idiosyncrasy and individuality of literature puts certain 'literary sociologists' in a frame of mind which is the conceptual equivalent of bad temper (peremptory short cuts, sweeping assertions, refusal to let the victim speak).

I do not suggest that the writer must have the last word on the meaning of his own work, for what is the last word? And if Mrs Hennessy writes to me from 1305, Columbus Drive, Dayton, Ohio, to tell me that a novel of mine which I imagined to be about the English Revolution was really a wonderful, sad, moving depiction of the death of her first husband, then *je n'accuse pas*. Shaw painted Ibsen red and Sartre did the same to Genet. Shaw turned Ibsen into Shaw and Sartre turned Genet into Sartre: obviously a compliment was intended in both cases. In neither instance did one writer rob his admired colleague of his freedom, he simply enthusiastically tattooed him in the colours he liked best. It is the experience of creative writing itself which gives writers this mutual respect, and it is precisely this experience that the critics I have complained of so manifestly lack. It seems fair to point out that the longer Sartre has been distanced from the personal experience of creative writing, the more, in his capacity as critic, he has divested other writers of their freedom. In the high period of his own creative miracle, after the war, he explained Baudelaire in terms of a series of existential *choices*. But more recently a methodologically brilliant study of Flaubert drove itself by inexorable logic to the conclusion that the author of *Madame Bovary* was, in Sartre's own words, 'what was made of him'. A year or so earlier Sartre, reflecting on his own childhood, had reached an equally depressing 'discovery': 'I have not *chosen* my vocation: others had imposed it on me.'

Writers will blindly and stubbornly continue to insist on freedom to choose and freedom to know what they are choosing. They will not willingly abandon the capacity for criticism, rational analysis and conceptual thought to literary sociologists. If this were not so a dialectical literature would be impossible.

CHAPTER SIX

Towards a Dialectical Theatre

ONE

Theatre, yes; drama, no.

Broadly speaking, the theatrical form which conveys realism and towards which realist playwrights have been drawn is *drama*. But drama is older than realism. The tragedies and comedies of the Greek and Shakespearian periods were for the most part dramas. Racine and Molière were dramatists. Nineteenth-century realism is distinguished by specific qualities of its own (psychology, certainty, plot, action, resolution — the 'well-made play'). What realism shares with drama in general (and what we must now jettison) is mimesis, the myth of representation, empathy, illusion and magic. In short, the massive onslaught on the spectator's capacity to identify himself as a spectator seated in a theatre watching a play, a contrivance, an artifact. Modern realism has the distinction of carrying this attack to its extreme point. The alienating, epic and theatre-like tendencies so evident in, for example, Shakespeare, are winnowed out and rejected as the primitive or naïve failures of the early theatre to perfect its techniques. By this reasoning the most advanced theatre is that which most perfectly masks its own nature. But this view is correct in only one respect. It is true that the theatre of Shakespeare or even of the early nineteenth century (Goethe) lacked certain modern technical resources which convey a completely 'real' or naturalistic effect. No doubt some early playwrights regretted this deficiency and indicated their embarrassment by clumsy passages of writing which, when seen on the stage, are neither here nor there. But in general we can say that the vastly improved technical resources of the modern theatre led the realist dramatists up the garden path; it is only more recently that these same technical resources *have been turned against illusion*.

In the public, committed theatre, the movement from illusionist drama to alienated theatre is most clearly seen in the passage from Ibsen to Brecht. In this respect, Shaw is an important transitional figure. At the same time the impact of modernism and particularly of expressionism hastened the transformation. Nor can any kind of theatre, public or private, any longer afford to pretend that Antonin Artaud never existed.

A model of public, committed, dramatic realism is Ibsen's play *An Enemy of the People*. Or, alternatively, Galsworthy's plays *Justice* and *Strife*. Shaw both contributed to the perpetuation of the Ibsen tradition and to its destruction. Shaw inherited and developed all the certainties of the Enlightenment (while borrowing the Will from the anti-Enlightenment). But his preoccupation with *what* he wanted to say and his eclectic approach to *how* he said it, how he conveyed it on the stage, placed a package of dynamite on the pedestal of an apparently impregnable form of realist public drama. In *Mrs Warren's Profession*, he makes his social points by means of the 'well-made play', the great essential structure of modern realism; but Shaw was restless; the naturalistic, mimetic (smell it, see it, hear it as it is) element of realism was not of cardinal importance to him. In Shaw what Raymond Williams has called 'the tangible experience of life' is usually subordinated to an overt and avowed didacticism (prime example: *Back to Methuselah*, where Reason, exposition, the Will, the world-dominating ideas, run amok). In *Man and Superman* human behaviour is translated into a kind of algebra at the expense of realism.

Shaw lays the dynamite without really caring. He is not

mainly concerned with the theatre. He is concerned with ideas and society. For him the theatre is always a means. Others will light the fuse.

Brecht detects the dynamite laid by Shaw. Shaw admires Ibsen, Brecht admires Shaw, yet Brecht is radically opposed to Ibsen — a paradox explicable in terms of the giant leap-frog of genius. 'His world', wrote Brecht of Shaw, 'is one that arises from opinions. The opinions of his characters constitute their fates.' What Brecht admires in the Irishman is the emphasis on reason, on the conscious mind, on the intellect. In Brecht's didactic *Lehrstücke* the role of reason in man's ascent will be central. The very radicalism of Shaw's mind, his delight and expertise in dislocating stock associations, produced an intellectual alienation which carried in it the seeds of an aesthetic alienation.

But for Brecht, the consummator of this aesthetic aliena-tion, Shaw is no more than an interesting figure on the side-lines. Brecht inherits and develops an epic, expressionistic tradition whose early master is Büchner (notably his *Woyzeck* which makes explicit its social type-casting by calling its characters 'the Doctor', 'the Captain' and 'the Drum Major' — a minor but significant formal element which Brecht adopts). The influence of expressionism in the German theatre was in the ascendant before and after the First World War. Like the realists, Brecht searches out what is humanly and social typical; but unlike the realists, he does not wish to conceal his own didactic hànd or the medium through which he displays it. Not for him the confetti of naturalistic particularism. In 1930 Brecht sets down a classic exposition of the differences between dramatic and epic theatre. Plot gives way to narrative; the involvement of the spectator is replaced by the detachment of the observer; sensation and feeling are replaced by critical reason; sugges-tion by argument; emphasis on the outcome by emphasis on the course of events; the interdependence and 'necessary' sequence of scenes by the relative autonomy of scenes. Empathy gives way to alienation.

This is a schematic exposition. But the tendency is clear.

Brecht also makes other distinctions between drama and epic theatre which are more tendentious than illuminating. For example he attributes 'evolutionary determinism' and the notion of human unalterability to drama. But this is true only of ultra-naturalists and never of committed realists. It is also the case that Brecht claims to be a genuine 'realist', but then so also do Robbe-Grillet and Ionesco! Employed in this promiscuous way the word loses all descriptive value.

Meanwhile something else is happening which will eventually give an added propulsion to the replacement of drama by theatre. Artaud (a surrealist) demands that the theatre once more come into its own, discarding the psychology and plot so dear to dramatists, and fully exploiting its own resources. For Artaud a stage is not simply a place where a writer says something using actors and cardboard scenery. It is a place where music, dance, plastic art, pantomime, mimicry, intonation, gesticulation, architecture, lighting and scenery combine and coalesce. It is through them, as well as through the human voice, that theatre must communicate and must make its statement. The medium recognises itself.

At the same time Artaud offers a philosophy which the socially committed writer may view with suspicion. Artaud is intensely metaphysical; he wishes to revive the myths of Creation, Becoming and Chaos. He subscribes to the modernist notion that art and language are revolutionary in their own terms. He wishes to explode the spectator's conventional attitudes by an assault on the senses (hence the Theatre of Cruelty). As a surrealist he values what is latent rather than what is manifest; he prefers dream to formal reason; he eliminates the representational element of theatre almost entirely. That this cult is violently influential in the contemporary radical anti-theatre cannot be denied. I shall try to explain later its dangers. It was certainly foreign to Brecht and it is also foreign, I suggest, to a dialectical theatre. When the committed, public writer extends his hand to modernism he should wear rubber gloves.

The old drama of commitment, the old realism, is now dead in spirit but not yet buried. One recognises this in the dramatic work of Rolf Hochhuth. In both *The Deputy* and *Soldiers* there is a scattering of tributes to theatrical alienation but in terms of the total dramatic structure their function is superfluous and mannered. In *The Deputy* the author indicates that those characters grouped together in the cast list should be played by the same actors — an alienation device to convey the fact that in an age of universal military conscription it is not necessarily to anyone's credit that he wears the pyjamas of the victims rather than the uniform of the SS. *Soldiers* offers a prologue which indicates that the main body of the play to come is a play within a play — a play commissioned in the name of the Coventry Festival Committee by a Sculptor who himself 'inhabits the twilight zone of allegory'. It does not matter, says Hochhuth, whether this commissioned play is presented as reality or dream. I find none of this very interesting or impressive. It is significant that in the London production of *Soldiers* the prologue was altogether omitted and the curtain went up on a conventional, three-act realist drama. Dialectical theatre is integral; its principles work coherently throughout; certainly it is not a question of moistening a realist salad with a little alienation dressing. On the other hand, Hochhuth is a dramatist of considerable power and intelligence whose work reminds us of the formidable weapons for commitment possessed by realism. Hochhuth can actualise, give flesh and blood to historical characters, put them before us without ambiguity, evidence or hesitation. Before our eyes Pius III becomes his 'Pius III'. Churchill becomes his 'Churchill'. The process (weighing of evidence, motivation, interpretation) which the historian must display *in the course* of his published book is already resolved *before* the dramatised 'Pius' or 'Churchill' speaks his first word. Or so it seems and so the realist dramatist intends it to seem. Here he is, this is how it was! The character now *exists* as the author portrays him, our doubts are pushed away, one reality

supersedes another. This dramatic 'reality' is boldly employed by Conor Cruise O'Brien in his play *Murderous Angels*.
O'Brien's play has several qualities in common with those of
Hochhuth: a preoccupation with contemporary or recent
history; a left-wing perspective; a widely revered public
man as a target for deflation and exposure. O'Brien takes up
the theme of Dag Hammarskjöld's attitude to the capture, in
September 1960, of Patrice Lumumba by his enemies in the
province of Kasai. This, of course, was a real historical
situation: Lumumba's life was in obvious danger, yet there
were United Nations forces present in the area and these
forces being Ghanaian their commanding officer applied for
permission to free Lumumba from his captors and to give
him protection. In *Murderous Angels*, Act III, O'Brien depicts the character 'Asdal' (i.e., the Indian Special Repre-
sentative of the U.N. in Leopoldville, Dayal) telephoning
Hammarskjöld in New York and asking for authorisation for
the saving of Lumumba by the Ghanaian U.N. forces. In the
play we do not hear Hammarskjöld's replies, yet we can feel
them from the gradual stiffening of Asdal's attitude into one
of dignified but outraged obedience. Outraged, because at
the other end of the line Hammarskjöld, although fully
aware that Lumumba's life is in acute danger, is specifically
refusing permission for any U.N. intervention. How cold,
how murderous this saint! But wait: what is the relationship
of this theatrical situation to known historical fact? In an
appendix to his play, O'Brien comments: 'In Act III I
represent Dayal as having wished to intervene, and Hammarskjöld as having overruled him. There is no specific
documentary evidence for this.' But O'Brien further explains: 'While the historian must hesitate, lacking absolute
proof, the dramatist may present the hypothesis which he
finds most convincing.'

Present? Yes, but this 'present' in the realist tradition
means 'bring alive'. The *published* text of *Murderous Angels*
has both a preface and an appendix dealing with the relationship of the play to history. But when *acted on stage* there is

neither preface nor appendix, simply the 'action' itself. And this is because Conor Cruise O'Brien, although he employs a number of non-naturalistic stage devices, is, like Hochhuth, attempting to set his imagined characters 'in a dramatic situation matched as closely as possible to the historical situation of those figures.' Presumably, therefore, the aim is illusion and empathy. But with what is the audience being persuaded to empathise? The real Hammarskjöld? Apparently not, for the author comments in his preface: 'I never heard Hammarskjöld talk in this way, but it is quite clear that that was his habit of thought, and, the presentation of this was essential to the "imitation of the action" which I undertook.' In point of fact, Conor Cruise O'Brien as dramatist makes Hammarskjöld talk in a way which was unlike his actual talk — this is perfectly legitimate since we are forewarned of the method and motive of portrayal in the preface. But the preface is available *only to readers of the text*! What of the audience in the theatre? Perhaps the most powerful case for a dialectical, non-realistic form of theatre is that it offers the same necessary commentary on its own process-as-art *within the performance* that realist dramatists like Hochhuth or O'Brien offer *in the preface or appendix*.

My own objections to realism should by now be familiar to the reader and I will not repeat them. It does seem, however, that the very histrionic and assertive capacities of realist drama may ultimately backfire. The more spellbinding the magician, the more likely is the audience in retrospect to discount the portrait as one induced by magic. The dramatist achieves a Pyrrhic victory. The realist tradition encourages a certain 'gamesmanship' in the audience, which enters the theatre hoping to be hypnotised and seduced — but only for two-and-a-half hours. The more 'real' and mimetic the play, the more likely it is to be subsequently set aside and relegated to its proper place as just 'a play'. It fails to enter the bloodstream. But, to take a parallel example, Brecht's portrait of Hitler in *Arturo Ui*, alienated, ironical, blatantly attuned to the theatrical medium, a portrait observing its own creation and never aspiring to be the real Hitler caught in a butterfly net — this portrait becomes a central, long-term feature of one's composite image of the *Führer*.

TWO

The epic or episodic structure of a play breaks up and disperses the pseudo-realistic illusions evoked by dramatic plot and sequence. The play now emerges *as a play*, as an artifact creating its theme by a series of exemplary acts of theatre (scenes), just as a teacher demonstrates a lesson by means of examples which are related but not invariably joined. The epic structure itself is a necessary but not sufficient element of a dialectical theatre.

I have already suggested that the world of mimetic illusions conjured up by realism is a relatively modern convention — certainly in its more extreme forms. In drawing attention to the alienated and 'theatrical' tendencies of pre-nineteenth-century drama I am, without doubt, succumbing to that curious and recurrent desire of the Left to validate its aspirations in terms of ancient Tradition; the avant-garde comes full circle until it embraces a half-forgotten arrière-garde. (Note Grotowski on this.) This fascination with the past is apparent in both radical political thought and radical aesthetics. The notion of alienation itself reflects a desire to recover something good, pure and innocent which — whether in reality or myth — once existed and was then lost or corrupted. Thus Rousseau tells us that man was (anthropologically) born free, but is now everywhere in chains. Marx and Engels, with the help of Morgan and other scholars, discovered a kind of primitive, harmonic innocence in 'early communism'. The word 'revolution' itself means *re-volution*, a turning back to something wholesome, something lost in the mists of history — hence the Jacobin myth of the glories of Republican Rome. And although

William Morris's fictional English utopia was nominally set in the 1960s, the spirit of it was manifestly medieval.

In pointing this out, I pretend to empty my pockets.

Consider, for example, the Corpus Christi cycle which took place in the daylight in the streets and open spaces of the medieval town. No attempt was made to conjure up complete illusion. The actors presented not the total character of God (admittedly some task) but merely certain of his actions. No single actor performed the entire role of any single character — a blow to mimesis. Nor was the complete suspension of disbelief ever invited. And yet the Corpus Christi cycle, although a cult and a ritual, was also intensely didactic in its reaffirmation of a central proposition of medieval ideology — the Passion of Christ, His humiliation, torture and death.

Lionel Abel has drawn attention to the long historical lifespan of what he calls, very usefully, 'Metatheatre'. Here we find the frequent recurrence of the play-within-a-play and also of the self-referring, self-dramatising character such as Falstaff who, like an actor, finds himself now in this play and now in that one, but always of course in a play, on the boards of a stage. This is a form of theatrical alienation quite foreign to the age of Ibsen, Strindberg, Chekhov and Arthur Miller. As for Hamlet, he was alienated not only from his own personality and environment (*Entfremdung*) but also from his own dramatic portrayal (*Verfremdung*). Shakespeare, Calderon and many of the minor playwrights of the 'early modern' age display a persistent theatrical self-consciousness which is lost or rejected in nineteenth- and twentieth-century drama. It is true, of course, that the main reason that female roles were played by boys in the Elizabethan age was social rather than aesthetic. But wait: here speaks Shakespeare's Cleopatra:

> *and I shall see*
> *Some squeaking Cleopatra boy my greatness*
> *I' th' posture of a whore.*

Consider what happens in a modern school which is sexually exclusive. Either boys must play female roles or girls must play male roles. Either way, both actors and audiences are uneasy and blushing about the transvestite imposture. And this is not only because of the raging confusions of puberty but also because the children, being aesthetically naïve, are embarrassed by any departure from naturalism. But when the Royal Shakespeare Company presented Ronald Pickup as Rosalind before a mature audience the effect was revelatory: with the mimetic, illusionist element reduced by the presence of a male actor, the audience was granted a marvellous freedom in its relationship to the language itself, to what was being said, felt and acted. The play became a play and the audience an audience. (There are limits: I do not propose that Helen of Troy be invariably portrayed by an octogenarian male hunchback.) Genet wants the *Maids* to be played by male actors — the portrayal to be therefore an ostensible metaphor for what is portrayed; or, alternatively and in view of Genet's homosexuality, the reality (female maids) would be a metaphor for his dream of the portrayal.

I regard Brecht and Genet as the two geniuses of the modern dialectical theatre.

The direct or indirect impact of Pirandello on dialectical theatre is difficult to assess because his dramas are partly progressive in tendency and partly retrogressive. The theme of his trilogy 'The Theatre in the Theatre' is a familiar one: 'all the world is a stage'. When we first encounter Pirandello's Six Characters they already have a real drama of their own, but it remains an incomplete potential and they are anxious to complete and actualise it *in the theatre*; indeed the Father wants the Six Characters to play themselves. The Actor Manager is interested in them only in so far as he can create the illusion of a reality for the audience, but the Father replies that the Six Characters have no reality outside this illusion. The Father regards himself as a character created by an author who did not subsequently take the trouble to complete the drama — a Falstaff abandoned, so to speak, between Part I and Part II. Pirandello is certainly sticking needles into the realist tradition (the Father comments that 'authors, as a rule, hide the labours of their creations'), and he also shows a dialectical self-consciousness about his own anti-realism when the Manager accuses the Father of imitating Pirandello's style.

Pirandello, in effect, carries the Metatheatre tradition (a component or ancestor of dialectical theatre) to its virtual limit. But here an important, if often elusive, distinction needs to be made. The self-awareness of dialectical writing and theatre, its self-consciousness about its own nature and process as language and art, does not all mean that the only valid *subject* for the writer is the act of writing. Nor, in the theatrical metaphor, does it imply, as Pirandello often does, that 'all the world is a stage'. Very frequently writers interpret their anti-realist vocation in terms of writing about a novelist writing about a novelist writing about a novelist . . . *ad infinitum.* This is tedious, introspective and masturbatory. It also evades the real problem, the relationship of art to life to art. Far from proposing that all the world is a stage, dialectical theatre insists that a stage is a stage attempting to say something about the world while remaining conscious of its own nature as a stage. Here art constantly reaches out from itself without ever being able (or wishing) to escape from itself, any such escape being by definition a sham. In these respects Pirandello's work is somewhat foreign to dialectical theatre, and it also has to be borne in mind that Pirandello is a dramatic rather than an epic writer, a factor which lures him back into the heart of the realism he parodies. 'Every creature of fantasy and art,' he writes, 'in order to exist, must have his drama . . . the drama is the character's *raison d'être*, his vital function necessary for his existence.' This proposition is in flat contradiction to the basic philosophy of dialectical theatre.

The influence of Pirandello is wide and often productive of nothing more than an entertaining but shallow theatrical dexterity. In Tom Stoppard's *The Real Inspector Hound* — to take a recent example — the audience finds itself confronted by its own reflection in a huge mirror. What follows is a play in a 'theatre' within a *(the)* theatre; no doubt an ingenious parody of certain theatrical conventions but nevertheless entirely introverted and circular, a form of art which scarcely attempts to set the outer world in theatrical motion.

THREE

A Pirandello play, furthermore, generally requires utterly naturalistic and non-alienated acting. Alienated acting is not an invariable rule of dialectical theatre but it is nevertheless a marked tendency. It is quite false to assume that realistic acting is 'natural' and alienated acting 'stylised'. All acting is stylised. Only skilled, trained actors can appear 'natural' on stage or before a camera. Realistic acting, however, aims to conceal the contrivance while alienated acting exposes it. (Qualification: Sisyphus again; total exposure of a process is never possible because the actor has to *act* his exposure of acting just as the writer has to *write* his exposure of writing.) The contrived and conventional basis of all acting remains true of 'method' acting as well. In theory the method actor digs beneath the surface of stylised gesture and intonation to discover the real, naturalistic core of his character's be-haviour — to find the 'real' Peer Gynt behind the lines, the Peer Gynt who exists off-stage as well as on. But, as Peter Brook has commented, the method actor's observations of others are often observations or projections of himself filtered and monitored many times over with the medium — the stage or camera — always at the back of his mind. This is inevitable. Everyone deplores 'ham' acting; but 'ham' acting mainly involves the clumsy, exaggerated, affected exposure of the techniques employed by realist actors. Method acting, reacting against this ritualised expressionism, soon develops its own rituals and exaggerations.

This feeling was confirmed for me by a visit (under secretive, almost conspiratorial conditions) to Grotowski's Polish Theatre Laboratory production of *The Constant Prince* at St George's Church, Stepney. Highly controlled and austerely impressive as this ritual of agony in a cellar became, the final effect on this particular spectator of an intense, sadistic, white-heat hour of flagellation, pain and superhuman courage was precisely that of a dream — total impact at the time, ephemeral in the aftermath. I found myself strangely cut off from the performance I observed with such fascination. It is true that I understand no Polish — but it cannot be entirely coincidental that Grotowski's style as a director is most revered by these who share this deficiency. For in his hands the text is used as a mere 'trampoline'.

Stanislavsky, whose influence on the modern theatre is enormous, was the pitiless enemy of alienated acting and alienated theatre. He reached for the 'soul', to stir 'delicate and deep human feelings' with 'the direct cooperation of nature itself'. In one of his books, the Director (really Stanislavsky) tells two students: 'The difference between your art and mine is the same as between the two words *seem* and *be*. I must have real truth. You are satisfied with its appearance.' (Although the attack here is less on deliberately alienated acting than on clumsy, amateurish theatricality, the essential demand for mimetic naturalism is obvious.) It was Stanislavsky who urged actors to imagine what their characters did and had done when not on stage — the playwright only portrays a few crucial moments in their lives. But alienated and dialectical theatre argues the reverse: the characters have no life of their own outside of the play which is the sole source of their existence. According to Stanislavsky, the actor should say to himself: 'All these properties, make-up, costumes, the scenery, the publicness of the performance, are lies . . . But *if* they were true, then I would be this and this, and I would behave in this manner and this way towards this and this event.' This famous 'as if' is the core of naturalistic illusionism. Stanislavsky speaks of 'the magical, creative *if*'.

The child must believe in this imagined truth 'just as the child believes in the existence of its doll and of all life in it and around it'.

One could not get a clearer statement of the naturalist-realist philosophy of art, as well as an implicit confirmation of the qualities I have attributed to it. Note these key words: magical, child, doll, believe . . .

In alienated acting the 'if' is posed on a different basis. The actor indicates a certain illusion, a sketch, a first essay at representational mimesis *as if* the character were real. The actor then indicates the nature of the contrivance (with the help of the playwright and director), dissolving this first *as if*. The process is now reversed: we are invited to consider reality critically *as if* it corresponded to the artistic contrivance in a refracted form, bearing in mind how the particular artistic medium and its use on this occasion might govern the refraction. Picasso draws a crooked nose to force people to visualise a real nose.

How does this work? Only go to see the great modern exponents of mime, the silent Chaplin, Marceau and Fialka. Here you find a form of expressionism which stands back from what it expresses and also from itself. You discover life through art (no pretence of mimesis) and art through life. You are suddenly, after all those evenings spent in the company of elaborate pretence and pseudo-illusion, in the presence of authenticity. There are no lies. Fialka told me that he was not a political or didactic artist; if he had to point to any one influence on his work, it would be that of Kafka. But of course Kafka in Eastern Europe is political dynamite and Fialka's statement has to be understood in the context of the intense, systematic and dogmatic politicisation of official art in the Communist countries. I saw two of Fialka's productions in London and then, a couple of months later, during the Czech liberal summer of 1968, his new production *Buttons* at the Theatre on the Balustrade in Prague. At that time the appearance of any *apolitical* work of art was in itself a form of political eloquence. But *Buttons* was by no means apolitical; what it possessed was that shy, gentle, Schweikian cunning and modesty seen also in Havel's plays, an oblique, indirect, between-the-lines style evolved during decades of authoritarian government. In that liberal summer a plea for truth, freedom and integrity, far from amounting to a sanctimonious generality, was directly relevant to the concrete details of the contemporary political struggle. And this is what *Buttons* was about: truth, integrity and freedom. Fialka made his statement of commitment by and through a highly alienated and dialectical art form. Illusionism had been banished; consequently one's vision of life was permanently enriched.

Puppets and pantomime have the same potential. For the child, puppets pose the question: how close can art approach to life? For adults the question is reversed: how close can life approach to art? In the Japanese Bunraku theatre three puppeteers, much larger than the puppet (the character) itself, remain visible throughout. Thus illusion (the actions of the puppet) and counter-illusion (the visible presence of his manipulators) both create and explode empathy in a continual dialectical interaction. The effect is reinforced by the Joruri singer, highly emotional in his tone, pitch and tempo, yet alienating in his physical separation from the action, in his role as chorus.

The Bunraku tradition is of course inimitable. But what I have seen of the New York Bread and Puppet Theatre reinforced my belief in the political committed potential of this kind of art.

FOUR

In 1926 Brecht remarked: 'I aim at an extremely classical, cold, highly intellectual style of performance.' This raises a question already discussed in an earlier chapter. A tendency only . . . by no means true of all of Brecht's work, and not true at all of Genet.

Brecht is the genius of modern alienated theatre, the writer and director who more than any other confirmed its vital necessity as a medium of commitment. But some of Brecht's theoretical propositions indicate a kind of stumbling somewhere between first base (alienation) and second base (dialectical art). 'I give the incidents baldly so that the audience can think for itself . . . I don't let my feelings intrude in my dramatic work. I'd give a false view of the world.' Assertions such as these, quite unrealisable in practice, can be attributed to the struggle against illusion, empathy and catharsis, the recurring properties of what Brecht called Aristotelian drama. At first base (alienation) the artist says: we must utterly divest art of all pretences; we must no longer mesmerise and hoodwink the audience. This notion informs the spirit of documentary theatre and cinema, the idea of 'cinema-vérité', the naïve faith in a simple, unadorned, passive recording of things-as-they-are. *But* in the course of this first-wave assault on illusion, contrivance, empathy and dishonesty, the artist forgets that art *is precisely* illusion, contrivance and dishonesty. Therefore a mature dialectical art is not only one which alienates the spectator from the action by demonstrating its nature as theatrical contrivance, it also proceeds to penetrate from inside the nature of artistic contrivance as a form of communication (and therefore as a form of reality). Brecht's claim to 'give the incidents baldly' leads him back towards the naturalistic fallacy.

From the point of view of dialectical writing, the interest of Brecht lies primarily in his unsurpassed mastery of base one, alienation. He, like the socialist realists, set out to describe and denounce capitalist society; he, like they, regarded the theatre as a weapon for political agitation, as a means of dispelling false consciousness, of opening up new vistas of social action, and of pouring petrol on the flames of class struggle. Both Brecht and the socialist realists wanted to *represent* real life; but Brecht insisted, correctly, that this could only be done once the mimetic pretensions of naturalism and realism were stripped away and the audience was brought to recognise itself as an audience, as a kind of parliament weighing judgment on a debate presented in the theatrical medium. (Brecht shared with other Marxists a profound distrust of the modernist obsession with form, art, language and literature as ends in themselves. But this distrust, justified in certain respects, has all along reinforced the self-mutilating naïvety of Marxist aesthetics. The achievements and insights of modernist writing and structuralist criticism are formidable; to ignore them is to tread water rather than to swim. Without a discriminating and highly critical incorporation of many of these insights no dialectical literature is possible.)

To return to Brecht and alienation (*Verfremdung*). The basic devices and techniques he used are by now familiar: projections, films, non-naturalistic settings, alienated acting, characters moving between the first and third person, the explicit announcement of stage directions, and directorial alienating devices (while Brutus is accusing Caesar of tyranny, he, Brutus, is seen maltreating a slave).

At the beginning of Brecht's version of *Mother*, Vlassova describes her own predicament from the outside, as if she were someone else:

> *André:* . . . and when we asked where she was going, she
> said to us:
> *The Mother:* I'm going with you.

In *The Measures Taken* the four Agitators speak in unison and act out their story in retrospect to the Control Chorus. The Agitators portray not only their own rules but those of the various people they encountered at Mukden.

In *St Joan of the Stockyards* the unemployed outside the Lennox packing plant also speak in chorus:

> *Unshakeable above our heads*
> *Stands economic law, the not-to-be-known.*
> *Terrible is the cyclical recurrence*
> *Of natural catastrophes.*

But of course many of Brecht's plays do have a central figure, a 'hero' or 'heroine', and he was aware that this very structural centrality maximises empathy. Accordingly we find him altering the text of *Mother Courage* to make Courage herself less sympathetic. (Sympathy and empathy are not the same, but the one encourages the other.) The scarcity of positive heroes in Brecht's work attracted diatribes from Stalinist critics. Pessimism about the human personality was less responsible for this tendency of Brecht than his acute awareness that a romantically portrayed hero weakens the audience's critical independence and offers it a totem pole for catharsis rather than a yardstick for critical development.

A Man's a Man displays every kind and variety of aliena-tion technique. The soldier Uriah, for example, abruptly discards his persona in order to comment on the sequence of the play. Galy Gay first acts himself, then becomes an actor reflecting on Galy Gay and what is about to happen to him, and finally resumes his role and acts out the conclusion. No other play of Brecht is so riddled with deliberate physical and logical absurdities; indeed it is here that Brecht comes closest to modernism and the Theatre of the Absurd. But the social content, the political content, are strongly in evidence.

Epilogue to *Arturo Ui*:

> *If we could learn to look instead of gawking,*
> *We'd see the horror in the heart of farce.*

FIVE

Brecht was both an artist and theorist. Genet is an artist. He tells us very little; we have no other evidence than the plays themselves. But in my opinion Genet comes closer to an authentically dialectical theatre than does Brecht. With Genet alienation is achieved not only *by* art but also *through* art, through ritual, symbol and the allegorical dimension. The world, life itself, the writer, his beliefs, his dreams, his art, the play itself, are all wrapped round each other in a complex of interlocking levels.

The Maids, The Balcony, The Blacks and *The Screens* are all concerned with personal and political power, the relationship of the rulers to the ruled (a relationship, incidentally, of hate). Genet's subject matter becomes content through form. Now this, as I have suggested earlier, is always true, but the content assumes infinitely richer surfaces when the writer appreciates the process and makes of it a further dimension of content. Genet trades in myth, (structures of thought alienated from reality by desire) not only at the level of reality (the characters behind his 'characters') but also at the level of art (Genet's own myths transposed into theatrical terms). The two maids, the clients of the brothel and the blacks *perform*, acting out their lives for their own benefit and for that of others. They are both the subject and the object of art; art comes back at them, helping them (not always conclusively) to bridge the gap between their situation and their aspirations. But Genet is pessimistic. Art, the last resort of his characters, emerges from the plays of Genet bearing roughly the same relation to revolutionary action as masturbation does to copulation.

In *The Blacks*, a group of Negroes stage a play in order to divert a white audience from the real political struggle being waged outside the theatre. But the play they perform is not an escapist romance or a classical tragedy. On the contrary, it depicts a white colonial establishment threatened by black insurrection. So here Genet implies that art invariably diverts attention from the reality behind it by sublimation and by reducing it to the proportions of contrived entertainment. This impression is reinforced by Genet's use of surrealistic parody, as when the white Queen invokes the virgins of the Parthenon, the stained-glass windows of Chartres, Lord Byron, Chopin, French cooking, the Unknown Soldiers, etc., in the name of white civilisation. Would the real white Queen, seated in the audience, recognise herself in such a farce? Probably not. Therefore she will be alienated from the white Queen on stage, disbelieve in her, and consequently disbelieve that the nigger revolt on stage could be reproduced in the real world outside. However, the situation is even more complicated. Negroes are playing the parts of white dignitaries with the aid of masks; but what if, as is very likely, these Negroes are themselves played by white actors? Genet replies: let them continue to wear white face-masks, but let them also put on Negro wigs and blacken their hands in order to simulate Negroes. But worse: suppose these white actors are playing before an audience of black Africans! Right, says Genet, find one white man, or a white dummy, and put it in the front row of the audience. Let the play (the 'play' within Genet's play) be performed for this single white figure.

What emerges from all this chess? Essentially a highly dialectical self-consciousness about the relationship of art to reality. Genet sets up two structures: (a) 'actors' and 'audience' *within The Blacks*; (b) actors and audience *of The Blacks*. A shift in the racial composition of any one of these four elements automatically generates a modification of total meaning for the real audience. We therefore have not only multiple reinsurance against illusion and empathy, but a delicate commentary on the interplay of art and reality, of subject, form and content. But Genet is not simply playing clever theatrical games and masquerades in the manner perfected by Pirandello; the levels of his play structurally represent, by means of myth, symbol, ritual and allegory, levels of consciousness and aspiration in the outer world. What his play says is virtually identical with what it does.

The Screens raises very seriously the question as to whether Genet's dialectical method does not blunt the political radicalism which partly inspires it. At a time when the whole French left-wing intelligentsia was united in its detestation of the Algerian war, and when a large part of it was openly committed to the cause of the FLN, Genet resolutely dug himself into a deep trench of ambiguity. The white colonials are detestable, yes. But what of the Arab revolutionaries, the fanatics, the men who not only kill to live but also live to kill . . . ? Against them Genet offers an apolitical anti-hero, Said, an anarchist of the spirit who wishes only to be left in peace. And Said's unlovely anti-social mother, who supports her boy against those who insult him — she too has Genet's support. (Note the contrast with Brecht's judgment on Mother Courage.)

Genet is a peculiar fellow no doubt and he never did fit neatly into any ideological category. But his plays remind us of the problem of revolt and revolution. Art is revolt; it loves the singular not the plural, and without this love, whether fully consummated or not, it suffocates in the grip of expediency. The artist is an individualist; his sympathy naturally extends to others of the same kind. These are factors, I suggest, which have led so many committed writers to amputate this limb of their sensibility, to distrust 'art', to castigate themselves for their petty-bourgeois love of aesthetics, and to dragoon themselves into using the pen as a weapon, a means only, something always transitive and never intransitive, something which serves its highest social duty when it covers its own rib. Well, these gentlemen are not without reason at a practical level. But I should say tactical level. Dialectical writing is a strategy, a long-term, problematical enterprise, a contribution to a general cultural and intellectual reorientation. It is not designed to get taxes lowered or wages raised tomorrow.

The influence of Brecht, like that of other innovatory masters, is not without its dangers. Only a mature writer like Arthur Adamov can hope to absorb it and then exteriorise it in authentically personal terms. Thus Adamov was able to effect a brilliant transition from ultra-modernism (the big A Absurd) to socialist commitment without biting the banal banana of realism. (See his *Paolo Paoli* and *Le Printemps '71*.) But all too often alienation techniques are adopted as mere fashionable mannerisms, without developing any mature, dialectical point of view, the result being that the audience is deprived of the good, gripping and absorbing pleasures of

realism without any compensatory offering. Feiffer's *God
Bless* is a case. Even so richly talented and highly accomplished
a playwright as John Arden (a friend to me and a hero too),
seems to have made little sense of alienation techniques in
Left-Handed Liberty. 'King John' steps out of his role to explain the historical situation to the audience, and Pandulph
the Papal legate does the same. In Scene 7, John once again
drops his mask and declares: 'There comes a time in any
stage-play, when the stage itself, the persons upon it, the
persons in front of it, must justify their existence . . .' He
then justifies, using modern historical references unavailable
to the real, historical King John. He announces his forthcoming death, resumes his part — and meets it. A case of
heavy-handed liberty? It is not, I think, merely a question of
the renowned superiority of the subtle over the obvious, the
implicit over the explicit. Nor simply a fear of alienation-
fatigue among theatre audiences. Isolated from their proper
aesthetic context and employed primarily as abrupt shock-
treatment, alienation techniques retreat into an innocuous
and somewhat tedious convention like the old 'now, children,
are you warm and comfortable?' In fact *The Hero Rises Up*
by John Arden and Margaretta D'Arcy, an expressionistic
and episodic extravaganza about Nelson, comes much closer
to dialectical alienation than *Left-Handed Liberty*.

Footnote on a new play recently (1969) seen in London:
John Spurling's *MacRune's Guevara*, though not a work of
major talent, transcends fashionable but superficial alienation
and achieves a coherent structural exploration of the relationship of life to dream, reality to myth, revolution to
theatre.

SIX

I have said that art tends towards revolt, towards an uncompromising and uncompromised gesture aimed at the general
social (false) consciousness. When I say 'art' here I intrude

a value judgment; I mean art at its best, art fulfilling a function peculiarly its own. This function is not really a matter
of procuring more bread for less sous tomorrow. But this is
precisely the aim of the Agitprop (agitation and propaganda)
tradition first developed in Russia and later taken up in
America and Europe. Agitprop flourished in the late twenties and early thirties, then lapsed with the general discredit
of committed theatre at the onset of the cold war. Now, in a
new climate of radicalism and artistic commitment, it is once
again alive and kicking.

Declared the initial manifesto of the New York Theatre
Union (1934): 'This is a new kind of professional theatre,
based on the interests and hopes of the great mass of working
people.' Although the plays had individual authors, or a pair
of 'em, the scripts were also submitted to a committee for
approval as well as to genuine proletarians working in the
relevant industrial field. Some titles: *Black Pit*, *Stevedore*,
Peace on Earth. In point of fact the Theatre Union never did
succeed in building up a reliable, ticket-purchasing, working-
class audience, and the annual deficit ran to something like
$15,000 a year. I mention this because for radical writers and
theatre people the question is always inescapable; which
audience, which class, when, how — theatre, factory, street
. . . capital city or provincial town . . . regular travelling
company or *ad hoc* casting . . . ? I have no worthwhile opinions
on this. One keeps trying, aiming for audiences relatively
unexposed to theatre, trying not to take 'no' for an answer,
remembering that for every five disheartening collapses,
somewhere someone like Roger Planchon has pulled it off . . .

But Agitprop is by no means totally alien to dialectical
theatre. The American 'Living Newspaper', for example,
drew heavily on epic forms, alienation techniques, cinematic
documentary and the style of the political cabarets of the
Paris and Berlin cellars. Drama was out. A loudspeaker
might serve as a *raisonneur*, inquiring, cajoling, pointing the
moral of the action. Sometimes historical characters were confined to a documentary role (direct quotes only), sometimes

they were integrated into fictional scenes. In neither case
was illusion or empathy attempted. The action on stage
and the physical apparatus presented to the eye were likewise
blatantly symbolic rather than naturalistic and mimetic.
Thus in *One Third of a Nation* slum congestion was conveyed by the farcical yet relevant spectacle of a large number
of people crowding on to one small carpet.

The Agitprop is a hot medium. Today's problem, tomorrow's solution. Now move. This heat burns through the
alienation, burns it up, sacrifices art like a throw-away paper
plate. Take Clifford Odets' famous *Waiting for Lefty*. (Odets:
'art should shoot bullets' — remember?) The alienation
paraphernalia is all splendidly in evidence in overkill proportions: episodic structure, choral recitation, caricature,
blatant stylisation. There is no attempt at naturalistic
characterisation; the characters are cardboard cut-outs. But
then come the slogans, the hot gospelling, the rhetoric . . .
Harold Clurman recalls a Sunday night benefit performance
of *Lefty* by members of the Group Theatre: 'The first
scene of *Lefty* had not played two minutes when a shock of
delighted recognition struck the audience like a tidal wave
. . . The actors no longer performed; they were being carried
along as if by an exultancy of communication such as I had
never witnessed in the theatre before.' At the end a question
was fired at the audience; like one man they spontaneously
rose and chanted their response: 'Strike! Strike!' The theatre,
having held up a mirror to life, is blinded by the reflection.

Brecht wrote a number of *Lehrstücke* with close affinities
to the Agitprop tradition. But Brecht found it hard to
fashion the rough brute boulders of Agitprop out of his own
fine clay. In *The Measures Taken* we read or hear this: 'Who
fights for communism must be able to fight and not to fight;
to speak the truth . . .' The Control Chorus quotes Lenin:
'Intelligence is not to make no mistakes, but quickly to see
how to make them good.' Brecht failed to achieve authentic
Agitprop because the artistic style of Agitprop aims at transparency, aims to set the documented fact into active, rhetorical

motion. Language and art function here by attempting to obliterate themselves, to become subsumed: the *saying* enters what is *said* and shelters there, obsequious and self-effacing before the Categorical Imperative of Politics. Brecht could never achieve this abasement. As an artist, he could never obliterate his art, his language, his medium. So:

> *The Three Agitators :* The individual can be wiped out
> But the Party cannot be wiped out
> For it rests on the teaching of the class writers
> Which is created from acquaintance with reality
> And is destined to change it
> For the teaching will take hold of the masses.

These lines have only a superficial, contextual resemblance to Agitprop. Neither the Russians nor the German Communists were pleased by *The Measures Taken*. A lucid mind and a classical yet supple sense of language interposes and creates a symbol instead of an exhortation. Brecht takes an idea (the right political end justifies the means) and then carries it with perfect theatrical symmetry to its devastating literary conclusion. At Mukden the Party leader reminds the Agitators: 'One and all of you are nameless and motherless, blank pages on which the revolution writes its instructions.' Consequently a well-intentioned and good-hearted young comrade has to be murdered by his colleagues and buried in a lime pit because his good intentions repeatedly hinder the cause. Brecht achieves a kind of pure, dream-like logic by and through the process of writing for the theatre. Necessity becomes a pitiless poetry. But this was not at all what the Communists wanted! Where was the pious humanism, the romantic sentiment, the empathy . . . ?

Brecht's *Lehrstücke* had more generalised aims (theme: reason-in-action) than the Agitprop polemical tradition required. Agitprop is a kind of fertility dance or warpath ritual by which the group both prepares for and mythically assures its victory in the conflict ahead. It is a violent rehearsal in symbolic form — only the symbol must efface itself. It is a

cartoon rather than a painting. Brecht perhaps comes closest
to these aims and needs in his adaptation of Gorky's *Mother*.
He claimed that at least 15,000 working-class women saw the
production in the halls and clubs of the proletarian districts.
Says the Mother: 'Communism is good for us. What is this
talk of communism?' (Then she sings.) 'It is sensible, anyone can understand it. It's easy, you're not an exploiter, you
can grasp it.' Each scene is presented as an object lesson or
parable . . . ('I give the incidents baldly, so that the audience
can think for itself.') Here Brecht comes closest to this bald-
ness, to transparency, to the deliberate effacing of art.

Today Agitprop again thrives. The Californian Teatro
Campesino performs in market places, housing estates, factories, schools and small halls. Street theatre is once more in
vogue, yet I doubt its relevance. I doubt the relevance of any
form of Agitprop theatre — to us. Us? I am assuming an
unashamedly highbrow position and one directly related to
the 'grand' theatre. Take Peter Weiss's two most didactic
Agitprop plays, *Song of the Lusitanian Bogey* and *Vietnam
Discourse*; both are apparently designed to be played away
from the grand theatre, aimed at audiences with a relatively
fresh (or naïve) theatrical experience. Simple plays, crammed
with facts, devoid of complexity, they hammer home the
struggle of the oppressed against the oppressor. Yet most if
not all roads now lead back to the grand theatre. A black
American company brings *Lusitanian Bogey* (target: Portuguese colonialism) to the London West End. The company
play it very cool, setting sophistication (implicit alienation)
of portrayal against the brute didacticism of the message. It
can't be done. We can't divest ourselves of our intelligences,
our sense of contradiction and paradox, as if it were so much
petty-bourgeois guilt. You say that Portuguese rule in Angola
is neither complicated nor paradoxical. I agree. As citizen,
advocate, propagandist, fund-raiser or platform orator I am
one hundred per cent opposed to Portuguese rule anywhere
outside of Portugal (and ninety per cent opposed to it even
there). I realise this before I enter the theatre, and Weiss's

cardboard cut-out lashings and beatings, weeping choruses, monstrous white villains and sledge-hammer reiterations of the statistics of colonial life will not make me one hundred-and-one per cent opposed. On the contrary, if Weiss bores me stiff for two or more hours on behalf of the blacks, I am more likely to come away feeling that these blacks and their eternal misfortunes and our eternal white guilt about it is all a bore. I do not propose that playwrights should avoid such subjects as colonial Africa or Vietnam, but I do propose that they remember that what emerges is not the subject but the content, that is to say the subject mediating and mediated by the artistic form; and I propose also that they make the first target of their commitment the *structure* of our consciousness, the *way* we think, know, feel, listen and respond. For the committed writer, reinforcing the conventional left-liberal righteousness about this or that contemporary issue is both a waste of time and a lost opportunity. As writer and artist he will do better to commit his language and his art to the erection of new playgrounds in the cities of the mind, the imagination and the emotions.

SEVEN

There are many kinds of humour, aggressive or defensive, challenging or therapeutic. Humour alienates a man from the reality principle, permits him to step back into a new perspective, and affords him valuable space for intellectual and emotional manœuvre. But what characterises the cruder forms of political writing, notably Agitprop, is an indiscriminate reliance on wild lunges of the hatchet, on cartoon and caricature, on the depiction of monsters so deformed, gross and obscene that either we cannot take them seriously or, alternatively, we can only legitimate our delighted, partisan laughter in terms of the extravagant, self-indulgent codes afforded by art alone. Such excesses are foreign to the masterpieces of didactic literature. Here it is the rapier thrust

or nothing. A Dean Swift, an Anatole France, a Brecht, a
Havel, achieve their devastating effects with a straight face.
Their sensitive affinity to the possible enables them to trans-
fer the reality principle from one level to another, from the
'real' to the 'surreal', and so to pull off a sharp penetration of
our general consciousness. Parody is a crude and blunt
weapon; it attempts to destroy illusion by exaggerating
features to the point of the ridiculous. But from satire we
gain a sense of the absurdity of the familiar and the fami-
liarity of the absurd. The satirist's most precious weapon is
irony, the defeat of an opponent by pretending to accept his
(subtly) exaggerated reasoning. This is the method employed
by Swift's Gulliver when, with all apparent seriousness, he
records the official description of the six-inch-high Lilli-
putian Emperor as the 'delight and terror of the universe
. . . whose head strikes against the sun . . . whose dominions
extend . . . to the extremities of the globe . . .' And what
ardent Protestant soul could easily fend off Swift's depiction
of the Big Endians and the Little Endians — those Lilli-
putians who by tradition broke their eggs at the wrong end
(Catholic Recusants in England?) being legally ineligible for
a wide range of official employments. What battle-scarred
warrior could prevent a shudder on reading this in Anatole
France's *Penguin Island*? . . . 'One of them, Draco the Great,
attained great renown as a man of war. He was defeated more
frequently than the others. It is by this constancy in defeat
that great captains are recognised.' And some pages later:
'All armies are the finest in the world.' Discretion, restraint,
subtlety, an unfailing sense of the possible, these are France's
weapons. On the Dreyfus Affair: 'Fortunately the judges
were certain, for there was no evidence.' On modern bourgeois politics: 'Paul Visire and his collaborators wanted reforms, and it was in order not to compromise these reforms
that they refrained from proposing them . . .'

But to return to the theatre:

Two recent plays, very different in subject matter, style
and cultural tradition, are nevertheless joined by their

intense political commitment and by their uncompromising resistance to local forms of oppression and mendacity. Both are minor masterpieces of satire and irony, and both achieve their effects by alienating the audience from the action. Each discovers a central, relevant myth and then, with discipline and economy, works within the myth in order to explode it.

In *The Memorandum*, the Czech writer Václav Havel takes as his theme and target the bureaucratic authoritarianism of Eastern Europe. The action of this conventionally structured drama is set in three office rooms at a time when Ptydepe, a new office language, is being officially introduced and imposed. The principle of Ptydepe is this: if the similarity between any two words is to be minimised (at least a 60 per cent dissimilarity is demanded), then words must be formed by the least probable combinations of letters. Says the hack Party-liner Ballas: 'It is a paradox, but it is precisely the surface unhumanity of an artificial language which guarantees its truly humanistic function.' Chaos ensues. But justice is not done; the natural manipulators of the political system will survive every zig-zag of policy. When an official memo arrives condemning the new language, the ambitious Gross, who has climbed into the Director's chair on the ladder of Ptydepe, becomes instantly its most energetic opponent, finding scapegoats everywhere, including those who were originally the most sceptical. Havel thus sets up and effectively dramatises a logic of absurdity which emerges as only a minor distortion or refraction of the real, prevailing social logic under Czechoslovak neo-Stalinism.

In *MacBird!* Barbara Garson's intentions are close to those of Havel. Once again satire is employed with devastating success. Garson offers and then juxtaposes two myths; the mode of Shakespearian political sentiment and the mode of American machine politics; cutting across both is the cult of hero and villain. From the moment that a middle-aged man wearing a business suit and a sword declares, 'Oh for a fireless muse, that could descend . . .', Garson sustains the alienation-effect to the end. However passionate and heart-felt her rejection of the Vietnam war, American imperialism, racism and cynical political manœuvre, she succeeds in divorcing subject and form, emphasis and expression, so that the content of the play emerges at a critical, alienated level. High satire is the key.

The trouble with left-wing British satirical theatre is its lack of intellectual and artistic self-consciousness, its tendency to degenerate into crude parody, caricature and cartoon. Lords, monarchs, popes, bishops and politicians — time and again they are wheeled on-stage, grotesquely costumed and serenaded by patriotic music, peppered with easily flung darts and then hurried away to the morgue. No one is shocked, no one learns anything. Suburban ladies arrive in coachloads at the London theatres, conditioned in advance to associate an afternoon in the stalls with scurrilous, irresponsible and obscene pantomime. The Tory ladies, hangers, floggers and defenders of public morality who pass before their eyes on the boards of the stage are really themselves. But the self-indulgent excesses of the playwright, his jackdaw-like obsession with the obvious and farcical, ensures that no such self-identification will be made. The audience takes refuge in a defensive schizophrenia while the artistic community continues to congratulate itself on its own bold, no-holds-barred radicalism. The exotic and the excessive generate dissociation not alienation. Your average satirist will dress up a Chicago cabbage racketeer to look like Hitler; it takes a Brecht to dress down Hitler to look like a Chicago cabbage racketeer.

EIGHT

The theatre of the New Left, the 'third theatre' as they say, off-off Broadway, off-off-off everything, challenges the 'system' physically and morally, hurling dung at its ethical assumptions, at its pattern of language, at its false pretensions to coherence. Distrusting the mind, this experimental, anarchistic sub-culture is in constant motion, very American, always throwing away yesterday but loving the naked, uncorrupted man. A communal theatre, an anti-theatre, it mocks bourgeois values, the family-and-garden (B.A., Ph.D.) image of the old mandarin Left in its square trousers. The key terms are: pot, the cosmic self, underground, LSD, Being, dung, cop-pigs, identity, psychedelic, in, awareness, alienation, revolution, death-wish, kinky-booted pillheads (etc), sick, system, total dehumanization, feelings, image . . .

But make no mistake, however aggressively it may run naked from the auditorium into the street, this sub-culture is a withdrawal symptom, an enclave psychology, a polka dot pattern of monasteries marooned in the dark ages of the ad man's affluent society, the free communing with the free (while there is still time, man, while there is still time). Bohemian and radical here achieve one of their rare historical couplings, and obscenity becomes a form of freedom (see Mailer's *Why Are We in Vietnam?*), a surrealism of the subconscious more capable of undermining the established culture than the wise sayings of Karl Marx or Leon Trotsky. Your war is obscene, says Mailer to Johnson or Nixon, more obscene than all the dirty words that I and my fellow pornographers could ever dream up . . . but you keep them hidden beneath that creeping-jesus skin, I'm going to flush them out, fuck by fuck . . .

The mindless Left pities itself. Someone owes it something, but the delivery has aborted. Paul Foster writes a preface to his play *Tom Paine*, complaining: 'Who is Tom Paine anyway? A year ago I could not answer that question . . . Why is he hidden away and out of sight? Why have we as a nation practised un-think?' Then apparently Foster read twenty-one books on Paine (disregard the contradiction). But if un-think has been darkly perpetuated by the system, don't expect Foster or La Mama to clarify the past. As William Packer says admiringly of *Tom Paine*, it 'bears little resemblance to historic fact' and does not 'try to recreate the man as he really was' . . . no, on the contrary, it is 'something of a charade conceived in surrealistic terms . . . peppered with four-letter words' (*de rigeur*, naturally). As for the spectator, 'if he knows nothing of the life of Tom Paine he will not learn much from this play.' To grasp the essence of mindless Leftism, one need only quote Packer's reference to George III as 'an eighteenth-century Hitler'. (In which case Hitler was presumably a twentieth-century George III.)

The Living Theatre: messianic, wholesale rhetoric, evangelic hysteria, self-pity (always), parody dressed up in the rags of tattered passion, narcissism, violence. Language debased, virtually destroyed, the senses assaulted . . . The Living Theatre's *Frankenstein* teaches about the corruption of natural man by society, civilisation and language. Nothing less than total de-alienation will do. Okay. How? By an abrupt inner cleansing, by the volcanic re-emergence of LOVE, by a communal ONENESS of will and faith. If this were to happen, the prostrate girl would levitate. But she won't: so we remain a violent, corrupt, sick community. So the audience must be punished, must feel the force of the irrational and the inhuman, of violence and sadism. A powerful, strongly-muscled actor looms menacingly over a cringing spectator . . . vigorously ruffles his hair . . . 'Relax, man, relax.' Now he prises the spectator's folded arms apart, shakes him by the shoulders and then, quivering with rage, sets to work on his victim's thighs. Why? Because 'the revolution is a wheel spinning off living energy. Make it real! Do it now! *Begin!*'

The Living Theatre is the origin and the archetype of the leftist third theatre. It is characterised by stereotyped political assertions, glib formulations, simplistic nihilism, groupgropes, raw emotionalism, rejection of knowledge and of coherent thought, form and reason; by hymns to love and togetherness, obsessive, meaningless sexuality, violence for its own sake in the name of anti-violence. Form is distrusted because misunderstood. A pathetic belief (shared by witchdoctors) prevails that mimicry and parody will expose and destroy the enemy. Cheap laughter, guaranteed in advance, is achieved by means of a slack, sloppy assumption of virtue. A beautiful naked girl cries out, 'live, dance, strip!' They have told her that she is making the revolution . . . and the revolution is FUNTIME. As for the assault on the audience's separate identity, the attempt to create total creative communion and to destroy every inhibiting phobia and inhibition (hang-up) between actors and audience, this is just a charade. It's a lie, but a peculiarly unpleasant one because totalitarian in mood. Be sure of this; the wretched spectator 'participates' only so long as the actors permit him to. If he really gets carried away and takes things into his own hands, if he carries on after the whistle blows, then he can expect the actors at best to reassert their status and authority, at worst to stop him short with a rabbit-punch. I have seen both happen.

As an instrument of commitment this cult of pseudo-participation is worse than useless. It creates a new mystification. It is bogus. An alienated and dialectical theatre makes its first principle a sober recognition of physical reality: a theatrical event is a performance, *by* some, *for* others. Of course participation may have its uses in the theatre of therapy (T-groups, weeping in unison, relating from your feelings instead of your image, getting tribal, unzipping in public, finding an identity in an emotional commune . . .), but commitment and therapy are radically incompatible.

A young man in a G-string exhorts me to 'wake up and be free!' He seizes my neighbour's spectacles and screams, 'Fuck technology!' He smashes the spectacles, crushes them underfoot. Noble savage or naked ape?

In reality, this blind, affected mindlessness complements rather than subverts the de-humanising tendencies of modern society. I do not say that the third theatre has produced nothing of value; the energy, the sense of the physical, the restless innovations, the social courage of the activists, the sheer professional capability of certain groups — all these qualities are good, life-giving, exemplary. Likewise the sharp, nervous, probing reactions to contemporary events, crimes and horrors. But the third theatre is a child-like theatre supporting a king-size erection, a theatre of young actors suddenly liberated from their super-ego (the author, the playwright), a theatre run amok . . .

The Happening (no longer an isolated but an almost continuous event in the third theatre) is the antithesis of alienation. Working by shock treatment, the Happening leaps at the senses, the nerves, smothering the critical faculty. Calling for total involvement, indeed total immersion, it champions the uncorrupted id as the buried hero and denounces the super-ego (socialised reason) as the villain of the piece. The Happening is an orgasm: the event is the message.

It seems to me that actors need a super-ego. Of course I am a writer and you have to 'aim off for wind' in accounting for my vested interest in the matter. But if you had seen the Grand Théâtre Panique's Notting Hill Gate production of Arrabal's *The Labyrinth* I think you would agree that my reservations about self-determination for actors has to do with more than professional prejudice. What happens? Arrabal's five characters are joined by a dozen others, plus goat. Arrabal's notion of 'panic' (as so often Artaud's notion of 'cruelty') is misunderstood and vulgarised into terms of pure physical noise and chaos. Arrabal's text disappears under an avalanche of nudity, swinging on ropes, flushing lavatories, noise, flickering lights, incomprehensibly garbled snatches of language — and a good deal of meticulously rehearsed 'improvisation'. Plus a bit of pseudo-participation in the middle.

Now I have indicated the alienating and dialectical value of a movement from drama to theatre. The consequences of this include a certain diminution of the role of the playwright (indeed drama from Ibsen to Arthur Miller can be viewed as the tyranny of the writer). The more a text relies on the physical potentialities of the theatre and the less it relies on words, the more the creative balance swings from the writer to the director and the actors. I accept that. Jean-Claude

van Itallie's *Americah Hurrah!*, written for the Open
Theatre, took shape under the give-and-take, exploratory
conditions of a cooperative workshop. The results validated
the method. 'I'd like the audience to be assaulted with the
sound of these words, not particularly with their meaning',
says van Itallie of his *Motel*. Fine — up to a point. But if the
physical theatre runs amok, as did the Grand Théâtre
Panique with Arrabal's *The Labyrinth*, then the general,
retrogressive effect is bound to be to drive serious writers
away from the theatre or, alternatively, back into obsolete
modes of traditional drama, complete with illusion, empathy,
mimesis, plot and catharsis. However, if that smacks of pro-
tectionism or special lobbying, forget it. The crucial question
is posed by Peter Brook: Can the 'play', the event itself, the
'Holy Theatre', replace the text? 'Is there another language
just as exacting for the author, as the language of words?'
Is there, he asks, not a language of sounds, of word-as-part-
of-movement, of word-as-lie, word-as-parody, word-as-
rubbish, word-as-contradiction, of word-as-shock or word-
cry?' Grotowski and his collaborator Ludwik Flazen take
the same point of view. 'It was necessary to think radically of
that in the theatre which is not word *(parole)*; it was necessary to think of theatre.' That is to say, words are extraneous
to pure (or 'poor') theatre — a view which Grotowski
confirms when he defines theatre as 'that which happens
between the spectator and the actor'.

Let us hold back the answer for the moment.

The alternative to an author's theatre (drama) is either an
actors' theatre or a director's theatre (as with Grotowski,
Brook and others). Where the director is the big gun a new
script may be improvised or evolved cooperatively (as with
US) or a rotten old script *(The Tempest, Macbeth)* revamped
in terms of its potential for physical movement, gesture and
ritual. The influence of Artaud is once again clear here;
Artaud recommended as exemplary the Balinese theatre
because its director, or *metteur en scène*, replaced the
written text as the main genetical and creative force. Artaud

complained that authors worked on paper and in seclusion, abstracted from the live presence of the theatre; he himself wanted to see a theatrical language pitched somewhere between gesture and thought, the subconscious and the conscious. At the same time Artaud had no patience with an actors' dictatorship. He spoke of, 'the caprice of the wild and thoughtless inspiration of the actor . . . who, once cut off from the text, plunges in without any idea what he is doing . . .'

I am still holding back an answer to Brook's question. But the answer to it, perhaps, is implicit in his own work. In his handling of actors, Brook is the gentle dictator. He does not say, 'do this, do that', he encourages and coaxes actors into 'finding' an inner life which corresponds to or harmonises with his own overall vision. He forces them to be free. Now — in cases where the text is a negligible factor or reduced to a subordinate role, as in *US* or Brook's adaptation of *The Tempest*, the visible effects of this general authoritarianism are as alarming as they are brilliant. No doubt about it, the actor, the live human being on stage, is reduced, driven inwards, halted in mid-stride, subordinated to a wider choreography, rendered dumb and helpless before the music of the cosmos. This technique is alienating in one important respect: the 'part', the performance is never finished or rounded-off, it is always presented as an extension of a perpetual rehearsal. Thus the theatrical *process* is partially exposed. But in the hands of Brook or Grotowski this process involves a continual moving inwards, a restless introspection, a groping for the latent, buried realm of feeling; it is a religious process (Holy Theatre, Brook calls it), getting closer to God, to the Spirit, to an almost mystical communion, of man and nature. It would be wrong to equate Brook's ideas on acting with those of the method school; but there are noticeable analogies. Ritual as holy communion implies a high degree of empathy on the part of both actors and audience. Here Brook's style approaches that of the third theatre, the actors' theatre, with the important proviso that a single, controlled vision replaces the anarchy of multiple spontaneity.

The advantages, indeed the necessity of a literary text, the product of a single guiding intelligence, now become apparent. All experience indicates that it requires a particular type of talent or intelligence to combine two functions: the formation of a coherent and yet complex vision of reality, and the translation of this vision into dramatic or theatrical terms. It is not simply that writers are generally best suited for this task; more important, the *process of writing* is an integral and indispensable element of it. Once a text exists it provides director and actors not only with a model, a building-plan, but also with a linguistic structure to be resisted and transcended. Grotowski regards the matter differently. Historically, he says, the text was among the last elements to develop within theatrical art. In pure (or 'poor') theatrical terms the text is superfluous. In Grotowski's production of Wyspianski's *Acropolis*, the play is transposed to entirely different scenic circumstances and what is presented is a transplant of a verbal tissue (the poetic 'core' of the text) into a foreign organ (theatre starting from the demands of a particular *mise en scène*). 'We consider the text as a trampoline, not as a model, not because we despise literature, but because the creative part of theatre is not to be found in literature . . .' In fact there are many reasons for reacting to this assertion with suspicion. One can perhaps use or misuse classical texts as 'trampolines' (as Grotowski and Brook like to do), but no contemporary playwright worth his salt is going to put up willingly with such cavalier treatment. Grotowski begins with a modest disclaimer; we are not a theatre, he says, so much as an experimental laboratory particularly dedicated to exploring the *actor's* art. Ultimately, however, he grows so bold that the claims and definitions made on behalf of an experimental laboratory are foisted on the world as the final claims and definitions of theatre-as-such. Who can plausibly maintain that the text, literature, the written word, is never the generically creative element of authentic theatre? No one. In a truly dialectical theatre the text provides not only the general vision of coherence and the initial level of literary and semantic alienation from outer reality, it also offers at a second level a 'reality' of its own which in turn must be exposed and transcended as well as respected. But this implies a disciplined process, rather than using the text as a 'trampoline' from which director and actors leap into their own empty spaces. Left to their own devices, the director and his actors cannot achieve a genuine theatrical alienation.

As for language and the alternative, non-representational or non-verbal forms of language proposed by Brook as being ideally suited to the theatre, no categorical answer would be sensible. Pantomime, as I have said, makes the complete exclusion of verbal language, of the human voice, a viable jumping-off point for an alienated form of theatre. There is no harm in calling every form of communication available in the theatre a form of 'language' — except that it obscures the particular function of language, verbal and written, as man's most highly developed metaphor or code for achieving communicative coherence. The indirect political consequences of a radical fragmentation of language have already been discussed in an early chapter on modernism, and the pessimistic *Weltanschauung* of the anti-Enlightenment. I remain in general sympathy with the Marxist-realist philosophy in this respect; although language is a code not a mirror, although this code inevitably forces a hiatus between the signifier and the signified, the great and worthy struggle is and can only be that of Sisyphus, constantly to heave the boulder of coherence up the hill. Failure to do this not only generates a deep pessimism and lethargy, it also cuts the theatre off to an unnecessary extent from everyday life and discourse.

When Brook came to direct *US* he could not avoid the attempt at direct, significative language. It may have been an accident that the production lacked the services of a writer's text; on the other hand the absence of such a text apparently

coincided with Brook's instincts. So the director and the
actors read through the Fulbright Committee Hearings . . .
With what result? 'We begin to see the war as a collision of
dreams.' A bad start. Brook's method was to offer to the
actors material from which they could improvise and work
out a physical, expressive shape. A writer was then employed, more as a technician than as a creative intelligence,
to lend general coherence to what emerged. The results were
predictable (banality in politically committed theatre is the
short cut to death). Arnold Wesker afterwards commented:
'I can't understand how Peter (Brook) permitted himself so
much to the degree of obscuring what was being said.' But
in this kind of basically text-less theatre it is precisely the 'so
much' — the ritual, the groping for inner truth — which is
'being said'.

Brook's most rewarding productions *(Lear, Marat-Sade)*
are precisely those involving a strong, coherent writer's
text. In *Marat-Sade*, Weiss's text offers both cohesion and
a complex metaphor of primarily theatrical alienation: the
events of the French Revolution are seen as played by mad-
men who, to further complicate the relationship of the reality
to its representation, are directed by de Sade. Thus the
original events (post-1789), the moment of nominal dramatic portrayal (1808), and finally the act of totalising theatrical
presentation (Weiss's play itself), provide a brilliantly structured text on the inter-penetration of reality and art. But this
text too threatens an arbitrary finality unless — as was the
case — the director and his cast restore it to motion and self-
exposure. *Marat-Sade* represents a high point of modern
dialectical theatre, combining as it does vision with coherence, intelligence with intuition, reason with emotion, and
the viability of the spoken word with the full physical
resources of the stage.

'In the creative process there is the father, the author of
the play; the mother, the actor pregnant with the part: and
the child, the role to be born.' The words are Stanislavsky's.
They are not quite true, but almost.

NINE

Summary: Some principles of committed, dialectical theatre.

(1) Replacement of drama by theatre. Development of an epic and episodic structure rather than a plot. Exploitation of the full physical and aesthetic resources of the medium (which is not to say all of them all the time!)

(2) The necessity of alienation techniques in the writing, direction and acting of plays. Following this, a dialectical appreciation of the relationship of theatre to reality and of theatre to itself.

(3) Acceptance of only those aspects of the Agitprop tradition compatible with theatrical self-awareness (or intransitivity).

(4) Satire and irony good, cartoon and caricature bad.

(5) Rejection of mindlessness, chaos, the cult of spontaneity, and bogus audience participation.

(6) Restoration of the writer and the text to their vital primary role.

CHAPTER SEVEN

Towards a Dialectical Novel

ONE

Inside lecture room 508 (Eng. Lang. & Lit. Block, fifth floor, two elevators and one hot-and-cold drinks automat) a class of some five hundred freshers are expectantly gathered, pens poised, to receive the Critical Word from the college's brash and bright young star, Associate Professor of Creative Writing, Herbert Bug. (Meanwhile ten thousand other students follow his lecture on closed-circuit TV.)

Bug begins by laying down the Golden Rule of the Fictional Tablet, Contemporary Model:

'Good morning, ladies and gentlemen. I gather that you all aspire to be novelists, that you desire not only to read but also to write and even to publish works of fiction. In that case I must first counsel you to discover and develop the most modest aspects of your natures; whatever you may privately think about your innate abilities, do not, repeat not, get caught out behaving like God.' *(Bug pauses here. Ripple of nervous laughter from audience.)* 'The Lord Almighty makes His presence manifest in all His works. But you, my creative friends, must on no account make your own presence manifest in any of yours. I offer you only one Golden Rule. Never, repeat never, in your novels give any evidence, clue or inference that *you* have written what you have written. Banish yourself ruthlessly from your own pages. Remember that a great novel is born not written — or so it must seem to the reader. Nothing must appear in the narrative that is not seen, felt or described by one of the characters. You must create a universe which is entirely self-generating and self-contained. You, the creator, the puppet-master, must remain invisible. That supreme sacrifice is the highest calling of your art. The narrator is dead: every development of plot and character must take shape, must emerge, from a dramatised scene. As potential novelists I am duty bound to offer you this dire warning: let the reader only once catch a glimpse of you, pen in hand, and the illusion you have created with so much pain and sweat will lie shattered in the dust.'

Thus Spake Bug.

Whose debt to Henry James requires no elaboration.

TWO

What can be the rationale and justification of this abdication? Is it simply that man (the novelist), unlike God, is not omniscient, that he is victim not only of ignorance but also of his subconscious and transindividual nonconscious (*pace* Goldmann) as well? Or is it, as Lukács insists, that a novelist's characters quickly adopt an independent existence of their own? No, it is none of these things. For Bug, it will be recalled, was less concerned to challenge the novelist's god-like powers than to plead that these same powers *be at all costs concealed*. For Bug, Art is synonymous with Pretence. Literature becomes an exercise in Bad Faith. Personally, I utterly reject both the social implications of this doctrine and its artistic pretensions. As H. G. Wells put it: 'The important point that I tried to argue with Henry James was that the novel of completely consistent characterisation arranged beautifully in a story and painted deep and round and solid, no more exhausts the possibilities of the novel, than the art of Velasquez exhausts the possibilities of the painted picture.'

This concealment, this creation of a self-contained fictional illusion, is not practised by realists alone. Not only James but Joyce as well made it a cornerstone of the high novel. The intrusive authorial hand is as absent in Faulkner as in Hemingway, in Robbe-Grillet as in Farrell. Indeed Robbe-Grillet, along with some other exponents of the *nouveau roman*, is at great pains to eliminate any sign or shadow of an exterior, privileged voice from his work. Even those writers like Balzac, who revealed such a shadow implicitly and unintentionally rather than explicitly, as a conscious theory of alienation, are taken to task and reprimanded. One notices that Michel Butor, despite his brilliant experimental perceptions as novelist and critic about the process of writing, about the relationship of writing to experience and of pre-verbal impressions to verbal expressions — despite this, Butor adheres to the hallowed tradition of confining the narrative voice to a strictly internal circuit. Neither Gisela Elsner in *The Giant Dwarfs* nor Christine Brooke-Rose in *Between* — two modernist novels — ever releases the hermetic seals from the jar of illusion and interiorisation.

Consequently the *nouveau roman* retains the worst and discards the best of the realist tradition. It retains self-containment, the magical, empathy-inducing illusion, while throwing overboard man, psychological coherence, morality, politics, the human capacity for action. But I exaggerate; much depends on whom you are reading. The tendency, however, is clear.

In the theatre, on the boards of the stage, the elimination of the playwright's guiding hand is greatly facilitated by the medium. Banish the soliloquy, dispense with the monologue addressed in confidence to the audience, heed the rules of the *pièce bien faite*, and the rest takes care of itself. The characters are visibly there, of flesh and blood, they speak, they act, they pursue their own destiny, the illusion is complete. But the novelist refines himself out of existence only as a result of painstaking skill, restraint and craftsmanship. The richer, more varied possibilities of the medium, and the fact that the narrative itself constantly provokes exegesis and exposition, have to be contained and transcended. A stage character (leaving aside alienation techniques) must speak for himself; we know and judge him purely on the basis of his own speech and behaviour, or on that of other characters. But the novelist can tell us *about* his characters; and what he can do he is naturally tempted to do.

One sees this with Henry James himself — how frequently he succumbed to the very vices he denounced. Take, for example, *Washington Square*. We have not gone two pages before we read this: 'It will be seen that I am describing a clever man . . .' Immediately the smooth skin of illusion is scarred; the author has admitted his narrative presence. But he is not yet God, he can still save the illusion by presenting himself not as the creator of his tale but as its recorder or chronicler. This convention takes care of a sentence like the following: 'It is uncertain whether Mrs Penniman ever instituted a search for unfurnished lodgings, but it is beyond dispute that she never found them.' The novelist introduces the word 'uncertain' in such a context at his peril. An illusion is sustained by persuading the reader not to ask too many questions, to suspend disbelief and to keep it suspended. As soon as an exterior voice says, 'it is uncertain', this same voice reveals itself and threatens the whole fragile edifice. But now James falls deeper into the pit; he commits unpardonable errors: 'I doubt, however, whether Catherine was irritated, though she broke into a vehement protest.' What's all this? Why should the person who has hitherto enjoyed such privileged insights into Catherine's mind suddenly be uncertain about the inner mood behind her outward action? The effect, inevitably, is once more to bring the reader out of his trance and to make him question how this narrative 'I' could *ever* have been certain about Catherine's inner life. But James's deviations from his own creed are not yet exhausted: '. . . and, though it is an awkward confession to make about one's heroine, I must add that she was something of a glutton.' What, what, what! 'One's heroine?' In the smoothly polished, finely manicured modern illusionist novel such a word is pure heresy, sheer hara-kiri. Identified now as an author's 'heroine' Catherine forfeits our empathy. And this same alienation inevitably follows, to give one last example, from James's sudden intervention to the effect that, 'it must be remembered in extenuation of this primitive young woman, that she held these opinions in an age of general darkness.' The whole illusionist technique, when transferred to the historical novel, demands that the reader be persuaded to live *inside* and only inside the age depicted. I am reminded here of the occasional clumsiness of Theodore Dreiser who was capable of shattering his own illusion of nineteenth-century Philadelphian society with the observation: 'the telephone had not yet been invented.'

Sartre praised Hemingway for restricting his perspective to those enjoyed by his characters alone (it is easier to do if the hero is an 'I' rather than a 'he'), but even the master sometimes slipped up. Almost every passage and episode in *For Whom the Bell Tolls* is related by or from the point of view of a character, and when the hero Robert Jordan is on stage we know virtually nothing that he does not know. As a result we begin to feel that this is Robert Jordan's true-life experience set down by Jordan but with his own figure cast in the third-person in order to swing the balance from the individual to the social whole, to Spain in torment. The shock is therefore considerable when we suddenly read: 'It would have been very interesting for Robert Jordan to have heard Pablo speaking to the bay horse but he did not hear him . . .'

I mentioned Sartre; it was he who, some thirty years ago and in the course of an attack on François Mauriac, offered one of the most formidable and explicit defences of the self-contained novel. Defining (somewhat arbitrarily!) the novel as 'an action related from various points of view', he castigated Mauriac for unwittingly assuming the mantle of God by oscillating his narrative perspective between the interior life of his heroine Thérèse and externalised judgments on her. One moment an absolute Subject, the next she becomes the objectified victim of a conspiracy between

writer and reader. Insisting on a theory of literary relativity
— there is no more place for a privileged observer in the
novel than in the world of Einstein — Sartre denied Mauriac
the right to call his heroine 'a cautious and desperate woman';
indeed to call her anything. Influenced as he was by the
literary style of Dos Passos and Hemingway, Sartre but-
tressed his position with an existentialist philosophical proposition of his own: to pass judgment on your characters, to
objectify them, he said, is to determine their actions in
advance and so to rob them of their freedom.

I do not wish here to enter into a discussion about Sartre's
concept of freedom. Unless one reverts to Lukács' proposition about characters leading independent lives of their own,
the notion of a fictional character's 'freedom' is strictly
absurd. In any case how can an invented, unreal image of a
non-existent person, an image created out of the artificial
convention of language and typography, have any sort of
'freedom' or 'independence'? As for Sartre's own fictional
characters, they are often schematically presented in terms
of their creator's own phenomenology of mind: freedom,
evasion, bad faith, the for-itself, the in-itself, etc. Whatever
choices these imaginary creatures enjoy he, Sartre, has given
them and he, Sartre, can take away. (If he sleeps badly he
may well do so.) We can call people in novels 'people' or
'persons' but we prefer to call them 'characters'. Why? Because their authors endow them with qualities, actions and
reactions which have a certain coherence and consistency,
which endow these imaginary persons with what we call a
character. And every stroke of the author's brush represents
an act of determination and domination. Sartre struggles
against this inexorable logic by contrasting 'character' to an
imposed, deterministic destiny, and by defining character as
'the combination of mild forces which insinuate themselves
into our intentions and imperceptibly deflect our efforts,
always in the same direction'. Oh yes? Why 'mild', why 'insinuate', why 'imperceptibly' if, as Sartre admits, 'always in
the same direction'?

The fact is that the technique of interiorised narration, if defended as representing any kind of freedom or self-determination for fictional characters, is a complete sham. It is a lie. A basic principle of dialectical writing is to lie as little as possible. This does not preclude interiorised narration, it simply demands its exposure as contrivance. Camus also chose to project his fictional narratives from a subjective perspective, from 'inside' the action. In *The Plague* we learn only at the end that the character Dr Rieux is in fact the author of the book. But we 'learn' this only within the framework of a suspended disbelief; we know perfectly well that Camus, not Dr Rieux, wrote the book and was ultimately and exclusively responsible for all the subjectivities, egos and alter egos within its pages. Nor do the techniques of Sartre himself always conform to his own principles. In *La Mort dans l'Ame*, for example, he refers to the character Boris first as 'he' and then as 'I': 'He heaved a sigh and relapsed into silence ashamed at having talked about himself. What I can't face is leading a mean, obscure existence.' *Eh bien!* An alienation technique *par excellence*, and one which automatically draws the reader's attention to the manipulation of Boris by his private Lord Almighty — Sartre.

The absence of alienation indicates a double danger. In the realist vein, the self-contained, illusionist novel fosters the impression of a real slice of life mirrored without distortion and without an active intervening agency. In the modernist vein, the same fictional technique implies, or can imply, the opposite myth — that the reality of the world is synonymous with language itself. Here the book does not claim to reflect the world, it claims to constitute the world.

The plain truth is that fictional narrative, unlike dramatic dialogue, offers the author every opportunity to comment, judge, compare, intrapolate, extrapolate and generally display his hand. So why not? Why mystify the operation? Why conceal the fact that we, the writers, are driven to write fiction largely because we are hungry for a small parcel of divinity? The illusionist novel not only deceives, it fails to deceive. Any reader can guess that Richard Wright was a wiser man than his own creation Bigger Thomas. But, disturbed by the danger that Bigger might momentarily cease to come across as a pure, self-propelled subject, Wright ties himself up: 'Though he (Bigger) could not have put it into words, he felt that not only had they resolved to put him to death, but that . . . they regarded him as a figment of that black world which they feared and were anxious to keep under control.' What has happened here? The central notion of the sentence is Wright's and his alone. But, Bigger being a simple, unlettered nigger, this same notion would seem 'out of character' if it emanated straight from his own brain. Yet Wright is anxious not to intrude, not to show his own hand. So he resorts in good faith to the bad-faith formula 'though he could not have put it into words . . .' (Something you can't put into words is never the same as something that another person can.)

THREE

What does Associate Professor Bug make of *Don Quixote*?

It is curious, viewed from the prevailing Jamesean House of Fiction, to recall that the great foundation stone of the modern novel is one of the masterpieces of dialectical alienation.

'But the unfortunate thing is that the author of this history left the battle in suspense at this critical point, with the excuse that he could find no more records of Don Quixote's exploits than those related here.' Here Cervantes (tongue in cheek) presents himself not as the sole creator of Don Quixote but rather as the chance discoverer of a work written in Arabic by the historian Cide Hamete Benegali — a work which he subsequently had translated and then set down in his own words. So we are forced to remember that Don Quixote, whether real or not, has reached us not only *by* but also *through* the medium of writing. In posing his own authorial reality at the level of an illusion, Cervantes prepares us for the de-realisation of his hero.

'Notice that this second part of *Don Quixote*, which I place before you, is cut by the same craftsmen from the same cloth as the first . . .' Here, a reaffirmation at the level of myth, of the literary process. Cervantes continues: '. . . and that in it I present you with the knight at greater length and in the end, dead and buried.' Poor quixotic knight, robbed of his 'freedom' at a single stroke of the pen! Now I have a few lines back drawn attention to Richard Wright's attempt to reconcile his own intelligence with Bigger Thomas's simplicity. Notice how easily Cervantes disposes of the same dilemma (which he deliberately creates in order to dispose of it): 'When the translator of this history [Cervantes himself according to Cervantes' convention] comes to write this fifth chapter, he declares that he considers it apocryphal, because in it Sancho's style is much superior to what one would expect of his limited understanding . . .'

Don Quixote is epic not only in scale but also in structure. While there is a discernible sequence of events, one thing leading to another, the structure is sufficiently episodic to permit a shuffling of the chapters like a pack of cards. Dramatic plot, with its causal and psychological implications, is invariably an agent of illusion and empathy. So too is that holy triad, the unity of time, place and action — something which Cervantes, with his love of the tangential and his direct, non-illusionist style ('in a calm and clear voice she began the story of her life . . .') does everything to avoid.

Cervantes contrives to remind us, while straight-facedly maintaining the opposite, that Don Quixote is a creature of fiction. He achieves this by drawing attention to the process of writing, and by casting the knight's adventures in a structural mould which dispels empathy and illusion (or, rather, which creates empathy and illusion only to destroy them). But Cervantes now takes a further major step towards a dialectical depiction of the inter-penetration of literature and reality. Literature itself is an integral element of social consciousness and to that extent creates what it expresses. Cervantes grasps this firmly. In the second part of *Don Quixote*, Don Quixote learns that he is already the subject of a book by Cide Hamete Benegali. 'He could not persuade himself that such a history existed, for the blood of his enemies he had slain was scarcely dry on his sword blade.' Had some sage given his adventures to the press by magic art? Originally Don Quixote's adventures had been stimulated by his indiscriminate absorption of tales of knight-errantry, but now, in Part Two, he will henceforward attempt to justify and exceed his own literary image, while naïvely accepting it as the real image.

Cervantes turns the assumptions of the Renaissance upside down. Writing ceases to be the coherent, expressive prose of a coherent world. Things live obstinately in their ironic identities, words are no longer immanent to things. Cervantes explores the relationship of words to the world and of words to themselves, to their own nature as signs. Analogy — a crucial element of alienation — is employed to reinforce the dialectical structure of the book. What at first appeared to be a case of madness (loss of contact with the reality principle on the knight's behalf) is ultimately conveyed analogically in terms of literature's own internal contradictions. Don Quixote says as much when he repents on his death bed of having given the author of the book about him the occasion 'of publishing so many gross absurdities as are therein written'.

Don Quixote was published in 1604. More than a century later Sterne and Fielding wrote under its shadow. In the 1750s, as in our own times, minor writers resolved their interest in the process of writing by writing about writing. *Tristram Shandy*, a major work by any standards, reveals a fascination with the problem of artistic deception and what kind of credibility art can carry. The hidden God is purged: Sterne insists not only on the limitations of language but on the nature of art as artifice. Fielding, a crucial figure with

one foot in the seventeenth century and one in the nineteenth, was attempting to reconcile the influence of Cervantes with the emerging bourgeois demand for illusion and
certainty. Thus *Joseph Andrews* has a discernible plot yet
yields to Cervantes' epic structure by setting up a series of
partially disconnected adventures on the road between
Somerset and London, complete with interpolations like the
tale of Leonore. Fielding discards Cervantes and anticipates
naturalism when he comments, apparently without irony,
that everything in his novel 'is copied from the book of
nature'. Yet in his preface he initially dispels illusion by
remarking that he decided to make Parson Adams a clergy-
man because no other office would provide so many oppor-
tunities to display his worthy inclinations. Book Two
begins with a chapter discussing the devices employed by
authors and pointing out that the spaces between chapters
are like an inn where the reader may take refreshment. A
chapter here or there, says Fielding, could be skipped without injury to the whole — a remark which reflects a double
alienation: the episodic structure of the novel and the
author's willingness to discuss it. In passing, Fielding draws
attention to the novel-as-book by commenting that separate
chapters enable the reader to remember where he left off
without spoiling the book by turning down the pages.

With Fielding alienation is already a conceit, cream on
the cake. Cervantes' profound dialectical sense is lost. Henceforward the author's voice will be progressively eased out,
art will perfect techniques for concealing its own nature as
artifact, and Henry James will complain in 1884 how painful
it is for those who take fiction seriously to observe how certain novelists idiotically 'gave themselves away'. Trollope is
chastised for conceding to the reader, by way of disgressions,
parenthesis and asides, that he is only 'making believe', that
the events he sets down are untrue and, worst of all, that he
as author is capable of turning the narrative in a number of
alternative directions. 'Such a betrayal of a sacred office',
wrote James, 'seems to me, I confess, a terrible crime.'

So the novel enters the era of sanctity, magic and mysticism. It becomes its own false consciousness.

Within the realist tradition, attempts to reverse this inexorable process inevitably prove to be half-hearted. In the works of Thomas Mann the narrator tends to weave in and out of his own narrative. Joseph and his brother remind each other that they are in a story. In *Felix Krull,* the narrator abruptly comments: '. . . I know very well that a storyteller ought not to encumber the reader with incidents of which "nothing comes", to put the matter bluntly, since they in no way advance what is called "the action".' But after the first seventy pages these alienating intrusions disappear and the government of illusion rules unchallenged. Lukács, although misunderstanding the German writer, will accord him his *licet.*

The recent publication of John Fowles's *The French Lieutenant's Woman,* a novel set squarely in the realist-illusionist tradition, yet self-consciously alienated from that same tradition, perhaps presages an important breakthrough, or rather break-*back*, in the development of fiction with a capacity for coherent social comment. On page 99 the novelist abruptly intrudes: 'I have disgracefully broken the illusion?' he asks. 'No. My characters still exist, and in a reality no less, and no more, real than the one I have just broken.' Fowles then plunges us back into the story, but the illusion is constantly and deliberately sabotaged by a variety of means. The novel is located in nineteenth-century England; according to ultra-Jamesian theory we, the readers, should be persuaded to 'live' totally inside the temporal setting of the action. Yet Fowles frequently thrusts in front of us footnotes comparing nineteenth-century attitudes and behaviour to their twentieth-century counterparts. He not only alienates us from the action or subject-theme of the novel (e.g.: 'While conceding a partial truth to the theory of sublimation, I sometimes wonder if this does not lead us into the error of supposing the Victorians were not in fact highly sexed.'), but also from the novel as a genre, as literature.

Having followed the story to a legitimate and credible climax, we are told: 'And now, having brought this fiction to a thoroughly traditional ending, I had better explain that although all I have described in the last two chapters happened, it did not happen quite in the way you may have been led to believe.' More concretely, of the 'hero': 'Charles was no exception, and the last few pages you have read are not what happened, but what he spent the hours between London and Exeter imagining might happen. To be sure he did not think in quite the detailed and coherent manner I have employed . . .' At the end of the novel, Fowles offers two alternative climaxes and then confesses to what it is in his own philosophy as a writer which determines his preference for one over the other.

The French Lieutenant's Woman is clearly a landmark in contemporary fiction.

FOUR

The modernist novel — and here I am using the term very broadly indeed, in a manner fit to unnerve any discriminating critic (always supposing that he has pursued me this far) — the modernist novel performs sterling service in its occasional refusal to accept passively the totalitarian world of illusionist fiction . . .

. . . Molloy: 'Shall I describe the room? No I shall have occasion to do so later, perhaps.'

Borges's character Pierre Menard, a modern Frenchman, sets himself the task of producing pages which coincide word for word with those of *Don Quixote*. He learns Spanish, becomes a Catholic, fights Moors and Turks, endeavours to forget European history from 1602 to 1918. At the conclusion of his exquisite investigation of the literary process, Borges comments: 'The text of Cervantes and that of Menard are verbally identical, but the second is almost infinitely richer.'

And here is Alexander Trocchi, deep in despair (but a rich, fertile despair): 'I always find it difficult to get back to the narrative. It is as though I might have chosen any of a thousand narratives.' Trocchi then firmly grasps the alienation principle: 'For a long time I have felt that writing which is not ostensibly self-conscious is in a vital way inauthentic for our time . . . I know of no young man who is not either an ignoramus or a fool who can take the old objective forms for granted. Is there no character in the book large enough to doubt the validity of the book itself?' It is reasonable, I think, to applaud these lines without inevitably accepting the iconoclastic pessimism of what follows: 'I shit idiocy and wisdom, turd by turd, thinking impressionistically, aware of no valid final order to impose.'

Meanwhile Michel Butor, whose experimental spirit is always worth pursuing, has attempted a kind of internal alienation within a framework which has two features noticeably associated with illusionism: an emphasis on the novel as an exploration of 'facticity', the physical texture of the external world, and a disciplined restriction of the narrative point of view to that of a character *(personnage)*. In *La Modification* the narrator refers to himself as *'vous'* — an attempt to discover an interior monologue below the level of the language *(langage)* of the character himself. This *'vous'* is intended to allow the author to describe both the actual situation of the character-narrator and the manner in which language expressing this situation is born within him. Thus the novel which for its fictional author (the narrator) is a fragment of autobiography, is for the real author (Butor) a fiction which retraces in transposed terms the experience which led to its creation.

Of all contemporary novelists, Butor has made the most far-reaching methodological contributions to the dialectical novel. Too often in modernist writing the A-effect appears as no more than a decorative and superfluous conceit — as, for example, in Le Clézio's *Terra Amata*: 'You've opened the book at this page. You've turned over two or three pages, glancing idly at the title, the name of the author, the publisher . . .' And later: 'I'll begin by saying what kind of landscape it was' (reminiscent of Molloy's 'Shall I describe the room?'). Subsequently Le Clézio, rather in the manner of Fielding, portrays the reader as perhaps putting down the book, chatting to his wife, looking for diversions and so on. But these interruptions are not part of a wider, cumulative and integrated system; having more to do with the *épater les bourgeois* state of mind, they don't even enjoy the casual humour of Grass's terrible dwarf Oskar: 'You can begin a story,' ruminates the three-feet tall narrator, 'by striking out boldly, backward and forward. You can be modern, put aside all mention of time and distance . . . Or you can decide that it is impossible to write a novel nowadays, but then, behind your own back so to speak, give birth to a whopper, a novel to end all novels.'

It is understandable but regrettable (because narcissistic) that novelists preoccupied by the process of writing so frequently find a solution in terms of writing about a writer. This occurs in Uwe Johnson's *The Third Book about Achim* (a book about a man who writes a book about a man who tells him how to write a book!), in Trocchi's *Cain's Book*, in Thomas Hinde's *High* and in Philippe Sollers's *The Park*. Sarraute pursues a similar theme in *The Golden Fruits*. The danger here is that alienation will be discredited by association — as being invariably linked to an introverted, élitist, 'art for art's sake' sensibility divorced from wider social, moral and political preoccupations. There are, however, at least two (probably more) classics of this genre which signify fundamental break-aways from the Jamesian-Joycean syndrome of self-contained illusion.

First, Gide's *The Counterfeiters*: 'I am not sure', says the author (Gide himself, not a fictional narrator) 'where he dined that evening — or even whether he dined at all.' Compare this with James's 'It is uncertain whether Mrs Penniman ever instituted a search for unfurnished lodgings, but it is beyond dispute that she never found them.' In terms of pure Jamesianism this sentence represents a lapse, a heretical inconsistency: but for Gide the irony is purposeful. In point of fact the illusionist novelist is a Hidden God; he fully exploits all the available superhuman powers and prerogatives while striving to disguise his labours. Gide blows this open: how can the novelist *not* know whether his character dined or not? Gide's central character Edouard is keeping a journal with a view to writing a novel (called *The Counterfeiters* of course) which will depart radically from realism, from 'the kind of dialogue which is drawn from life and which realists take so much pride in.' The novel, complains Edouard, has been a slave to resemblance. The 'pure' novel must erode the contours of real life to find a particular style. Edouard clearly speaks for Gide himself when he says: 'The subject of the book, if you must have one, is just that very struggle between what reality offers him [the novelist] and what he himself desires to make of it.' To illustrate this process Gide employs the familiar device of the box-within-a-box-within-a-box. Edouard's notebooks contain a running criticism of the novel he is writing within Gide's novel but also, implicitly, *of* Gide's novel. Gide frequently explodes illusion: Part Two, Chapter Seven, is entitled: 'The Author Reviews his Characters.' Edouard, says Gide, 'has irritated me more than once ... I hope I haven't shown it too much ...'

Moravia's *The Lie*, a minor masterpiece of self-referring, dialectical writing, also exploits the myth-like theme of writing a book. The central character (once again) keeps a journal of his life in order to write a novel based on his experiences. Moravia intersperses the 'real' events of the day with the character's diary version of them, a version frequently diverging from the 'reality' in emphasis, detail and ascription of motivation. But we soon learn how the character's project of writing a novel about himself influences his actual behaviour — he lives his own intended literary image. So far so good. Yet Moravia has baffled us. Things are not what they seem. We have been caught out in our conditioned assumptions about the mirror-like, representational nature of literature, of the novel we hold in our hands, even as we are accepting how the act of writing distorts experience when we consider the character's (fictional) journal. We have taken Moravia's convention at face value: if the actual events of the character's day are real, what he writes about them in his journal (where there is a divergence) must be distorted. But wait: are not the 'actual' events of the day also written down? Of course! Everything we are reading is in fact the novel which the character finally produced! Experience has governed expression but so has expression governed and distorted experience.

FIVE

The mild and limited modes of alienation mainly employed by committed public novelists during the present century are those of allegory, utopia (or dystopia) and history. But nine times out of ten this initial displacement or sustained metaphor is offset by a strict adherence to realism. Thus from the moment we accept the surreal, temporal and spatial conventions of *1984* or *The Time Machine*, no effort is spared to gain and secure our empathy, our transfixation and the suspension of our disbelief. This also holds good for left-wing historical novelists like Romain Rolland, Reinrich Mann and Leon Feuchtwanger. In *The House of Desdemona*, Feuchtwanger maintains that the past sheds an alienating and illuminating light on the present. True enough. But history as a form of displacement is in itself an extremely restricted one, confined to the subject matter of the novel and having little bearing on the literary process itself. Even so, the point is worth considering. A play about the Vietnam war which takes the Vietnam war as its literal subject runs the immense risk of appealing only to the converted. (In fact a good deal of committed writing has precisely this aim; not to convert the badmen but to drum up enthusiasm and indignation among the goodmen. It is an altogether easier task.) If on the other hand the writer chooses a more oblique, allegorical approach, by way of historical parallel, he runs the opposite risk: everyone will agree with him!

Why is this a risk? Let us revert for a moment to the theatre, for there you gain an insight into audience reaction which is out of the novelist's reach. In London's West End, the R.S.C. are performing Arthur Kopit's play *Indians*. The audience is mainly middle class, with a heavy splattering of American tourists, ladies in mid-Western spectacles, rinsed hair and rheumatism. Kopit, the playwright, shows us how atrociously the white man treated the American Indian. The audience laps it up, secure in their consciences, insulated by the costumes and the passage of historical time against pain, doubt and self-awareness. Everyone, devoted patriots and enemies of Vietnamese Communism alike, entertains impeccably enlightened opinions about 'da way dem poor Injuns was treated back then'. Custer of the West a modern marine or Green Beret colonel? I doubt whether the thought crosses more than half a dozen minds . . . So Kopit wins battle after battle, scene after scene, only to lose a war which is never properly engaged.

History is a generous rope on which to hang yourself. John Arden takes a national hero, Nelson, and strenuously debunks him in the course of a ballad opera staged in the Punch and Judy style of travelling melodrama. The effect is artistically brilliant but who at the end cares about the actual hero of Trafalgar? Once again elapsed, historical time — and a conditioned acceptance that the theatre is a place where patriotism is debunked — stacks the cards too predictably on the playwright's side. Almost everyone except a few military historians and descendants of Field-Marshal Haig rejoiced in the savage satire of *Oh What a Lovely War!* (Perhaps the English are peculiarly relaxed about their past — I doubt whether a French writer could get away with so unrestrained an attack on Foch, Pétain and the spirit of the *union sacrée*.) Just because it was the *First* World War prostrate on the operating table, an experience outside all but a few living memories, the *bien pensant* public easily absorbed the proposition that the British war effort of 1914–18 was an unmitigated saga of wickedness, bungling, imperialism and useless slaughter. (The Kaiser? No worse than Lloyd George.) Here history-as-art and art-as-history indulgently anaesthetises an audience to its own basic chauvinism. But when Charles Wood wrote *Dingo*, a brilliant, pain-racked hymn of hatred against war, all hell broke loose. For Wood had audaciously taken the *Second* World War as his target and that, as my incensed, middle-aged companion in the theatre clearly intimated, was neither history nor a laughing matter. Wood had come up with one of the finest contributions to both the political and aesthetic avant-gardes ever seen on the English stage: a magnificent synthesis of commitment and dialectical writing. But do not attribute the anger of my companion in the audience to reactionary philistinism; he just happens to have served in *that* war and he knows why.

So how does the historical playwright or novelist fight and win his own war? I don't know. When the whiskies have been too numerous and the night too short I see no alternative but a cheap, valueless victory or a predestined defeat. Such was the case last night, the foregoing six or seven pages having been written, pushed onto the page, slowly, haltingly, with grim, unimaginative resolve during a day of emotional torment. The cause? See Strindberg.

In the political novel, the allegory is the most commonly employed metaphor of alienation. Concentration, exemplification, exaggeration — these are the key didactic weapons of the allegorical novel. In *Erewohn* and *Penguin Island*, they are employed to reveal the extent of human folly and pride; in Well's *The Island of Dr Moreau*, Rex Warner's *The Aerodrome*, Orwell's *Animal Farm* and Golding's *The Lord of the Flies*, to delineate man's unquenchable lust for power. Butler, Orwell and Golding all make the folly and conformism of the mob an important related theme. The allegorist proposes general statements about human behaviour, statements which embrace but also transcend the particular

experiences of particular communities. The writer alienates
the reader from the dust cloud of the immediate environment by erecting a mythical, unreal world — very often an
island or a previously undiscovered country lying beyond
distant mountains. Alternatively the allegorical mode is
achieved by injecting an unforeseeable and improbable element into an apparently normal situation; Wells does this in
The Invisible Man, Kafka in *The Metamorphosis* and Orwell
in *Animal Farm* This last book is surely the classic of the
genre — all inessentials pared away, a literary form precisely disciplined to its didactic purpose, achieving an almost
exact parallel between the events and characters of the farm
and those of Stalin's Russia, the totally effective alienation
from man to pig, from historical reality to myth. The form
of the novel itself so strongly juxtaposes myth and reality
that the reader is afforded an implicit critical insight not
only into totalitarianism but into the process of its literary
transposition. *1984* is markedly inferior in form although
perhaps more imaginatively penetrating in social vision:
having offered us his hellish dystopia, Orwell henceforward
strives with all the weapons of the illusionist novel to persuade us to live within it, within this literary world, this
book of printed pages, without critical detachment. When
Winston and Julia unzip in the forest we, the male readers
. . . I can't speak for the other half.

In terms of the collective social consciousness, the dystopia
or anti-utopia takes pride of place as the authentic political
allegory of our age. At some moment, perhaps in the 1920s,
with the petrification of the Bolshevik Revolution, the
utopia, the dream of a Bellamy or a Morris, became impossible. The future of man assumed nightmarish proportions
— authoritarianism, science run amok, de-humanisation,
total alienation *(Entfremdung)*. The three classic dystopian
novels (representing also a linear sequence of influences)
are Zamyatin's *We*, Huxley's *Brave New World* and Orwell's
1984. (Wells's *Time Machine* has more in common with science
fiction. Jack London's *The Iron Heel* is less a dystopian

novel, elaborating in detail the future structure of hell, than a warning of a brutal fascistic repression yet to come.) And these three novels reveal a remarkable recurrence of theme: an obsessive fear of the eradication of all human individuality, of the political manipulation of the sexual impulse (by means of licence in Zamyatin and Huxley, by way of repression in Orwell), of the absolute banishment of love, of the destruction of the family, of the overriding power of the state, and of the systematic distortion of history. The regime equates happiness with slavery; the imperialist impulse between states has been carried to its extreme conclusion and the Cult of Personality is given unbridled rein (Zamyatin's Well-Doer, Huxley's World Controller and Orwell's Big Brother). Oligarchy and élitism have reached hideous proportions in all three novels and so too has the degradation of the lower orders, the masses — Epsilons (Zamyatin), Proles (Huxley), Proles (Orwell).

These allegories are didactic because they are warnings as well as prophecies. They say 'this will happen' in order to persuade us not to let it happen. It may be a depressing thought, but these pessimistic documents outstrip in political and literary authenticity almost all the socialist, forward-looking novels of the age. The reason has less to do with the inevitability of a horrendous destiny than the fact that literature, as an act of *revolt*, is historically structured and attuned to represent the *individual* constituent in the parliament of the collective culture. Here we notice again how the form, the structure of the novel as a genre naturally proposes, if not imposes, a certain political content. *We, Brave New World* and *1984* each offers us a hero, a singular individual who has not yet succumbed or been crushed or been totally absorbed by the prevailing totalitarianism. I have never been convinced by Sartre's assertion that there can be no great literature which does not contribute to the liberation of man by man; but I cannot conceive of a great or even a good novel which celebrates the totalitarian ethic of happiness equals slavery. The singular hero, the last individualist, is born not

only out of the logic of liberalism, but out of the very womb
of the novel. And it is undoubtedly a deficiency in Huxley
and Orwell that they conceal this, that they confine their
alienation effects to the single level of allegory and then pro-
ceed to employ the full resources of illusionism to blind us
to the fact that the form of expression is a factor of what is
expressed.

I refer, above, to 'the very womb of the novel'. In point of
fact, as I have tried to show in an earlier chapter, this innate
individualism is shared by the novel with other modes of
creative literature, particularly drama. In the general context
of the twentieth-century writer's obsession with individual
rights and the dangers of totalitarian dystopia, Mayakovsky's
play, *The Bedbug*, provides a further confirmation of my
point. Unlike Zamyatin, Huxley and Orwell, Mayakovsky
was a dedicated Communist whose play begins not by celebrating individualism but, on the contrary, by indicating in
the person of Prisypkin its parasitical decadence. Prisypkin
appears on-stage as the social villain, a bedbug-infested,
guitar-strumming, vodka-soaked vulgarian who exploits his
Party card and proletarian pedigree for private advantage.
But in the second half of the play a startling metamorphosis
takes place. Mayakovsky envisages a communist millen-
nium — it is 1978 — in which Prisypkin has been preserved
as a kind of historical-zoological curiosity. Here again literature, in setting the singular against the plural, finds itself
coaxed into the sympathy with the singular even where the
original political orientation was in the opposite direction.
In Mayakovsky's communist paradise all of Prisypkin's vices
and temptations — sex, vodka, tobacco, romance, laziness,
dirt — have been banished. Without changing character
this fellow has suddenly become the object of our sympathy
and compassion; he has become, furthermore, a deliberate
metaphor for Mayakovsky's own tortured predicament in
the Soviet Union. And when this Prisypkin, this figure of
fun and horror, finally cries out, 'Alone! Alone!', who
would not reach out to him and embrace him?

Zamyatin's *We* is a novel which anticipates, stimulates and indeed transcends the modern dystopian tradition. As a novel, as a work of literature, it has a profound dialectical quality. Of course one can arbitrarily abstract the 'content' from the form and pay exclusive attention to the author's gruesome prognostic vision: the organic has given way to the inorganic, informing has become a sacred duty, people have numbers not names, life is regulated by mathematical tables, freedom is extinct, etc. But, beyond this, Zamyatin's use of the notebook format, his compressed similes and metaphors, his ability to shift the narrative between extreme subjectivity and extreme objectivity, all this contributes to a literary style — functional expressionism, if you like — which 'relives' the nightmare at the level of literary existence as well as at the level of literary expression. It is not a question of form matching content: that is always a meaningless formula — rather like saying, 'the way you have cooked this soufflé perfectly suits the soufflé you have produced.' It is a question of a literary construction of dystopia recognising and exploring by means of internal alienations its own nature as sign, symbol and book.

SIX

A novel is a book, and the book is a form of communication which has shown a remarkable resistance to technological change. This fact governs everything we write and therefore everything we say. The scenes of a play may be presented in any order (if suitably written) or simultaneously; but you cannot read two chapters or two pages of a novel simultaneously. As for the order or sequence of reading, a novel can be sold loose-leaf, unbound, in a cardboard box, but in that case don't expect the libraries to take any notice of it. All sorts of experiments have been tried, boring holes through the pages, clipping margins, mucking about. But the linear sequence of print of our linguistic family, left to right left to right, down the page, over the page, carries an irresistible logic. And this logic naturally dictates a certain view of the world, and a certain blindness. Blindness because the novel is in fact less a sequence than a surface on which certain linguistic patterns are inscribed. It is often forgotten that the book *as a material object* also yields its own meaning, different from that of a play and partly dependent on the quality of its intrusion into the reader's general activity. How long does it take him to read it, how frequently does he break off, how extensively does he explore the possibilities of reading as an activity? I mean this: a book will wait for you; you read, it moves, you stop, it stands still. You decide to retrace your steps, to re-read earlier passages, the book accepts this passively. It would be futile for the writer to try and anticipate all the permutations and combinations of possibilities; at the same time the writer ignores at his peril the particular mode of production to which he contributes and by which he is defined.

But the novel-as-book raises a further possibility. The boundaries between literary and artistic forms are in a constant state of flux and erosion. Does the dialectical novel potentially involve the replacement of 'fiction' by the wider concept of the Book? Accepted that any art form has an arbitrary or conventional basis, you can nevertheless distinguish broadly between basic forms and compound forms. The lyric poem, the sonata and the act of mime are all basic, whereas opera is obviously a compound form, involving music, singing, acting, the plastic arts, ballet and so forth. Historically the novel is a less basic form than many of its proponents and practitioners suppose — the word 'novel' simply means 'new' and was, for example, not used by Fielding who referred instead to the 'comic epic poem in prose', a good if rough indication of the novel's varied ancestry. Consequently the novel remains to this day an extremely fluid, open-ended literary form, sharing a lot and borrowing a lot from history, biography, philosophy, journalism as well as from other art forms like the drama and the cinema. This whore-like, open-legged personality is both a charm and a virtue of the novel; but the illusionists, the refiners and polishers, the magicians and conjurors, the mimetic realists and the salesmen of empathy, the hidden Gods — they would all have us believe that our coarse and rugged courtesan is in fact a porcelain princess without debts or duties. How a particular writer will explode this fragile myth must depend on his interests and temperament. But it is at least safe to indicate, very generally, that he will not be ashamed of his debts to neighbouring literary states the other side of the frontier of 'art'; that he will no longer hold to the absurd fetish that obliges his neighbours to lay their cards face up on the table while he shields the sacred muse by keeping his own face-down; that he will no longer invest fiction with holy properties it does not possess. The dialectical novel must inevitably de-mystify fiction by recognising its fictitious nature and by using it as an operating principle within literature, within the Book and within the general field of linguistic communication.

SEVEN

I have indicated certain approaches, yet obviously the journey remains uncompleted. The radical novel has fallen behind the radical theatre in terms of authentic innovation and self-awareness. Alienation in the modern novel is for the most part the achievement of modernists and, if for this reason alone, is almost automatically associated with the private or apolitical sensibility. And where committed novelists, public novelists, have departed from realism, it has nine times out of ten been in the direction of political pessimissism or despair. Where is the Brecht of the modern novel? I do not see him. Hašek perhaps. Mailer's *Why Are We in Vietnam?* is good but not good enough to provide a model for the committed, dialectical novel. Put the picture in reverse; by and large the radical, committed impulse

among novelists remains stubbornly harnessed to the realist,
illusionist impulse. And whereas in the theatre many of the
writers and artists whose work is of genuine *aesthetic* importance are men and women with an obvious *political*
orientation to the Left, the most interesting or influential
contemporary novelists are almost without exception writing
about 'private' lives. Today's young radical student finds
voices speaking to him and for him in the theatre; but if he
has a passion for novels he must either accept kitchen-sink
naturalism (or worn-out socialist realism) or else stare into
space. Clearly that space ought to be, must be, filled.

So what is to be done? More than a century ago the
Russian radical N. G. Chernyshevsky wrote a novel with
precisely that title, *What Is To Be Done?*, a title later used by
Lenin himself. No more avowedly didactive novel can be
imagined; Chernyshevsky made no bones about the fact
that his prime purpose was to canvass the virtues of utilitarianism and materialism, and of the 'new men' in Russia who
incarnated these virtues. As a theorist, Chernyshevsky was a
firm proponent of mimetic and realist fiction. Furthermore
he was a clumsy novelist, and there are more worthwhile
ideas on a single page than there are examples of artistic
talent or sensibility in the whole book. Yet for some reason,
I don't know what, clumsiness perhaps, or bad temper, or
sheer aesthetic idiocy, Chernyshevsky in his crude way
blazed a path which was soon to be throttled by the strangu-
lating creepers of Jamesian illusionism. Take this, for example: 'Yes, the very first pages of this tale reveal that I
have a very poor opinion of the public. I have employed the
ordinary trick of novelists. I have begun with dramatic
scenes.' Chernyshevsky accumulates alienation effects:
'There will be no more mystery; you will be able to foresee
twenty pages in advance the climax of each situation . . .'
Pages? Who ever dared suggest that the self-contained, self-
generating life of a nineteenth-century Russian town *could be
divided into pages*? But what is even more startling in this
philosopher of mimesis is the cavalier manner in which he

addresses his own characters, robbing them of every kind of bogus 'freedom', Sartreian or otherwise. The woman Maria Alexevna, having served her fictional time, is abruptly kicked out of the novel with the judgment: 'Your methods were bad, but your surroundings offered you no others.' I offer one last example of Chernyshevsky's astonishing leap-frog from realism into alienation: 'I have shown Rakhmetov in order to satisfy the most essential condition of art, and simply for that. Well now, find out if you can what this artistic condition is.'

I still don't know what to make of N. G. Chernyshevsky. Fifteen years ago, as a schoolboy armouring himself for an Oxford scholarship examination, I discovered a volume of his essays in Collett's bookshop in the Charing Cross Road. Printed in Moscow, it was naturally excellent value for money. I had never heard of Chernyshevsky. A few months later I travelled to Oxford for the examination and managed to work his name and opinions into virtually every essay I wrote. The tutors who invigilated me *viva-voce* wanted to know *who* the hell this Chernyshevsky was. They were apprehensive in case I had invented him. Had I made him up? No. Did I really think he was an important philosopher? Yes. Today I know a little more about him (he suffered for his beliefs with years of exile in Siberia) and I am convinced he was a lousy novelist. One wouldn't dream of imitating him. Yet I mention him now, fifteen years later, because it is clear to me that as a novelist he stumbled *on to something* which has a lively relevance today; and the best that can be said of my own generation of radical novelists is that we are trying to get on to this something — which eludes us.

About the Author

David Caute was born in 1936 and took a First in history at Wadham College, Oxford. He pursued graduate studies at Oxford and Harvard and took his D.Phil. at Oxford in 1962. He has been Fellow of All Souls, 1959–65; Visiting Professor at New York and Columbia Universities, 1966–67; Reader in Social and Political Theory, Brunel University, 1967–70.

His novels: *At Fever Pitch* (Authors' Club Award and John Llewelyn Rhys Prize, 1959); *Comrade Jacob* (1961); *The Decline of the West* (1966); *The Occupation* (1971). His plays: *Songs for an Autumn Rifle* (Edinburgh, 1961), *The Demonstration* (Nottingham 1961, Unity Theatre 1970). His political studies: *Communism and the French Intellectuals, 1914–60* (1967); *The Left in Europe since 1789* (1966); *Essential Writings of Karl Marx* (editor, 1967); *Fanon* (1970).

He has been widely published in periodicals, the most celebrated of his articles being that in *Encounter*, March 1966, explaining his reasons for resigning from All Souls. His political sympathies have always been with the Left, and have carried him in and out of such phenomena as the Free School of New York and the Anti-University of London. In 1965 he was co-organiser of the Oxford Teach-In on Vietnam.

COLOPHON BOOKS ON LITERATURE, DRAMA & MUSIC